W9-BCK-385

Civil War in Russia

DK265
F578
1962

Civil War in Russia

DAVID FOOTMAN

76464

FREDERICK A. PRAEGER, *Publisher*
NEW YORK

1962

NOV

BOOKS THAT MATTER
Published in the United States of America in 1962
by Frederick A. Praeger, Inc., Publisher
64 University Place, New York 3, N.Y.
All rights reserved
Printed in Great Britain
by Ebenezer Baylis and Son, Ltd.
Worcester and London

Library of Congress Catalog
Card Number: 62-17560

This book is Number 114 in the series of
Praeger Publications in Russian History and
World Communism

© *David Footman* 1961

TO THE
WARDEN AND FELLOWS
OF
ST. ANTONY'S COLLEGE
OXFORD

Contents

9

Acknowledgments

That this book was undertaken and completed has been largely due to the encouragement of the Warden and Fellows of St. Antony's College; and, apart from St. Antony's, I have had advice and help from more friends in this country and in America than can be listed here. I am especially indebted to Dr. George Katkov, Mr. Leonard Schapiro and Dr. S. V. Utechin; and Mrs. Valerie Jensen has given valuable technical assistance. The sole responsibility remains of course my own.

Shortened versions of a number of the episodes here described have appeared in *History Today*, and the chapter on Nestor Makhno first came out in *St. Antony's Papers Number VI*. These passages are now republished by courtesy of the editors of *History Today* and of Messrs. Chatto and Windus Ltd.

Acknowledgments are also due to the Department of Slavic Studies, Indiana University, which printed an article of mine in *Indiana Slavic Studies* (Vol. II, Bloomington, 1958) based on much of the material here used for the chapter on Kolchak.

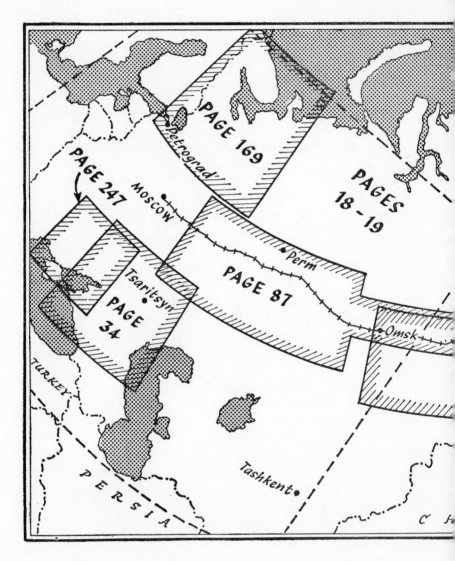

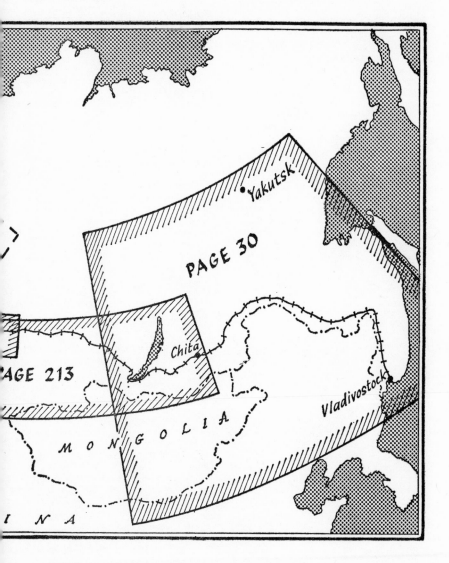

PAGE 30

Yakutsk

PAGE 213

Chita

Vladivostock

M O N G O L I A

I N A

Introduction

The Russian Civil War was, more than once, like the Battle of Waterloo, 'a damned near thing'. But in the end the victory of the Reds was complete, and the Bolshevik régime established absolute control over all European and Asiatic Russia. The experience of the Civil War had a profound influence on the régime and on its driving force, the Bolshevik Party; and thus may be said to have played a substantial part in the shaping of the Party-dominated Russia of today.

Little has been written in the West on the actual course of the war. There are several books on the diplomatic history. But admirable and important as many of them are, it must be remembered that the decisions of statesmen in the Western capitals, often profoundly influencing world history, were mostly taken with very imperfect knowledge of what was actually happening in Russia: indeed, Lenin and Trotsky were at times ignorant of developments in front line areas. The Civil War was seldom what world leaders of the time imagined it to be, and for lesser beings was obscured in a fog of ignorance, partisanship, self-justification and myth—a fog that to some extent still persists.

This book makes no claim to be anything like a full history of the Civil War. For one thing, as explained in the bibliographical note, much of the essential material is still not available. For another, the complexity of the struggle on all the many fronts—the wide variety of personality, motivation and circumstance—would need an inordinately long book to explain what was happening and why it was happening. What is here attempted is merely to state briefly the main established facts of the Civil War, and within that framework to give a more detailed account of some of the more important phases. It is written in the belief that the main concern of history is what happens to human beings.

(ii)

Certain milestones in the revolutions of 1917 had bearing on the Civil War that followed them.[1] Ever-growing demonstrations and disorders in Petrograd in the second week of March led to a breakdown of the local administration. On March 12th members of the State Duma present in the capital set up a committee; and leaders of the revolutionary parties—the Socialist Revolutionaries (S.R.s), the Mensheviks and the then less numerous Bolsheviks—brought into being the Petrograd Soviet of Workers' Deputies, including deputies from the factories and units of the Petrograd garrison. At midnight, March 14th–15th, the Emperor Nicholas abdicated in favour of his brother, the Grand Duke Michael. On the 16th Michael also abdicated, and the monarchy in Russia thus came to an end.

The liberal members of the Duma set up a Provisional Government—the leaders of the Soviet refusing to participate except for the Socialist Kerensky, who came in as Minister of Justice. There then ensued the so-called period of Dual Power, an uneasy partnership or rivalry between the 'bourgeois liberals' of the Provisional Government as representing parliamentary

[1] See the table of dates on pp. 311–317. Dates are given in New Style throughout. (Russia adopted the New Style calendar, to come into line with the rest of the world, early in 1918. The Old Style calendar previously in use was thirteen days behind—e.g. January 1st Old Style is January 14th New Style. Both revolutions of 1917 came towards the end of the month, so that the 'February Revolution' took place, according to the New Style, in March, and the 'October Revolution' in November.)

legality, and the 'revolutionary democrats' of the Soviet as representing the popular will, with neither side willing to recognize the supreme authority of the other. The famous Order No. 1 issued by the Soviet on March 14th, whatever the motives of its originators, had the effect of undermining discipline and embittering the breach between the officers and the rank and file. In the surge of liberal optimism the old police powers were swept away. At the end of March the Soviet appealed to the peoples of the world for a peace without annexations or indemnities.

Lenin returned from abroad in mid-April and four days later issued his *April Theses*. At this period defeatism, as preached by Lenin, had no very wide appeal. To the Right, the continuance of the war was bound up with Russia's honour; to the moderate Left, the new democratic Russia must be defended against German imperialism. But in early May a note to the Western Allies from Milyukov, Minister of Foreign Affairs, reaffirming Russia's treaty obligations and claims, provoked strong opposition from the Left. There were large-scale demonstrations; Milyukov resigned and the cabinet was reorganized to include moderate Socialists, Kerensky, now Minister of War, emerging as its most prominent personality.

Early July saw the opening of the so-called Kerensky offensive against the Central Powers. Later that month there were more troubles in Petrograd: sailors from Kronstadt and Petrograd soldiers and workers (with Bolshevik backing) attempted a rising. But public opinion was on the side of the Government. The disorders were suppressed, and official accusations of Bolshevik complicity with Russia's enemies[1] brought the Party loss of influence and prestige. Lenin and Zinoviev went into hiding and Trotsky (in late July) was arrested.

On July 21st the cabinet was again reorganized with Kerensky as Prime Minister. But, at the front, the July offensive had

[1] German relations with the Bolsheviks and other Russian revolutionary parties have yet to be finally elucidated. See G. Katkov in *International Affairs* of April 1956, and Z. A. B. Zeman, *The Germans and the Russian Revolution* (Oxford, 1957).

by now been halted and turned into an increasingly disordered retreat. In view of the urgent need for discipline General L. Kornilov was appointed Commander-in-Chief. The Kornilov-Kerensky negotiations and the subsequent fiasco of the Kornilov 'revolt' are briefly touched on in Chapter I. Suffice it to say that as a result of the episode, the now largely socialist Government finally lost the backing both of the Left (for its alleged failure to defend the Revolution) and of the Right (for its failure to promote an ordered Russia). There was disintegration in the army and growing anarchy in rural areas where the Government had failed to deal with the land problem. The Bolsheviks and their sympathizers increased rapidly in numbers and influence. In spite of vacillation in the Bolshevik Central Committee (during Lenin's absence in hiding) the Party had, by late September, a majority in the Petrograd Soviet. On October 23rd the Central Committee took the decision to stage an armed rising; and on November 7th (the 'October Revolution') the Bolsheviks seized Petrograd. By the 15th they were masters of Moscow and within a few days they had extended their control to most of the provincial centres. Supreme Headquarters at Mogilev was occupied by a Bolshevik detachment on December 3rd. By this time the Left wing of the Socialist Revolutionaries had agreed to participate in a Bolshevik government, an alliance that was to continue for two months. A preliminary armistice was agreed with the Central Powers on December 5th and formally concluded on the 15th. A week later peace negotiations started at Brest-Litovsk.

Meanwhile the Constituent Assembly, which was to shape the pattern of the future Russia, had been elected with a clear majority for the moderate anti-Bolshevist S.R.s. The Assembly met in Petrograd on January 18th, and was dispersed by the Bolshevik authorities the following day.

(iii)

At the time of the Bolshevik *coup d'état* Russia was in a state of administrative and emotional exhaustion. The Provisional Government (and, indeed, the Soviet) had attempted to rule by exhortation: seldom has history seen a spate of such unceasing rhetoric as in the Russia of 1917. With the end of the old police force and the progressive disintegration of the army, the enforcement of law was ceasing to be the prerogative of government. There had come into being a variety of gangs and groups who found violence feasible and advantageous: the borderline between politics, administration and thuggery was growing hazy. In wide areas life continued, albeit untidily, much as it had been before; elsewhere there was violence and privation. But the peasants, or most of them, were still bringing in their produce to the markets, in decreasing quantities as the incentives became less. The railways still functioned, after a fashion, as did the postal services and factories—all of them progressively less efficiently.

Likewise the emotional atmosphere was patchy and confused. Myths, in the sense of passionately held concepts with little factual foundation, held powerful sway; and Marxian theories were by no means the most potent. The idea of Revolution as something inherently good was of prime importance. This myth dated from long before 1917, but after February its hold increased enormously. Associated myths were those of the mission of the proletariat or the innate virtues of the Russian peasant. The term 'counter-revolutionary' acquired such stigma that opponents of Revolution were forced to find other slogans. Order was one: to some it might mean the restoration of privilege—though most of those who fought for it had little privilege to reassert. Order and Freedom was another—the two being quite incompatible in the Russia of that time. And then there was the image of Russia, a Russia that must find its soul. A powerful factor was the class hatred that the Bolsheviks and their conscious and unconscious allies had been so sedulously propagating.

But for most of the time and for most of the mass of the people the prevailing mood was one of exhaustion, ignorance, anxiety and inertia. Hard times had bred cynicism and *je m'en fichism*.

The black market boomed, and where liquor was available men got drunk. There were many who hoped that some force, somewhere, was working towards whatever future order the individual concerned aspired to; but comparatively few were prepared to take positive personal action. The prospects were not good enough to offset the risks that positive action would involve.

(iv)

The fighting began untidily and haphazardly. In November there was Kerensky's futile counter-attack against the capital with General Krasnov and a small force of half-hearted Cossacks. In Moscow and elsewhere sharp resistance to the Bolshevik take-over came from officers and army cadets, but this was crushed promptly and bloodily. Throughout the empire the Cossacks refused to recognize the new régime: in the Orenburg area the local Cossacks under their Ataman, General Dutov, seized the provincial capital, and for five months were engaged in a little private war against Red Guards detachments organized by the Bolshevik-dominated Soviets of the neighbouring cities. Another private war was started at the turn of the year on the Manchurian frontier by two Cossack captains, Semenov and Ungern-Sternberg, with five companions.

The first round of the Civil War proper dates from January, 1918, when the Bolsheviks, with such troops as they could scrape together, launched a two-pronged offensive against the Ukraine and the Don, whose locally established governments had proclaimed their independence. In the Ukraine the Red forces under Muraviev pushed back the army of the Ukrainian *Rada* and occupied Kiev; but when the *Rada* made peace with the Germans the position was radically changed. Events on the Don will be described in more detail in Chapter I. Briefly, the Reds, under the overall command of Antonov-Ovseenko, proved too powerful for the Don Cossacks and the little

Volunteer Army that had been formed on the Don territory by Generals Alekseev, Kornilov and Denikin. In late February the Don régime collapsed, and the Volunteer Army set out on a precarious trek to the Kuban—culminating (in April) in an unsuccessful attack on Ekaterinodar and the death in action of General Kornilov. With Bolshevik régimes established in Rostov and Novocherkassk, the first round of the Civil War appeared to have ended in a decisive victory for the Reds.

(v)

In the next stage it was the German Army that played the dominating role. After the breakdown of the early Brest-Litovsk negotiations the Germans resumed their advance. Lenin had no choice but to insist on the signature of the Brest-Litovsk Treaty on March 3rd. Under this treaty it was agreed that the Ukraine should, in effect, become a German satellite. The Germans soon dispersed the *Rada*, installed Skoropadsky as their puppet *Hetman*; and German and Austrian troops proceeded to occupy the whole Ukraine. In the North the Germans completed their military occupation of what later became Latvia and Estonia. Brest-Litovsk confirmed the independence of Finland, and during April Finnish Whites under Mannerheim and Germans under von der Goltz effectively crushed the Finnish Reds. In the flurry occasioned by the German threat Trotsky authorized the Murmansk Soviet to co-operate with the small Allied naval forces operating in the extreme North.

The Brest-Litovsk Treaty did not end the fighting in the Ukraine. The Ukrainian Communists, technically independent of the centre, together with their Left-wing associates, put up a show of resistance to the advancing Germans, Austro-Hungarians and Hetmanite Ukrainians for the next two months until finally called off by Moscow. Their efforts were futile; and the main results of this forgotten little war were to give further proof to Moscow of the worthlessness of the Red armed forces, and to undermine any effectiveness or prestige that the first Bolshevik régime in the Don had ever possessed. In early May the Germans occupied Rostov, and about the same time a Cossack rising drove the Bolsheviks out of Novocherkassk. General Krasnov, the newly elected Ataman, established friendly relations with the Germans and proceeded to build up a Don Cossack state. On his southern border the Volunteer Army, back from the Kuban expedition, were able to refit and prepare for further operations. In the Far East, Semenov had now got together a little army on the Manchurian frontier, obtained some help from the British and French and more permanent backing from the Japanese, and was starting his incursions into Soviet territory.

(vi)

The third round, which will be described in Chapter II, occupied the summer of 1918. The Czechoslovak Legion of some 40,000 men, strung out over 5,000 miles of the Trans-Siberian Railway between European Russia and the Pacific port of Vladivostock, revolted against the Bolsheviks on May 25th. By the end of June the main stations along the line were in Czech hands except for a large gap round Irkutsk, where a well-meaning American Consul had persuaded the Legionaries to proceed on their way without fighting. Following the Czech successes a number of anti-Bolshevik governments came into being, including an S.R. régime at Samara and one rather more to the Right at Omsk. In the same month of June an Allied force landed at Murmansk; and at the other end of the empire, in Transcaspia, a revolt against the (Bolshevik) Tashkent Soviet established a rival régime in Ashkhabad.

In July and August the Reds suffered a series of major set-backs. Encouraged by hopes of large-scale Allied intervention, the Czechs and the Samara anti-Bolsheviks made rapid advances in the Urals and along the Volga, culminating in the capture of Kazan and the huge State Gold Reserve on August 12th. In the far north the Archangel Bolsheviks were ejected by a bloodless *coup* at the end of July (see Chapter IV), and the port and city occupied by Allied military. In the Far East, United States and Japanese detachments landed in Vladivostock in August, and within the next few weeks the last vestiges of Bolshevik authority in Siberia and the Far East were wiped out by Czech, Omsk, Japanese and Semenov troops. Semenov establishing his headquarters at Chita. In Transcaspia in July the Ashkhabad régime signed an agreement with the British Military Mission under General Malleson. In August the 'Dunster-force' landed in Baku. In the same month Denikin and the Volunteer Army captured Ekaterinodar and Novorossisk—thus gaining an outlet to the sea.

(vii)

In the next stage, from the autumn of 1918 to the spring of 1919, the tide began to turn. An important factor was the determined effort by Trotsky and his associates to build up a battle-worthy Red Army (see Chapter III). Meanwhile the Czech and Samara troops on the Volga front, disappointed in their hopes of Allied aid, became war-weary and demoralized. Kazan was recaptured in September, and during the next few weeks the Reds advanced steadily towards the Urals, reaching Ufa at the end of the year. Of perhaps greater import was the final German defeat in the West and the armistice of November 11th. The withdrawal of the German troops from Russian soil left a power vacuum which the Western Allies had neither the means nor indeed the will effectively to fill. In the north-west the young Estonian state proved capable of defending its frontiers, but the Reds overran most of Latvia, including Riga. By January they were marching on the main Ukrainian centres, although Odessa had been occupied by a mixed Allied force under French command. Only in the north-east and south-east did the Bolsheviks suffer appreciable defeats. Kolchak had assumed power as Supreme Ruler at Omsk (to the indignation of the Socialists) in mid-November; six weeks later his young

Siberian Army captured Perm. And in the south an attempted offensive by the Red North Caucasus Army was broken, and Stavropol lost to Denikin.

In late March it was confidentially agreed among the Western Allies that their contingents should be withdrawn from Russian soil; but even before that decision was taken trouble broke out in the Odessa expeditionary force under French command. Weak Red detachments advanced from the north, and the French and other units refused to fight. Discipline rapidly disintegrated, and the whole force was hurriedly embarked and removed in April.

(viii)

The ensuing round, from the spring of 1919 until December of that year, was the decisive period of the war and marked with sharp vicissitudes of fortune.

On the Archangel-Murmansk fronts the British, together with the new local White Army, staged a limited offensive in the late summer. Its object was merely to prevent the Reds interfering with the British evacuation. All British and Allied troops were embarked in September, and the fate of the Northern Provisional Government then became dependent on the outcome on the other fronts.

In the Baltic sector, von der Goltz's Balt and German volunteers cleared the Bolsheviks out of southern Latvia in the spring, and went on to capture Riga in May; thereafter the position was bedevilled by bitter conflicts of policies and personalities among the British, German, Baltic and Russian elements involved. In October a small White Army (which had for months been fighting a minor war on the Estonian frontier) went over to the offensive under General Yudenich. They advanced to within a few miles of Petrograd, were defeated by hastily assembled Red reinforcements, straggled back westwards, and the survivors were disarmed by the Estonians and set to work in forced labour camps.

Of far greater importance were events on the southern section. In March a Communist régime under Bela Kun was set up in Budapest. This—coinciding with the fiasco of the French expedition in South Russia—raised Bolshevik hopes of an extension of Communist power throughout south-eastern Europe. Urgent preparations were improvised for a drive into Roumania. But at the critical moment the local Red commander renounced the Bolshevik cause and proclaimed himself Ataman, and a further internal war broke out between the Communists and the peasant guerrilla army under Nestor Makhno (see Chapter VI). Within a very few weeks Bolshevik military power in the south-western sector had fallen to pieces. To the east of this sector the Whites were gathering their strength. In April Denikin assumed supreme command in the south, and in May launched a major offensive and broke into the Donets basin. Kharkov was captured on June 25th, and Tsaritsyn five days later. In July he developed his three-pronged drive against Moscow. Poltava was taken in late July, Odessa and Kiev in August. In the same month a large-scale cavalry raid behind the Red lines penetrated as far north as Tambov. In September picked units of the Volunteer Army captured Kursk. In October the Whites reached the furthest limit of their expansion by the occupation of Chernigov in the Northern Ukraine and of Orel, less than 250 miles from Moscow. But by now reserves were exhausted and supply lines had become precariously long. Denikin's military staff and his Special Conference which functioned as government had taken on too ambitious a task for their resources. Lack of organization and lack of adequate personnel had brought chaos and confusion throughout the enormous area occupied. When the Reds counter-attacked near Orel the White effort had been spent. In a matter of days they were decisively defeated, and by early November were in full retreat.

Operations on the minor Transcaspian front call for little comment. A small contingent of mostly Indian troops, sent up by the Malleson Mission, had enabled the Ashkhabad régime to hold their own in the intermittent and fluctuating fighting of the winter and spring. When these were withdrawn (in early summer) the end of the anti-Bolshevik government was merely a question of time. Ashkhabad was evacuated in mid-July, and Krasnovodsk on the Caspian, where a last stand was made, was stormed by the Red Army a few months later.

The eastern front, on the other hand, was of decisive importance. In February of 1919 both sides were preparing for a spring offensive. Kolchak's so-called Western Army was the first to strike. Ufa was retaken in mid-March; by mid-April the Red front seemed broken, and the Whites were confidently predicting a triumphal march to Moscow. But once again the Whites paid the penalty of faulty strategy and dissipation of effort. Instead of supporting the main thrust to the Volga, Kolchak's Northern (Siberian) Army pressed on beyond Perm, in the futile hope of a junction with the British at Archangel; and the advance, inevitably, petered out in the empty wastes of northern Russia. And so when a hastily concentrated Red Army group under Frunze launched a counter-drive between Samara and Orenburg at the end of April the Western Army had neither the reserves nor the cohesion to withstand it. The Reds reached the Urals and took Ekaterinburg in mid-July; and the collapse of a desperate White effort round Chelyabinsk a few days later meant that the issue on the eastern front had been decided. A stand by the Whites on the Tobol was brief and unavailing. In early November Omsk, the White capital, was evacuated.

The final phase in the East is described in Chapter V. During the two months of the Supreme Ruler's uneasy journey along the Trans-Siberian Railway from Omsk to Irkutsk his empire fell to pieces—not so much from the pressure of the depleted and typhus-ridden Red Army as from desertion, mutiny and revolt and its own inherent impotence. On arrival in Irkutsk in mid-January Kolchak was handed over to his enemies by the Czechoslovak Legion and executed three weeks later.

(ix)

Early in 1920 it might seem that for all intents and purposes the
Civil War was over. Kolchak was dead. In February a peace
treaty with Estonia stabilized the position in the north-west
and the White régime at Archangel was liquidated. By March
the Red Army had occupied the Don and Kuban. In early
April (when Denikin handed over the command to Wrangel)
the White cause in the south was confined to some 40,000
beaten and weary troops, and a horde of refugees, all crowded
into the Crimean peninsula. But in late April the Poles attacked,
and reached Kiev in early May. In June Wrangel's army,
reorganized and re-equipped, broke out of the Crimea and
occupied the Northern Tauride. That same month saw the
beginning of the Polish reverses. By late July the Soviet forces
were approaching Warsaw. In August came the spectacular
Polish counter-offensive. Wrangel meanwhile launched expeditions into the Don and Kuban. When both these failed he
renewed his offensive to the north in the hope of making
contact with the advancing Poles. However, the Russo-Polish
armistice was concluded on October 12th; and this enabled a
greatly superior Soviet force to be concentrated against the
Whites in the south. The decisive battle began in late October.
Ten days later the Reds stormed the isthmus of Perekop.
Wrangel had no choice but to order the total evacuation of his
army, and the Civil War on Russian soil was over.

(x)

Events in the Far East form an epilogue to the Russian Civil
War. By April, 1920, when all the American troops had withdrawn, there was no White element between Lake Baikal and
the Pacific capable of maintaining a government without strong
Japanese backing; and the Japanese were, in the long run,
unable to resist the persistent American pressure to evacuate.

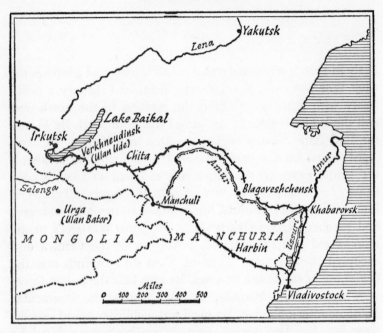

The vacuum created by successive Japanese withdrawals was filled by the first Soviet satellite—the Far Eastern Republic, founded at Verkhneudinsk at the end of March, 1920, and officially recognized by Moscow almost immediately afterwards. In the autumn the last Japanese units pulled out of Chita. Semenov's régime collapsed and the Ataman himself escaped by plane. His nominal subordinate, Ungern-Sternberg, started off with his little army on a grim and lonely expedition to Mongolia, where he captured Urga (Ulan Bator) in February, 1921, but was defeated and himself killed by the Reds before the end of the year. Of the rest of the Chita forces such units as maintained their cohesion fought their way through partisan bands to Manchuria. Here they were reorganized, with Japanese help, and later launched an unsuccessful invasion across the frontier. But the Far Eastern Republic, with Soviet backing, had by now built up an army of some military value, and was profiting by the anti-Japanese feelings of the very great majority of Russians in the Far East. When the Japanese finally evacuated Vladivostock in the autumn of 1922 the Maritime Province was at once absorbed into the Far Eastern Republic; and the Republic, its task completed, proclaimed itself to be dissolved and incorporated into the Soviet Union.

(xi)

The reasons for selecting the particular aspects and episodes that make up this book should perhaps be briefly summarized. Chapter I describes the beginnings of the Volunteer Army that was to become the *corps d'élite* of the White forces in the South, and gives an account of the first serious campaigns of the Civil War against the background of the moods and waverings of the local Cossack communities; it also attempts to show how it was that, in those early days, neither anti-Bolsheviks nor Bolsheviks could establish a stable régime in the southern areas. Chapter II deals with the Czechoslovak Legion, whose revolt brought about the collapse of Soviet authority from the Volga to the Pacific; and also with the early partnership of the Legion with the Socialist Revolutionaries. It gives an account of the Samara People's Government and of S.R. participation in the short-lived Directorate at Omsk—the only occasions on which non-Bolshevik socialists played any appreciable role in the affairs of post-Revolutionary Russia; and goes on to describe the final eclipse and humiliation of what had been the largest of the Russian political parties. As to Chapter III, no explanation is needed for the inclusion, in any work on the Civil War, of a study of the building up of the Red Army. The far north, the subject of Chapter IV, was admittedly a minor sector, but it was the only theatre where significant Western Allied forces remained for any length of time on Russian soil or took any appreciable part in the actual fighting; and what happened at Murmansk and Archangel brings out a number of the problems that intervention entailed. Apart from the personal fate of Kolchak, Chapter V is an account of the collapse of the only anti-Bolshevist All Russian authority ever to be established, and also describes the circumstances of the reimposition of Bolshevik rule on eastern Siberia. Chapter VI deals with the career of Nestor Makhno, the peasant leader who was in closest touch with the feelings and aspirations of the Russian peasant masses, and whose more spectacular campaigns coincide in time and place with the final phases of the Civil War in European Russia.

CHAPTER I

The Don and the Volunteer Army

(i)

The Kornilov affair of September, 1917, was, in some respects, a prelude to the Civil War that was to flare up four months later. It is a curious episode, of which no really satisfactory account has yet been given. It arose from the ever-increasing demoralization in the army following the collapse of the July offensive. Kerensky himself recognized the need of appointing to supreme command a general with a toughness and a force of personality to carry through the drastic counter-measures that had become so necessary. His final choice was Kornilov; and for some weeks there were confidential exchanges between the new Prime Minister and the new Commander-in-Chief on the scope and nature of the steps to be taken both at the front and in the rear. Any long-term partnership between two such incompatible personalities is unthinkable; but, by early September, complete agreement seemed to have been reached on an immediate programme—including the dispatch of a task force to Petrograd (where the garrison was quite unreliable) to quash any anti-government rising that the new measures might well have provoked. This is not the occasion to attempt to unravel the tangle of suspicions, hidden reservations and misunderstandings that led to the last-minute break. Kerensky convinced himself that he, his government and the popular cause for which they stood were about to be swept away by a military dictatorship. He

C

denounced Kornilov as a traitor and issued impassioned appeals to the nation to defend and preserve the Revolution, appeals that were exploited to the full by the Bolsheviks and their allies. The move to restore order and discipline foundered, to the bewilderment of its supporters, amid the upsurge of revolutionary emotion. The commander of the task force forPetrograd shot himself, and his troops melted away. Kornilov was arrested, together with his Chief of Staff, Lukomsky, and a number of junior officers and civilian sympathizers, and confined in a monastery turned prison at Bykhov in north-west Russia not far from the Supreme Headquarters at Mogilev. Here they were shortly joined by Generals Denikin and Markov, who had been arrested by their rank and file at the H.Q. of the South-West Army Group.

Kerensky and his cabinet seem to have had no clear idea of what was to be done with the prisoners. A Commission of Inquiry was appointed and its proceedings postponed the need of making a decision. There were, of course, soldiers' committees and extremist local Soviets who demanded that the class enemies should be shot forthwith: indeed, Denikin and his party were in real danger until their transfer to Bykhov. But here the sympathies of the Tekintsi regiment, on guard at the monastery, were with the generals; on at least one occasion they used force to drive off a gang who had come to seize the prisoners. In theory the inmates of Bykhov were supposed to be cut off from the outside world, but visits from wives were allowed between 10 a.m. and 6 p.m., and there was little difficulty over correspondence with friends outside. Throughout, the prisoners were in touch with the Supreme Headquarters (the *Stavka*) at Mogilev, where first Alekseev and then Dukhonin held the post of Commander-in-Chief under Kerensky. Escape from Bykhov would have been possible at any moment. But the generals did not want to escape. Their consciences were clear. What they required was full, public and official exoneration, either by means of trial and acquittal or else by a formal declaration on the part of the Government. Escape was only envisaged in the event of a serious danger of lynching. The question of formal exoneration did not apply to the juniors, and successive appeals were made to the *Stavka* and the Procurator for their release. By the time of the Bolshevik *coup* nearly half the Bykhov prisoners had been set free. By December 1st only Generals Kornilov, Denikin, Lukomsky, Romanovsky and Martov were left.

These five, together with Alekseev, were to play leading roles in the opening stages of the Civil War, and it has been suggested that Bykhov served as conspiratorial centre for the Counter-Revolution. This is hardly true. These middle-aged and eminently respectable generals were not conspirators; nor does the idea of a large-scale underground network ever seem to have been seriously considered. False papers and civilian clothes were got ready against the possible need of flight; and efforts were made to collect funds to help the families of junior officers—all pay had been stopped from the day of arrest—and to provide winter clothing for the faithful Tekintsi. But it was not till late October that 40,000 roubles were received from Kornilov sympathizers in Moscow, and this seems to have been entirely spent on welfare.

There was, of course, continuous discussion on political themes. There was a natural deference to Kornilov in view of his position: but when he left his private quarters to join in the general conversation the talks remained free and uninhibited. There was no serious suggestion of a return to the old régime: that, to Kornilov and Denikin, would have been unthinkable. (In view of their portrayal as arch-reactionaries it is worth remembering that their home backgrounds were considerably poorer and harder than those of either Lenin or Trotsky.) Some of the juniors favoured a restoration of the monarchy: here there was a wide cleavage of opinion. But on one point, the essential one, there was unanimity. The 'movement' was to be continued. That is to say steps must be taken to restore discipline in the Army both at the front and in the rear; to continue the war on the side of the Allies; to organize military supplies and industry generally; and to ensure that the central government, the provincial administration, and the courts should function without the interference of 'irresponsible organs'. There was no precise programme for the subsequent settlement of affairs, though hopes were set on a Constituent Assembly.

It seemed clear to all that the Army must be the instrument of the movement. But there was, at that stage, no inkling of the scope or nature of the civil war that was to develop. Clearly a rot had set in over wide areas of Russia; but, it was confidently hoped in the isolation of Bykhov, there were other areas as yet unaffected where a disciplined force might be assembled to deal with the opposing rabble. Hopes were set on South Russia: Lukomsky urged Dukhonin to concentrate reliable troops at Mogilev and then transfer the *Stavka* to the area of the South-West Army Group. And when Dukhonin seemed unwilling or unable to act thoughts were turned more and more towards the

Don, where General Kaledin was believed to have established a stable Cossack régime.

(ii)

It was Alekseev, rather than the Bykhov generals, who engaged in work of organization. After his resignation as Commander-in-Chief he moved to the capitals and contacted the various officers' associations. These had started to be formed in the early summer as self-protection against the increasing risks and humiliations to which officers were exposed. By the autumn there were ten of them in Petrograd alone, and others in Moscow and other centres. An immediate concern was to look after those who had become destitute. Approaches were made to the wealthy for help, and a number of contacts developed between the officers' associations and bourgeois civilian groups such as the Moscow Union of Social Activists. Inevitably these contacts took on a political aspect: all concerned were aiming not so much at the restoration of the old régime as at the establishment of some ordered way of social life which seemed only possible with military help.

It was in this field that Alekseev became busy. His position and reputation made him a natural patron of officers' associations. His contacts with Milyukov and others brought him into the councils of the bourgeois groups. His self-imposed task was to organize, to co-ordinate and to collect funds. It is uncertain when he first conceived his idea of a Volunteer Army; but right from the beginning he seems to have thought of the Don as the one safe area where officers could be sent and funds accumulated for the inception of a movement that would bring stability to Russia. Like so many others he was taken by surprise by the Bolshevik seizure of power. To remain in Petrograd would have been dangerous; and in any case there was nothing he could usefully do there. So he left for the South, and, travelling alone with his A.D.C., he reached Novocherkassk in early November.

Meanwhile in Bykhov the full implications of the Bolshevik *coup* were not immediately apparent. But the departure of the junior inmates was expedited, and by the end of November only the five senior generals were left. They continued to impress upon Dukhonin that he should form a strong point by concentrating reliable troops around the *Stavka*. There were, of course, no 'reliable' troops for such a purpose; and the unfortunate Dukhonin, torn between his professional distaste at what was happening and his pedantic loyalty to whatever régime was in power, did nothing at all; he even felt it inconsistent with his responsibilities to accede to a request from Kaledin to send the five generals to Novocherkassk.

With the growing certainty that nothing could be expected from the *Stavka* it was natural that the hopes of the Bykhov prisoners should be focused on the Don. It is true that recent letters from Kaledin were full of reserves: he could offer the generals asylum but would make no further promises. However, not much weight was attached to these reserves. Few went as far as Zavoiko (Kornilov's A.D.C.) who maintained that the party was eagerly awaited by all in the Don except Kaledin, who was afraid of being overshadowed by the formidable ex-Commander-in-Chief. But the traditional faith in Cossack loyalty, Cossack integrity and Cossack stability persisted.

The position round Bykhov deteriorated. It was rumoured that the Bolshevik Krylenko was on his way with an armed detachment to take over the *Stavka*. Dukhonin at last sent a message that the prisoners must leave. It was agreed that the *Stavka* should provide a special train, but the train was not forthcoming. So when the five generals left the seclusion of Bykhov for the harsh realities of the world outside they did so individually, each along a route of his own devising, on December 2nd (a few hours before the unhappy Dukhonin was murdered in his headquarters), with a rendezvous in Novocherkassk. Denikin travelled as a Polish official, Lukomsky as a German colonist, Romanovsky as an army ensign and Markov as a common soldier. Kornilov, in the fond belief that his presence would make for the safety of his Tekintsi, rode off in full uniform at the head of the regiment. In the next few days they were repeatedly attacked by Red bands and suffered severely from lack of food and from the bitter winter cold. There was no choice but to part company. What was left of the regiment went west towards Kiev, and Kornilov continued his journey with one attendant, eventually reaching the Don, disguised as a peasant, some days after his fellow-generals.

(iii)

One other general was also making his way to the South. This was P. N. Krasnov, who had led Kerensky's hopeless venture to recover Petrograd. When his Cossacks refused to fight, he was taken under escort to the capital and spent five days in inconclusive argument with his Bolshevik captors, who seem to have hoped to induce him to serve the Soviet régime. He later obtained a genuine or bogus permit to leave Petrograd; and conceived a scheme to transfer the whole of his former command, the Third Cavalry Corps, to the Don. He realized there was little chance of inducing the rank and file to fight: but the corps equipment, supplies and funds would be a valuable addition to the strength of the independent Don Government. He wrote to Kaledin explaining what he had in mind, but the Ataman's reaction was so cautious and pessimistic that Krasnov received the impression that Kaledin was swimming with the tide, and that the tide was flowing in favour of the Bolsheviks. The scheme for the transfer of the corps inevitably came to nothing; there were too many practical difficulties, and the young Bolshevik régime was beginning to exercise some sort of control. In the end Krasnov set off alone with a false passport. He eventually reached the Don frontier only to hear the news of Kaledin's suicide.

(iv)

1917 was an eventful year for the Cossack areas. Following the February Revolution there was a movement among Cossacks generally to reassert the rights they had enjoyed up to the time of Peter the Great, and in South-East Russia the Don and the Kuban Cossacks did, for a time, establish their autonomy. There was talk, from late 1917 onwards, of setting up a Cossack Confederation, but the negotiations and the conferences came to nothing; and in the end the history of each of the Cossack communities was to follow its own confused and unhappy course.

The Don was by far the most important area in population and resources. Like the others it was mainly rural, half the inhabitants being Cossacks, the rest more recent settlers from Russia proper. The latter, the *inogorodni*, were in comparison poor relations, with small land holdings, meagre resources and no organized community to compare with the Cossack *Voisko*; they were bitterly jealous of Cossack privileges. In Rostov the province contained the one big town in any Cossack area, with a flourishing bourgeoisie. Taganrog also had factories and shipyards, so that the working-class element was appreciable. Of the political parties, the Socialist Revolutionaries had the greatest hold on the non-Cossack countryside, and the Mensheviks on the town workers. Initially the Bolsheviks were weak; in the spring of 1917 they had only 450 members in all Rostov.

In June, 1917, the Cossack *Krug* or council elected as Ataman General A. M. Kaledin, formerly in command of the 8th Army on the South-West front. In August Kaledin attended the State Conference at Moscow and made a speech demanding order and discipline. On the break between Kornilov and Kerensky he came out on the side of Kornilov. Kerensky thereupon dismissed him from the post of Ataman and ordered his arrest. No attention was paid to Kerensky's orders in Novocherkassk, the Don capital, and Kaledin remained in office—though he narrowly escaped being kidnapped by a group of revolutionaries when visiting Voronezh, on the fringe of his territory.

In spite of the break over Kornilov, when the Bolsheviks seized power Kaledin and the *Voisko* announced their loyalty to the Provisional Government and endeavoured to locate and contact what remained of that already non-existent body. The Bolsheviks were declared criminals, martial law was proclaimed and the *Voisko* Government assumed full powers throughout the Don. There was no active resistance. There was pro-Bolshevik sentiment in some of the military units; but these were disarmed with the help of the army cadets. The independence of the Don appeared to have been established.

But it was a precarious independence. The Bolsheviks, particularly since the Kornilov affair, had been rapidly increasing their influence. In the November elections to the Constituent Assembly they secured more votes in Rostov than any other single party;[1] and close contact was established between the Bolsheviks of Rostov and Taganrog and the revolutionary sailors of the Black Sea Fleet in the Crimean ports. The S.R.s and the Mensheviks vociferously opposed any step by the authorities which could be regarded as counter-revolutionary, in particular the disarming of the pro-Bolshevik military units. They were not against the independence of the Don; but their leaders, with their ideals of peaceful coexistence, insisted that independence should be established by friendly negotiation without any suggestion of the use of force. Some support for the Don Government was forthcoming from the Cadets; but most of the bourgeoisie remained passive, waiting to see how the new régime would fare. The Right-wingers were strongly critical. Of more importance was the discontent of the *inogorodni*, numbering nearly half the population and resentful of Cossack tutelage. The Ataman, sincerely anxious to broaden the régime, arranged in late November for a combined

---

[1] The complete figures were: Bolsheviks 25,000, Cossacks 14,000, Cadets 13,000, S.R.s 7,000, Mensheviks 4,000. In the Don province as a whole, however, the three leading parties were Cossacks 640,000, S.R.s 480,000, and Bolsheviks 250,000.

conference of Cossack and *inogorodni* representatives. But it was weeks before any agreement was achieved and then only with reservations. Meanwhile there had sprung up a complex of articulate and unco-ordinated councils, committees, congresses and associations. In many ways the Don was a continuation, in miniature, of the Russia of the Provisional Government.

The Ataman himself was a man of complete integrity, moderate, progressive, with a strong sense of responsibility for the well-being of all the peoples in his province. He was not the stuff of which dictators are made; in any case he lacked that first essential of a dictator—a strong-arm squad to enforce decisions. He had been elected by the Cossack *Krug* to lead the Cossack *Voisko*. The Cossacks (to the disappointment of old-fashioned Russian conservatives) were found to have little interest in the Russian monarchy or in the rest of Russia. They intended that Kaledin should uphold Cossack traditions and prevent Bolsheviks or other outsiders from interfering with Cossack privileges; they had little sympathy for Kaledin's concern for the *inogorodni*. Meanwhile, it should be remembered, it was the older Cossacks who had elected Kaledin and who had approved his anti-Bolshevik stand. The young men back from the army, the *frontovniks*, were war-weary like the rest of the Russian Army. They were suspicious of an Ataman whose avowed pro-Entente attitude involved the risk of the war flaring up again and their return to the front. They had no quarrel with the Bolsheviks who had brought them peace and the chance to go home. As the units arrived in the Don the men went back to their settlements or *stanitsas* where they formed an ever more vocal and active opposition to their pro-Kaledin seniors. As Krasnov had diagnosed, the tide was flowing in favour of the Bolsheviks.

To the south of the Don province lay the Kuban, which, in the autumn of 1917, seemed the most stable of the Cossack areas. The towns were small, industrial workers few (apart from the railway workers) and the area remote from the centres of disturbance. Some weeks before the Bolshevik *coup d'état* the Kuban Cossack *Rada* (an assembly corresponding to the Don

Krug) declared itself, in spite of the disapproval of the Provisional Government, to be an independent republic and 'a sovereign member of the Federation of Russian peoples'. A government was formed on the basis of Cossack votes (although the *inogorodni* here too amounted to half the population). Filimonov was elected Ataman. Pokrovsky, a junior Cossack officer, was deputed to form a corps of volunteers, mostly army officers and army cadets, and the disaffected old army units in Ekaterinodar were disarmed. Later, under pressure from the *inogorodni*, the Government was reorganized to include a proportion of non-Cossacks. As in the Don there was a profusion of self-appointed committees and councils. And here again in the weeks following the Bolshevik *coup* the tide began to flow in favour of the Reds, revolutionaries in the towns and railway centres becoming more belligerent, and returning *frontovniks* gradually swamping the older and more conservative Cossacks in the *stanitsas*. A Revolutionary Military Committee started to function in Armavir. Red fighting squads came into being and Pokrovsky's detachments were engaged in minor battles. But the main threat to the Kuban régime was to come from the Black Sea Province to the west. In Novorossisk the Bolsheviks were strong and had organized the dock workers. Soon after the overturn in Petrograd they were in effective control of the town and port and three months later could start to invade the Kuban. In the Stavropol province (east of the Kuban and south-east of the Don) there confusedly emerged a Provincial National Assembly under a temporary and precarious Bolshevik leadership. But there were continued quarrels within the Assembly, and in any case its authority, such as it was, was disregarded outside the town of Stavropol. Eastward again, towards the Caspian, the Terek area lapsed into anarchy. The Ataman of the Terek Cossacks was killed in a skirmish, and the various Terek National Congresses convened under Left-wing auspices spent their time and energies in internal disputes. North of the Caspian, the Astrakhan Cossacks and groups of officers and military cadets took to arms, but by late January and after some sharp fighting the Bolsheviks

43

established permanent control over the town of Astrakhan and the lower Volga.

Such was the position in the southern Cossack areas, on which Alekseev in Petrograd and Kornilov and Denikin in Bykhov had been building their hopes. Their few weeks' respite, on arrival in the South, was due not to Cossack strength but to Bolshevik weakness—to the small numbers and poor quality of the local Party cadres; to the irresponsibility of the Party's Left S.R. allies; to poor communications with the central leadership, so that little direction and no control was possible from Petrograd; and, finally, to the lack of discipline and organization in such military forces that the Reds could put into the field.

(v)

When Alekseev arrived in Novocherkassk in mid-November Kaledin explained the trouble that might arise in the Don if a counter-revolutionary movement was organized, and pressed him to go south to the Kuban. Alekseev did in fact visit Ekaterinodar, but finding the Don a more suitable base he went back to Kaledin and in the end secured his acquiescence. But it was stipulated that Alekseev's status was to be that of a guest of the Don Cossacks, that the movement was to be regarded as a purely private organization of Alekseev's, that it was to have no publicity and no overt support whatsoever from the Don Government. Kaledin did, however, provide certain sums, camouflaged as aid to refugees; and Alekseev started to form the Volunteer Army.

The Bykhov generals were, of course, more notoriously associated with counter-revolution than was Alekseev, and their pressure in the Don was therefore more embarrassing. Denikin, who arrived in early December, has left a moving account of his call on Kaledin, whom he found sitting alone in a huge office, exhausted and depressed. He told Denikin that the Cossacks were sick, affected with the malady that had spread over all Russia. Here in the Don he had no administration and no armed force. He believed the Bolsheviks were organizing an invasion. There were threats from the Donets Soviet Republic and from the Black Sea Fleet. Black Sea sailors were infiltrating into Rostov, where a Revolutionary Committee was openly calling for an overthrow of the régime. Meanwhile the Cossacks refused to fight. From time to time during the interview the telephone went and Kaledin answered it. 'I give orders,' he said, 'and nobody carries them out.' Finally he urgently begged that Denikin and his fellow-generals should leave for the Kuban or the Caucasus.

When Lukomsky arrived his first visit was to Alekseev. He records: 'M. V. Alekseev told me that he had decided to form a Volunteer Army on the Don; that in Petrograd and Moscow he had organized societies for the assistance of officers; that these societies maintained very close contact with social organs who were affording material help, and would direct to the Don all officers, cadets (*junkers*) and senior members of military schools who so wished; and the Federation of Officers' Associations was taking all steps to facilitate passage to the Don for any officer who wished from any part of the country.' Lukomsky made the suggestion that Alekseev should issue a resounding public appeal, so that officer volunteers would pour in in thousands. In reply Alekseev (quite apart from the conditions imposed by Kaledin) had to admit that the material help he was hoping for was, so far, only a trickle. He had, he said, the greatest difficulty in feeding and clothing such recruits as did arrive. Lukomsky made the point that money was not coming in because potential benefactors were unaware that there was in existence a movement which was worth their support. One must take a risk. Otherwise there would be a vicious circle—no money because there was no army, and no army because there was no money.

Lukomsky subsequently saw Kaledin, who reiterated his appeal that the newly arrived generals should leave the Don. In consequence, on December 9th Denikin and Markov set out for Ekaterinodar and Lukomsky for Vladikavkaz. Romanovsky, a less controversial figure, remained in Novocherkassk. But between the date of the departure of Denikin, Lukomsky and Markov and the arrival of Kornilov some ten days later the position and status of the little Volunteer Army in the Don had undergone a change.

(vi)

The preoccupied and hard-pressed Bolshevik leadership in Petrograd does not seem to have paid much attention to Cossack affairs until early December. Then came news of the Bykhov escapes, and the certainty that the former prisoners were making for the South. Reports, too, had been accumulating not only of the stand in the Don and Kuban, but also from the Urals, where Dutov, Ataman of the Orenburg Cossacks, had occupied the town of Orenburg, thus cutting rail communications between Russia proper and Russian Turkestan. On December 7th Trotsky sent a message by direct wire to Krylenko, instructing him to assemble a force 'sufficiently strong to be able in the shortest possible time to wipe off the face of the earth the counter-revolutionary rebellion of the Cossack Generals and Cadet Bourgeoisie'. On December 9th *Sovnarkom* issued a proclamation denouncing Kaledin, Dutov, the Cadet Bourgeoisie, Kornilov, the Ukrainian Central Rada and the 'capitalists of all countries who have brought about this world of butchery'. The proclamation declared that the Don and Ural areas were in a state of war, and that local revolutionaries should act at once. No negotiations whatever should be conducted with the counter-revolution. Its leaders were outlawed, and all affording them any support would be ruthlessly punished. On the other hand, those Cossacks who took steps to throw off their yoke must be greeted as brothers.

The two most important areas of opposition appeared to be in the Ukraine and the Don. Accordingly, Bolshevik military plans envisaged a double offensive—the one, under Muraviev, against Kiev, the other, under the general direction of Antonov-

Ovseenko, against the South, so as to cut off the Don from the Ukraine and establish direct contact with the Caucasus. Meanwhile, whether or not in consequence of the *Sovnarkom* appeal, the Rostov Revolutionary Military Committee decided to act. With the help of some sailors infiltrated from the Black Sea Fleet risings were staged in Taganrog and Rostov, and by the evening of December 10th Rostov was in revolutionary hands. Kaledin's Cossack units refused to move against the insurgents and the Ataman had to appeal to Alekseev for the help of his Volunteers. The latter retook Rostov on December 15th. The impact of the Red revolt, the evidence of the complete ineffectiveness of the local forces and the threats from Petrograd had some effect. Progressive intellectuals still proclaimed peaceful coexistence with the Bolsheviks, and the *inogorodni* congress still demanded that the Volunteers should be disarmed. The Cossack *Krug*, however, held that 'the Volunteer Army may remain in existence, but if it should turn against the people it must be reformed'. The final agreement reached between the Cossack and *inogorodni* representatives was to the effect that the Volunteer Army might remain if it protected the Don from Bolshevik invasion and fought on behalf of the Constituent Assembly, but it must be under the control of the Don Coalition Government; and if counter-revolutionary elements were to appear in its ranks they must be expelled from Don territory. These provisos provoked sarcastic comments from members of the Volunteer Army. But the resolution did at least amount to official recognition.

(vii)

After the suppression of the rising in Rostov in mid-December there was no serious threat to the Don until the development of the Bolshevik offensive a month later. The delicate internal discussions over the organization and command of the Volunteer Army accordingly took place in a comparative lull. Kornilov arrived in Novocherkassk about December 20th.

Denikin, Lukomsky and Markov were summoned back to meet him, Alekseev and Romanovsky being already on the spot.

Seniority, prestige and achievement marked out Kornilov and Alekseev as leaders, and it at once became apparent that the tough and temperamental fighting soldier and the elderly professorial administrator were going to be uneasy partners. Kornilov insisted on a single commander (which could be none other than himself). Alekseev was unwilling to relinquish control of finance and politics. It was not only that Kornilov understood little of either: his personal advisers (Zavoiko in particular) inspired no confidence in the other generals. But Kornilov maintained that the position of a C.-in-C. with no control over finance or politics would be impossible. Alekseev then suggested two Volunteer Armies, he himself to continue in the Don and Kornilov to organize a second army in the Kuban. Kornilov felt that would make them like two hucksters competing at a village fair. In any case, the more Kornilov saw of conditions in the South the less he liked them: he formed the plan of leaving for Siberia where he had spent his youth and where he could, he felt, build up a strong and unified movement far away from the intrigues and quarrels of the Don and the Kuban.

The deadlock was eventually solved by the arrival from Moscow of a group of Alekseev's civilian associates, including P. N. Milyukov, P. V. Struve, and M. M. Fedorov. These insisted that the movement as yet was too 'brittle' to afford to lose either Kornilov or Alekseev; furthermore, that Kaledin must be associated with them. Denikin and Lukomsky accordingly drafted proposals whereby Kornilov should be Commander-in-Chief of the Armed Forces, Alekseev to take charge of administration, finance and foreign relations, and Kaledin to handle all matters concerning the Don—the supreme authority to be a Triumvirate of these three men. A formula on these lines was eventually signed by the three generals and a copy sent to the National Centre in Moscow. Kornilov told Lukomsky he had signed the agreement reluctantly as he did not think it would work.

All this time Kornilov was living incognito and in mufti—in view of local susceptibilities and his reputation as arch counter-revolutionary. All kinds of schemes were being devised by his entourage, that Kornilov should start off on a crusade to Astrakhan, that he should 'dismiss' Alekseev, that he should even stage a *coup d'état* in Novocherkassk and depose Kaledin (this last was an idea of Zavoiko's, and when Kornilov heard of it he ordered him to leave the area within forty-eight hours). The atmosphere surrounding the Volunteer Army was full of intrigue and of rumour—that Kornilov was a 'democrat' and Alekseev a 'monarchist'; that there was a plot to assassinate Kornilov. Meanwhile, local Don politics continued in a spate of polemics and rhetoric. It is not surprising that Kornilov felt that this was not the place to build up that disciplined anti-Bolshevik and anti-German front that was his ambition.

There were others, notably Lukomsky, who believed that Kornilov would find greater scope in Siberia. But the Moscow politicians were dead against it. They feared (with some reason) that if Kornilov went east the cream of the officer volunteers would follow him, leaving Alekseev with little material with which to build. Kornilov let himself be persuaded, but he continued to feel his sojourn in the South was only temporary. He sent off couriers to Pepelyaev and other leading Siberian personalities. He put pressure on Alekseev to detach officers on missions to contact underground officer groups along the Volga; and his was the initiative behind the dispatch of General Flug on a mission of investigation, recruitment, organization and co-ordination in all the main centres along the Trans-Siberian Railway.[1]

Towards the end of the year a complicating factor arose with the arrival of Boris Savinkov, ex-revolutionary terrorist, ex-Provisional Government Military Commissar, principal intermediary in the abortive Kornilov-Kerensky negotiations and now active in the anti-Bolshevik underground. He was not very welcome in Novocherkassk. Kornilov, in view of what

---

[1] General Flug's account of his mission is in *Arkhiv Russkoi Revolyutsii*, Vol. IX.

D

had happened in September, refused at first to receive him. In the end he let himself be persuaded and discussions took place. Savinkov's point was that it was necessary to form a Political Council including himself: otherwise the movement, led exclusively by generals, would give an impression of being purely counter-revolutionary. This was a valid point and was accepted, albeit in some quarters rather reluctantly. The Council was formed, consisting of the top generals and Milyukov, Struve, Fedorov and Savinkov. At the latter's insistence the Council worked out the first public statement of the aims of the Volunteer Army. These aims were firstly to oppose anarchy and Bolshevik rule, secondly to protect free institutions in the Cossack areas and in South-East Russia, and thirdly to build up a force that would eventually establish freedom and order and hand over power to a (or the) Constituent Assembly. This last phrase as drafted left some doubt as to whether the Constituent Assembly was to be that elected in November or a new one: the intention of most of the Council was that it should be a new one.

(viii)

Meanwhile the Volunteer Army was growing, but growing only slowly. Don political susceptibilities had prevented an early appeal by Alekseev, and had also caused the rejection of a suggestion, made at the time of Kornilov's arrival, that he should issue a formal order instructing all officers to report to Novocherkassk. The first general appeal came with the publication of the Volunteer Army's programme at the turn of the year, but by that time the Bolsheviks had tightened their grip on the railways and on communications generally, and it had become more difficult for potential volunteers to get through.

During the early weeks of the V.A.'s existence the flow of recruits amounted to eighty volunteers a day. About half of these were officers—the rest were *junkers*, students, boys from the higher forms of military and civilian schools, a sprinkling of Army N.C.O.s and a very few privates. Considering that some 300,000 officers had served in the Russian Army in World War I this meagre response—even allowing for the difficulties of travel—was a great disappointment to the generals. Of course, at that time, many officers had not yet heard of the Volunteer Army. Others had no reason to think of it as other than just another ephemeral adventure. Others wavered (Brusilov at one stage wrote to Alekseev offering his support but afterwards changed his mind). In any case it would be quite wrong (though some of the generals clung to the illusion) to think of the Russian officers of 1917–18 as a close-knit professional body with common loyalties and the *esprit de corps* of an officer class of 1914. When war broke out the Russian Army contained some 55,000 regular officers. Casualties, especially among junior officers, had been very heavy. Replacements and additions had come from all walks and conditions of life and all shades of political opinion or lack of it. The one common bond was the experience of humiliation and danger following the promulgation of Order No. 1 back in March, 1917. For many officers such loyalties as still persisted were mostly to their families or to their own survival. Denikin sadly refers to the scores of officers sitting about in cafés in Rostov and Novocherkassk who not only did not volunteer but later on, when the Reds took over, hurried to report to the Bolshevik authorities that they had had nothing to do with the Volunteer Army.

There was no financial inducement to join up. For the first few weeks there were rations but no pay. From December 17th those serving as officers were paid 100 roubles a month, those in the ranks 30. These rates were raised from January 18th to 150 and 50 roubles respectively, and raised again in February to 270 and 150, with a small family allowance in addition. Alekseev was continually complaining of lack of funds. Next to nothing came through from his contacts in the capitals, on which he had built such hopes, till late December when 80,000 roubles (in two instalments) were received from Moscow. No more came through from this source when the

Bolsheviks had tightened up their control. Wealthy circles in Rostov and Novocherkassk promised 8,000,000 roubles, but only a quarter of this was, in fact, forthcoming.

Hopes were laid on financial help from the Allies. Approaches had been made to various Allied representatives in Petrograd and Moscow, and in late December French and British military and an American consular representative arrived in Novocherkassk. Colonel Hucher (of the French Military Mission to Roumania) promised on behalf of the Allies a subsidy of one hundred million roubles. But nothing had been received up to the time of the evacuation in February. The one substantial contribution was fifteen million roubles from an advance by the Rostov branch of the State Bank to the Don and to the Volunteer Armies: without this the formation of any appreciable force would have been impossible. At one stage agreement was reached with the Don Coalition Government that 25 per cent of the Don revenues were to be devoted to the needs of the armies, but very little materialized. Ekaterinodar refused an appeal by Alekseev for a similar contribution from the Kuban. Preparations were made for the printing and issue of a special Volunteer Army currency, but the notes were not ready by the time of the fall of Rostov.

As to arms, some were captured in brushes with the Reds and there were occasional raids into the Stavropol province for this purpose. Otherwise weapons and equipment had to be bought either from the Don Government's military stores or from returning Cossack units, the latter source of supply being cheaper. Denikin notes that Cossacks would sell anything, up to and including their consciences. From time to time a field gun was purchased; two were stolen from the 39th Division coming back from the Caucasus; two more were borrowed from the Don Government for the ostensible purpose of firing salutes at funerals and never returned.

Lukomsky records that by mid-January the Army totalled some 5,000 men. Denikin, more likely to be accurate, gives the figure of 3 to 4,000. A fair proportion of those were required to keep order in restive areas like Rostov. The leaders reckoned that the force must reach at least 10,000 before any offensive operation could be considered. By late January there were, on paper, three infantry regiments; three officers' battalions and a *junkers* battalion; two cavalry 'divisions'; two batteries of artillery; a small Czech pioneer unit that had been cut off from the Czechoslovak Legion; a Caucasian 'Division of Death', and a few partisan detachments. Many of these units were merely cadres. The force as a whole was top-heavy, with far too many officers finding excuses to install themselves in staff posts. Kornilov had his staff (with Lukomsky as C. of S.); so had Alekseev; and so had Denikin at his Divisional H.Q.

The period of service for which V.A. recruits engaged was four months. Discipline was patchy, as was only natural after the experiences of the past ten months. There was too much drinking, and Rostov and Novocherkassk were full of bars, brothels and gaming-houses. More serious was the fact that the hurry of extemporization and the inevitably insufficient knowledge of the personalities involved had led to unsuitable appointments to posts of command; this in a force with officers serving in the ranks, with junior captains as battalion commanders, and colonels under them commanding platoons, led to extreme bitterness. There were jealousies and intrigues and all kinds of potential sources of trouble, as when the *junkers* refused to serve alongside university students because university students must be Socialists. It was a class army because its members, whether or not they had possessed money or position (and most of them had not), had been in some way the victims of the Revolution; and not the least important factor of its morale was hatred of revolutionaries, the reverse of that class hatred which the revolutionary parties had been so sedulously propagating. The Volunteer Army included some idealists, some careerists and not a few adventurers and thugs. Man for man it was a far more effective fighting force than any that the Bolsheviks could put in the field for the next six months.

(ix)

The Don Government continued to cling to the hope of peaceful coexistence. A statement of policy proclaimed freedom of the press, release of all political prisoners, control over the Volunteer Army and the removal from Don territory of counter-revolutionaries. A delegation was formed to negotiate with the advancing Bolsheviks. It was, however, still maintained that the Government would resist any attempt by *Sovnarkom* to enforce its will upon the Don. How far the Government could in fact resist was another matter. The Cossacks (or such of them as had not gone home) refused to go into action. Kaledin appealed for volunteer partisan detachments. The appeal deflected a number of potential volunteers for the Volunteer Army: Kaledin offered better pay and less discipline. But there was no machinery for the scrutiny or control of partisans, and while some bands fought well against the Reds, many others, once they had received their arms and their subsidies, went back to their *stanitsas* or took to banditry.

In mid-January the Volunteer Army was transferred to Rostov. By agreement with Kaledin the Army undertook the defence of the western sector. This, with the garrisoning of Rostov, was a serious commitment for so small a force in all the teething troubles of its hurried improvisation. But Kaledin further asked for detachments to stiffen his own forces and for the policing of Novocherkassk. By the end of January the Volunteer Army had not a single unit in reserve.

A secret report from a Bolshevik agent in the Don is quoted by Antonov-Ovseenko, the Red Commander-in-Chief: it claimed that the local Party members and their sympathizers could deal with the Cossacks with very little aid from outside, but they could do nothing against the *junkers*. In the event it took the Reds two months of (at times hard) fighting to overrun the area. They had very great numerical superiority. They had competent commanders in Antonov-Ovseenko and in Sablin and Sivers (respectively in charge of the advances on Novo-

cherkassk from the north and on Rostov from the west). They
had a large and active fifth column behind the enemy's lines.
What they lacked was a proper fighting force. The Soviet
invaders were made up of unbattleworthy units of the old
army, of local Red Guards and a few volunteers from the two
capitals. The men were undisciplined and without staying
power. There were refusals to obey orders and frequent
desertions. There was no organized supply system, and food
and fodder had to be requisitioned locally. This led to trouble
in the villages, where there was no proper liaison between the
military and the local civilian soviets, and offered scope for
chicanery and thieving. It was to be several months before
the Bolshevik Party was in a position to curb these evils.

On January 23rd at Kamenskoe, some forty miles north of
Rostov, a congress of Cossack representatives repudiated
Kaledin and formed a Military Revolutionary Committee
whose aim was to liberate the toiling Cossacks from the yoke
of the counter-revolutionists of the *Voisko* Government. The
Don appeared to be breaking up. As the Red offensive
developed the Volunteer Army units suffered heavy casualties
and became physically exhausted. The need for reinforcements
was paramount. A mission was sent south to recruit Caucasian
mountaineers, and in early February a Prince Devlet Girei
arrived in Rostov with an offer to produce 2,000 Cherkess in a
fortnight and 8,000 more within six to eight weeks if provided
with arms and an advance of two million roubles. It was an
unconvincing story, but so great was the need that Kornilov
was prepared to risk the money. The more cautious Alekseev
would only offer two hundred thousand and nothing more was
heard of the Cherkess. Alekseev appealed to the head of the
French Military Mission in Roumania: 'I selected the Don
region,' he wrote, 'as the place to form the Volunteer Army
because it seemed to be a territory well supplied with bread
and because it formed part of a rich and powerful union of the
South-East. It seemed that its powerful political organization
would easily manage to defend its independence against
Bolshevism and that with the aid of the Cossacks we might

succeed in forming a new and strong army to restore order in Russia and renew the front . . . In this I was mistaken . . . We could go to the Kuban, but the Kuban . . . Cossacks are also in a state of moral dissolution. A mere glance at the map will show that the Kuban territory cannot be used as a base for future operations . . .' The point of the letter was to urge the French to direct the Czechoslovak Legion, then in the Ukraine, to make its way to the Don. It is a sign of the isolation of the Volunteer Army leadership that so unrealistic a plea could have been sent. The French had other plans for the Czechs, and the Czechs themselves would never have agreed. In any case it was too late.

The best of the Don partisan leaders was killed in action and his force dispersed. The Volunteer Army was driven out of Taganrog; Bataisk, across the river from Rostov, was occupied by Sivers. There were reports of further Red formations moving up from the south. It appeared to Kornilov that the only alternative to being trapped in Rostov was to get his army away. He issued orders to prepare for evacuation, which brought a desperate appeal from Kaledin to remain: without the Volunteer Army there would be nothing left. A meeting was hurriedly summoned at Novocherkassk with the Don Coalition Government and the Cossack *Krug*. Kornilov made every effort to persuade Kaledin to collect such fighting men and supplies as were available and withdraw with the Volunteer Army. As, for Kaledin, to leave the Don would have been to desert his post, he refused. But by this time he had lost all hope of being able to make any further personal contribution to the cause; after addressing the assembled conference on February 11th he retired to his room and shot himself.

He may have felt that his dramatic death might arouse some of that spirit which while alive he had failed to inspire; and it did in fact bring about a flicker of the romantic Cossack tradition. There were brave words about determined resistance to the Bolshevik invaders. A new Ataman (Nazarov) was elected. A resolution was passed for the call to the colours of all Cossacks between the ages of seventeen and fifty-five. There was an appeal for volunteers which met with a warm response. A suggestion was made to appoint Kornilov as C.-in-C. of all the defence forces of the area. Kornilov for his part cancelled his arrangements for evacuation and appointed Lukomsky as liaison officer in Novocherkassk.

But in fact the position had not changed. What was required was an army at the front, not eager little crowds in the recruiting offices in Novocherkassk. Antonov-Ovseenko had recorded that news of Kaledin's suicide was interpreted (rightly) at Red Headquarters as a sign of the collapse of the Don régime. Red pressure was intensified. Kornilov had hurriedly to change his plans again and order immediate evacuation. On the night of February 21st–22nd the Volunteer Army moved out of Rostov, and the underground Revolutionary Military Committee took over. Two days later Sivers' advance guard arrived in the city.

(x)

The Volunteer Army in late February numbered less than three thousand combatants. At its peak, a month previously, there had been some five thousand. The wastage was due to casualties, to sickness and to the desertion of some of the married men, who refused to leave their wives and families in a town about to be occupied by the Reds. Those of the school-boys with relations in Rostov had been ordered to leave the Army and go home, but many of them disobeyed the order and came back to the ranks. As a fighting force the Volunteer Army was remarkable for the high proportion of boys in their teens and of middle-aged and elderly officers. Non-combatants numbered nearly a thousand; indeed, Lukomsky suggested that the fighting men were hardly enough to act as escort for the others. There were two hundred wounded, there were wives and dependants—a number of whom had set out in the freezing winter in their town clothes and thin shoes. There were a few civilian politicians, felt by some of the officers to be a useless encumbrance.

As they left Kornilov marched on foot. He was offered a horse, but declared he preferred to march. The haste of the evacuation led to all sorts of muddles over transport and supplies. Denikin, now Kornilov's second-in-command, was down with bronchitis and had to be carried in a cart; for the first few days when he recovered he had to wear mufti, his uniforms and baggage having been lost. Funds were very short. Kornilov had wished to take over and bring out all the cash and valuables in the Rostov branch of the State Bank, but Alekseev and Denikin were insistent that to do so might tarnish the good name of the Volunteer Army; so the valuables were transferred to Novocherkassk, soon to be taken over by the Bolsheviks. Such financial resources as there were were carried in a wooden box on a peasant cart along with Alekseev, now a very sick man and destined never fully to recover. On the eve of departure he had written to a friend: 'We are moving out into the steppe. We can return only by God's mercy. But we must light a torch so that there will be one gleam of light in the darkness enveloping Russia.'

The Volunteer Army, at that moment, had no base, little ammunition, no source of supply, no allies and no fixed objective. Antonov-Ovseenko had foreseen the evacuation of Rostov, and had issued orders for the interception and liquidation of the Army on the outskirts of the city. When he learned that owing to the incompetence of his detachments in the South the opportunity had been missed, he decided that after all no further action was necessary; the Volunteer Army would probably disintegrate in the winter steppe, and could in any case be annihilated as soon as convenient. He turned his attention to the southern Ukraine, and directed the bulk of his forces against Ekaterinoslav.

Meanwhile, the Red forces were steadily closing in on Novocherkassk. There were some there who still clung to the hope of a peaceful settlement. On February 23rd a committee of Cossacks addressed an appeal to Sablin; Kaledin was dead, they wrote, the non-democratic leaders had gone, so why should the Red offensive continue? Sablin replied curtly that the reason was that the Cossacks did not recognize the rule of the *Sovnarkom* of Lenin, Trotsky and their colleagues.

With the departure of the Volunteer Army the only anti-Bolshevik force left was the Don 'Army', consisting of some 1,500 dispirited Cossacks under a General Popov, who was preparing to evacuate. Lukomsky, as Kornilov's representative, urgently pressed the new Ataman to withdraw with them, but Nazarov maintained, just as Kaledin had done, that his duty was to remain in his capital. (He was shot by the Reds on their arrival in Novocherkassk on February 26th.) All that was left for Lukomsky was to do what could be done for the Volunteer Army wounded in hospitals in the town. Those who could walk were given money and told to fend for themselves. Those for whom no safe houses could be found were left in the hospitals and told to make themselves out as private soldiers.

Lukomsky left Novocherkassk on the morning of February 25th and made his way to the Volunteer Army column then at the Cossack *stanitsa* of Olginskaya. On the 26th they had a visit from Popov. Kornilov pressed him to bring his Cossacks and join forces with the Volunteer Army, but Popov refused: his men, he said, would not be willing to leave the area of their homes and he proposed to move further into the steppe, organize partisan warfare and await events. On Popov's departure, there was held a council of war to decide on future action. The generals by no means shared Kornilov's views on the desirability of the Kuban as an objective, or his optimism on the prospects of recruiting Cossacks *en route*. Alekseev played with the idea of dispersing the force altogether, its members to make their way individually or in small groups, in mufti, to some prearranged rendezvous in the Caucasus. Lukomsky maintained that a move to the Kuban would be pointless and dangerous, and pressed for a withdrawal into the steppe. A few hours later a second council of war was held to which Lukomsky was not invited and at which Kornilov imposed acceptance of a march on Ekaterinodar.[1] So began what came to be called

[1] Lukomsky was piqued at his treatment, and in consequence accepted another liaison mission to Ekaterinodar. *En route* he was arrested by the

'the icy campaign' across the frozen steppe. The little force suffered under serious handicaps. At the top there was continued friction between Kornilov and Alekseev; Romanovsky, now Chief of Staff, had to use all his tact and patience to keep the peace. There had been a hurried reorganization on leaving, and again the new appointments led to bitterness and jealousy. There were complaints at Markov's excessive severity. Six weeks of gruelling defeat had left their mark on the rank and file. Morale was patchy, with violent swings between exultation and near panic. Discipline, too, was patchy. In the villages and *stanitsas* there was all sorts of trouble with the inhabitants. 'War and Revolution,' Denikin noted, 'are a bad school for an army's moral education.' And again: 'The Volunteer Army was not composed solely of Puritans.' What money there was was in large denominations; when the men were paid a thousand-rouble note was handed to a group of eight or ten. This factor complicated the procurement of food and fodder. In any case, many of the villagers, both Cossack and *inogorodni*, did not want to sell, and those that did demanded extortionate prices. So recourse had to be made to requisitioning, with all the friction and difficulties that requisitioning entails.

At the end of February the anti-Bolshevik Government of the Kuban was still in precarious existence in Ekaterinodar, engaged in the attempt to work out 'the most democratic constitution in the world'. In the other towns the Bolsheviks and their Left S.R. allies were now in control of the Soviets, and Bolshevik influence was paramount among the railway workers in the junctions, marshalling yards and workshops along the main lines. Armoured trains were improvised and manned by picked crews, and these became the most battleworthy element of the motley Red forces. In general it was the policy of the Volunteer Army to avoid the towns and railways, and indeed not to expose themselves to unnecessary fighting.

Their reception in the countryside was mixed. In the southern Don certain *stanitsas* made a pathetic attempt to 'observe

Bolsheviks, came within an ace of being executed, and only after many adventures escaped to the German-occupied Ukraine.

neutrality'. As one Cossack put it: 'Kornilov comes and rouses us up, and then he goes away and the Bolsheviks come. What about my farm and my wife?' The Volunteer Army command was well aware that their passage would provoke reprisals. Further south, in the Stavropol province, feeling was generally pro-Bolshevik and local Soviets were in charge of the settlements. The Army crossed into the Kuban in mid-March and here their reception was more friendly. Cossacks came out to meet them with bread and salt, and an appreciable number volunteered for service. These recruits added to the problems of discipline, as they systematically pillaged all *inogorodni* villages along their line of march.

(xi)

The first serious engagement came soon after they entered Stavropol province; the Volunteer Army captured a number of prisoners including some former officers. These were tried by court martial. Their pleas in defence varied: 'I did not give any orders to fire.' 'I served because I was forced to do so.' 'They are watching my family.' These pleas were accepted and the officers permitted to join the Volunteer Army. Thereafter fighting was almost continuous, and in one pitched battle the Volunteer Army lost 400 men in killed and wounded. But victory brought with it considerable booty, and stores were replenished.

A few days later came news that the Filimonov Government and its little army under Pokrovsky had been forced out of Ekaterinodar by the Red invaders from Novorossisk. The Kuban population, as Filimonov put it, 'were not in a position to defend their elected representatives.' At the end of March the Kuban leaders arrived at the Volunteer Army headquarters, and there were prolonged negotiations punctuated by the sound of gun-fire. Kornilov demanded complete integration of the Kuban forces under his sole command; Filimonov was jealous of any threat to Kuban independence and alarmed at the Great

Russian views of the Volunteer Army generals. In the end a compromise was reached. Kornilov assumed, for the time being, command of all troops, and the Kuban Government remained in being, undertaking to afford full co-operation in all military matters. The combined force then turned west for the climax of the whole campaign, the assault on Ekaterinodar. But here the Army came up against stiffer resistance than they had so far encountered. Three days' hard fighting made no appreciable impression on the defences, and then came tragedy: Kornilov was killed by a chance shell.

Denikin assumed command and called a council of war with Alekseev, Romanovsky and Filimonov. All agreed that the only course was to disengage and move north and north-east into the open steppe again, along a route parallel to and some fifty miles west of that of their original advance. Morale had been badly shaken; it was urgently essential to reach some quiet area where the troops could rest and reorganize. The need was such that the hard decision had to be taken to leave stretcher-cases behind with a doctor and nurses to look after them. The force had barely disengaged when it was attacked while crossing the main Black Sea railway near Medvedovskaya, thirty miles north-east of Ekaterinodar. There were critical moments. Denikin records that for the first time in three wars he saw panic. A group of White generals were nearly overrun by a Red armoured train: Markov shouted at the crew of the locomotive to stop firing at their own side and tossed a hand-grenade into the tender. V.A. field guns opened up on the train at point-blank range and the tide of battle turned. Medvedovskaya station was captured with a large haul of shells and S.A.A., and morale began to recover. But it was more than ever urgent to get the column clear of the area of the main railway lines. To increase mobility more baggage was jettisoned and it was decided, after some heart-searching, to leave behind all seriously wounded. The retreat continued, with only minor brushes with the enemy. By April 23rd the column was well clear of the railway area, having covered 220 versts in nine days. Men and horses were physically exhausted but morale was now buoyant.

As they proceeded further their reception in the *stanitsas* became more friendly, Bolshevik counter-measures weaker, reports increasingly reassuring. 'Light was dawning in the north.' It appeared that Don Cossack detachments were in the field, actively fighting the Reds, and information reaching Denikin seemed to show that mere partisan action was about to develop into civil war. When the Volunteer Army came to a halt in mid-May at Egorlytskaya some thirty-five miles south of Novocherkassk, they were in a Don province where Bolshevik power had been substantially broken. The Army's expedition had lasted eighty days, on forty-four of which they had been fighting the enemy. They had covered a total of 1,050 versts. Casualties had been 400 killed and 1,500 wounded. Thanks to the reinforcements from the Kuban, their net combatant strength had increased by one thousand. They had originally left the Don with some six to seven hundred shells in all, and with 150 to 200 rounds of S.A.A. per man. They returned with exactly the same provision.

(xii)

As we have seen, the Volunteer Army left Rostov on the night of February 21st–22nd. The Bolshevik Revolutionary Committee assumed control and sent a delegation to Sivers' headquarters at Bataisk. Sivers, however, feared a trap, and his troops did not come in for a couple of days; meanwhile the *Revkom* (Revolutionary Committee) appointed commissars and began to set up an administration. However, there soon arrived a certain Voitsekhovsky, appointed by Antonov-Ovseenko, as plenipotentiary Military Commissar of the Don province, and also representatives of the Cossack Military Revolutionary Committee, set up at Kamenskoe a month before. There were thus three separate authorities disputing the control of the city. Furthermore, in their hasty evacuation the Volunteer Army had left large stocks of arms and ammunition intact and unguarded, and for forty-eight hours all could help themselves who wished;

so that there came into being a variety of armed bands—anarchists, revolutionary sailors or merely thugs—who acknowledged no authority whatever. Much of the history of Rostov for the next two months is taken up with the repeated, drastic and quite ineffective efforts of the Bolshevik military and civilian organs to establish some relative security for life and for communal property. After two months of Soviet rule an order had to be issued forbidding Red Guards to go into the town unarmed. About the same time an English governess, stranded in Rostov, came to believe and continued to believe for the rest of her stay that the Bolsheviks had withdrawn altogether, and that the Anarchists had taken over.

During March, German and Austro-Hungarian troops were moving steadily eastward, against futile opposition, to complete their occupation of the Ukraine. On March 23rd the Rostov Military Revolutionary Committee proclaimed the Don to be the Don Soviet Socialist Republic, independent of, though closely associated with, the Russian Soviet Socialist Republic, one motive being the wish to deny to the Germans any pretext for entering the Don. For the moment the invaders were still some distance away; a more pressing embarrassment was the infiltration of defeated and demoralized Red Guards and partisans from the Ukraine. The Don Soviet Republic established a line of defence along the Ukrainian border and ordered, quite ineffectively, that the Ukrainian bands were to be disarmed on arrival. Before long, in the words of a Soviet historian, 'the whole *oblast* became a variegated military camp. In the towns there were dozens of different Red detachments, in most cases disintegrating, taking to banditry, with high demands for their food and lodging and refusing under various pretexts to go to the front. There was an increase in looting, pillage, attacks on civilians and thefts. There was a diversity of authority—one authority quarrelling with and even arresting another.' In the villages and *stanitsas* the Bolsheviks were impotent. They had no cadres and no security organs. 'In a number of places the inhabitants unobtrusively organized themselves, and counter-revolutionary officers endeavoured to take control of this tendency for their own ends. . . . The disorganization of the young administration . . . anarchist *putsches* . . . declassed elements rising under cover of the banner of the soviets . . . facilitated the almost legal activities of the counter-revolution.'

The air, inevitably, was thick with rumours in which the Germans figured largely. The Germans intended to remove everything that could be moved to Germany; the Bolsheviks were acting as instruments of the Germans. Confusion was the greater because no one, not even the top local Bolsheviks, knew what was the legal position of the Don Soviet Socialist Republic in the light of the Treaty of Brest-Litovsk. Indeed, the Treaty itself was a matter of controversy—at the April Congress of Soviets of the Don Republic over 40 per cent of the delegates were Left Socialist-Revolutionaries who did not recognize that treaty. At that Congress the Bolsheviks voted for an S.R. resolution calling for active military resistance to the Germans, presumably in the hope of scotching stories of a Bolshevik-German alliance. But the move was a mistaken one. Alarm at the prospect of having to fight the formidable German Army was far more potent than indignation over Bolshevik-German collaboration, and in many villages the resolution caused panic. A scheme for the mobilization of the 1914–17 classes against the 'irruption of the bandit-German hordes' had to be dropped. In Rostov an armed band, allegedly representing 'the Executive Committee of the Soviets of Workers, Peasants and Soldiers' Deputies of the Roumanian Front, the Black Sea Fleet and Odessa' started raiding public offices, confiscating the funds and arresting the Don Republic officials in charge. The workers became sick and tired of the continuing chaos, and began to listen to the Mensheviks. In late April the Bolsheviks passed a resolution to establish a Commune, confiscate all property, ration all foodstuffs and set the bourgeoisie to dig trenches. But publication was held up by obstruction in the office of their official newspaper.

(xiii)

Those officers working against the Bolsheviks in the countryside were mostly Cossack officers who, on the fall of Novocherkassk, had gone back to their *stanitsas* instead of following General Popov into the steppe. Two of them, Denisov and Mamontov, were later to become prominent in the Civil War, and Denisov has left a lively, if one-sided, account of his early experiences. Arms were available, and in early April partisan bands began to operate. On April 14th the Cossack bands staged a large-scale raid on Novocherkassk and held the town for three days until pushed out again by a numerically superior Red force sent up from Rostov. The Reds, however, had neither the will nor the means to follow up and destroy the retreating Cossacks, and the latter reassembled in the Zaplava area, some twenty miles east of Novocherkassk.

The experience taught Polyakov, the titular commander, and Denisov, his Chief of Staff, that better organization was essential, and they set to work to build up a new Army of the Don. Three thousand Cossacks had survived the raid. Other groups heard what was happening and joined up with them. There were also some five hundred former officers who had taken the opportunity to leave Novocherkassk with the retreating Cossacks. These last required firm and drastic screening; it was better, Denisov noted, 'to punish ten innocent than to let one guilty free.' In any case the officer problem was acute; a number were willing to serve in the ranks, but those both fit and willing to take posts of command were very few indeed. Denisov set himself to restore the old-time discipline and to make officers and Cossacks 'forget the past'. A weak Red attack was beaten off without difficulty and several Bolshevik agitators, who had infiltrated into the area, were apprehended and hanged. By late April numbers had reached five thousand infantry and one thousand cavalry. Equipment was woefully inadequate. There were thirty machine-guns, but of the six field guns two were unusable and two more lacked carriages

66

and harness. There were four motor bicycles, two cars and one broken-down lorry. There were two telegraph sets and two miles of wire, but all six telephones were unusable. There were three rounds of S.A.A. per rifle and five shells per gun. It was hoped that General Popov's force would bring adequate supplies with them when they returned from the steppe.

Popov made contact on April 25th, and as *Pokhodni* (i.e., campaigning) Ataman assumed overall command of all anti-Bolshevik Cossacks. Polyakov dropped out of the picture, and the period up to the final recovery of Novocherkassk was marked by a series of quarrels between Denisov and Popov. Denisov had disapproved of the withdrawal to the safety of the steppe while he, Denisov, had stayed behind to rally the *stanitsas*. Popov and his staff on their return were comfortably housed in a river steamer, and Denisov maliciously records the nickname of '*Parokhodni*' (i.e., steamboat) Ataman. Denisov disapproved of Popov's reorganization of the forces into a Northern Group, a Southern Group and a Trans-Don Group, and as commander of the Southern Group bitterly resented the removal of one-third of his force to take part in what he regarded as a senseless and costly offensive in the north. He demanded an immediate advance on Novocherkassk. On May 1st the Southern Group were attacked by the Reds in force; the Reds were routed, abandoning large stocks of ammunition and stores. The fact that the Southern Group became thus independent in the matter of supplies strengthened Denisov's hand, and after sharp exchanges with the reluctant Popov the assault on Novocherkassk was agreed.

Meanwhile, on May 1st the Germans occupied Taganrog. The Rostov *TsIK* (Executive Committee) sent a delegation to negotiate with the German commander, and in particular to ask why the Germans were invading the Don Republic. The delegation was informed that the Ukrainian Government had requested German help in establishing the frontiers of the Ukraine. The German commander did not know how these frontiers were ultimately to be defined. His instructions

67

included the occupation of Rostov, but this was not a matter of immediate urgency.

The Rostov Bolsheviks realized their weakness, and preparations were made for the evacuation of their various headquarters and key personnel; it was also planned to remove plant from the factories, but this the workmen refused to allow. On May 4th fighting broke out to the north-west of the town. Believing the Germans were attacking, *TsIK* hurriedly evacuated, and the Red Guards fell back in disorder. Then it transpired that it was not the Germans but a small force of Russian Whites under a Colonel Drozdovsky. The Reds were rallied, two armoured trains were brought up, and the Whites repulsed. Drozdovsky marched north, ran into the German advance guard, turned east and reached the outskirts of Novocherkassk on May 6th. His arrival coincided with a critical phase in the assault by Denisov's Cossacks, and his intervention was decisive. The Reds were driven out and Novocherkassk once more became the capital of the anti-Bolshevik Don Cossacks. On May 8th the Germans occupied Rostov without opposition. About the same time a directive from Moscow laid down that all hostilities against the Germans must cease. The local Red general staff was dissolved and the top Soviet military and civilian officials withdrew to Tsaritsyn.

(xiv)

The march of Drozdovsky's little army is an interesting episode in itself. At the turn of the year General Shcherbachev, in command of the disintegrating Russian forces along the Roumanian frontier, had refused a request from Alekseev that unemployed officers should be sent to the Don. He did, however, give permission for the formation of volunteer detachments to remain in the area. A few officers started to recruit, with rallies and speeches in defence of the Constituent Assembly. Response was poor, but Colonel Drozdovsky managed to collect a force of some nine hundred at Jassy, and General Belozor a slightly smaller one at Kishinev. Following Brest-Litovsk and the subsequent Roumanian peace treaty the Roumanians demanded the disarmament of these detachments. Shcherbachev issued the necessary orders and the Kishinev group was disbanded. But Drozdovsky announced his intention of taking his force to the Don. There were difficulties with the Roumanians, but departure was eventually agreed. The detachment crossed the Dniester, reached the Dnieper on April 10th and six days later were in the neighbourhood of Melitpol. They moved quickly, the infantry being carried in peasant carts; sometimes they covered as much as forty miles in twenty-four hours. At an early stage they were joined by a few officers from Kishinev, which brought the total strength up to 667 officers, 370 soldiers, 14 doctors, chaplains and military clerks, and 12 nursing sisters. From time to time they were attacked by Red Guards and Red partisans (sometimes by Hetmanite bands) but beat off their assailants without difficulty. As they neared the Don some peasants suspected they were landlords come to take away the peasants' land. But, as Drozdovsky noted, 'in general the masses are friendly; they ask for security, for the establishment of order.' When the column reached a village it was felt: 'At least we shall be at peace if only for one day.' The villagers would apprehend local Bolshevik bosses against whom they had grievances and bring them to Drozdovsky's headquarters for trial. Retribution was drastic. Drozdovsky noted: 'With these wild, depraved hooligans there is but one law which is still respected: "an eye for an eye". And I shall add: "two eyes for an eye, all teeth for one tooth".' And again: 'Gruesome as are our cruel punishments, gruesome is this joy, this exhilaration with murder that is familiar to some of our volunteers.'

Meanwhile German and Austro-Hungarian advance guards were pushing forward across the southern Ukraine. Feeling in the detachment towards them was mixed. On the one hand they were Russia's enemies; on the other they were chasing the Bolsheviks, and in any case it would be futile to go into action against them. And the Germans were perfectly willing to tolerate Drozdovsky as long as he did nothing to impede their operations; indeed it is probable that many German professional officers felt sympathy for the plight of their Russian opposite numbers. Drozdovsky comments: 'What odd relations there exist between us and the Germans. We behave like acknowledged allies, collaborate, treat each other in a severely correct manner, and in all cases of clashes between ourselves and the Ukrainians (i.e., the Skoropadsky troops) they always take our side. At the same time one German officer remarked, "Those who do not recognize our peace are our enemies." Probably the Germans do not understand our forced alliance against the Bolsheviks, do not guess at our hidden aims or else consider their realization impossible. We respond with meticulous civility. . . . The Germans are our enemies, we hate them but we have some respect for them. For the Ukrainians we have nothing but contempt as for renegades and demoralized bandits.'

News from other areas took long to reach the Drozdovsky force, and when it came it was often uncertain. It was not until mid-April that they learned that the Don province was under Bolshevik occupation. Kornilov was reported fighting in the Caucasus; then came the story of his death. Some days later, when the force was nearing Berdyansk, they heard that the Don Cossacks were rising and that the Volunteer Army was still in being. At the turn of the month the force passed well north of Taganrog (to avoid the Germans) and Drozdovsky took the bold decision to advance on Rostov. He realized the risk, with his inadequate strength, but he wished to forestall the Germans. As we have seen, his force was driven back, but two days later played a decisive part in the capture of Novocherkassk.

(xv)

In mid-May, 1918, the Germans were in Rostov. In Novocherkassk a Cossack assembly was in process of electing General Krasnov as Ataman to head a Right-wing Government; and the Volunteer Army, back from the south, was resting and refitting in the neighbouring steppe. Moscow had called off the war against the Germans. Some sporadic fighting still continued—there were a few stalwarts who fanatically refused to make peace with counter-revolution (an attack was even launched against Taganrog), but more often it was a case of Cossacks paying off old scores against the Reds. South of the Don frontier Soviet authority was acknowledged as far as the main Caucasus range. In Transcaucasia German and Turkish troops were advancing eastwards, and before the end of the month Georgia had proclaimed her independence and concluded an agreement with the Germans.

All those concerned with Russian affairs in the early summer of 1918 were demanding the establishment of order, but the Germans were the only party to use the term without social or ideological implications. Order was desirable for the purpose of obtaining the maximum amount of grain and other supplies with the minimum commitment of German armed force; and the German attitude is well illustrated in the directive on agrarian affairs issued by General Eichhorn, C.-in-C. at Kiev, on April 6th: The harvest belongs to those who have cultivated the land, and will be bought, for cash, at fixed rates by the German authorities; peasants must not acquire more land than they can cultivate; if any peasants have taken more land than they can sow, then the landlords must arrange for it to be sown and the peasant must not interfere.

On May 15th, soon after the German occupation of Rostov, Foreign Minister von Kühlmann suggested at a top-level meeting of German authorities in Spa that it should be announced once and for all that German armed action in Russia had come to an end. The General Staff representative agreed that the advance had been completed and that the demarcation line was being drawn; Ludendorff, however, added that there were still frequent attacks on German units by bands of Bolshevik and other Russian troops, and that 'fighting therefore kept breaking out again even against our wish'.

As the summer wore on, to the original German objectives of grain supplies and release of military man-power there was added a third: reinsurance against a possible Bolshevik collapse. In mid-May Mirbach reported from Moscow on a conversation with Lenin, in which the latter had admitted the many serious difficulties with which his régime was faced, and had said he was 'aiming at a speedy clarification of matters in the North and in the South.' The Kaiser's marginal comment on the last three words was: 'The Cossack Army will settle that soon.' In late May the revolt of the Czechoslovak Legion and the subsequent formation of local anti-Bolshevik and anti-German governments in the East were matters of serious concern. In early June a dispatch to Berlin from the embassy in Moscow discussed 'the possibility of the resurrection of a reasonably ordered bourgeois Russia with the help of the Entente'. It was therefore time to consider whether it were desirable to 'spin a thread reaching to Orenburg and Siberia over General Krasnov's head, to hold cavalry directed at Moscow but concealed, to prepare for a government with which we could agree, dipping as deep as possible into the ranks of the Cadets.' Within the next few days senior German officials were writing: 'As long as the Bolshevik Government remains in power we shall have to apply every available means to keep the Bolsheviks from orienting themselves in any other direction.' But 'we should at the same time entertain relations with other movements in Russia in order not to find ourselves suddenly high and dry . . . We have to acquire contacts with Right-wing monarchist groups.'

It is outside the scope of this book to go into the question of German reinsurance against a Bolshevik collapse or the factors making for the possibility of an abrupt switch in German policy towards the Bolsheviks. But in the large area between the Don, the Caucasus, the Black Sea and the Caspian, developments during the summer of 1918 did not point to the likelihood of permanent Soviet rule. It is true that, at any rate at first, Red troops under arms were far more numerous than any White force within reach of them. A step towards administrative consolidation was made with the establishment of the united Kuban-Black Sea Socialist Soviet Republic on May 18th. In Avtonomov and Sorokin (who had successfully defended

Ekaterinodar against Kornilov) the Reds had two competent military commanders. The direct line to Soviet Russia via Rostov and Novocherkassk was, of course, cut, but the railway via Tikhoretskaya to Tsaritsyn remained open for some weeks. The majority feeling in the towns, in the *inogorodni* villages and in some of the *stanitsas* was still, if not pro-Bolshevik, at least against the counter-revolution. And yet, in the late summer, the Volunteer Army's second campaign was to subdue the whole area.

In late May, when news reached Moscow of the loss of Novocherkassk, a proclamation signed by Lenin, Trotsky, Chicherin and Stalin declared that traitors had betrayed the Don to foreign landlords and capitalists: the toiling Cossacks should therefore rise and show that they remained as before in fraternal union with the workers and peasants of Russia. In the hope of appealing to Cossack loyalties *Sovnarkom* issued an order grouping all Cossack areas under a special Soviet. This, of course, was merely so much paper. On the spot was the confusion and dissension we have noted in Rostov during March and April. There was the same multiplicity of authorities. There were quarrels between the military and civil powers: Avtonomov staged a mutiny against the Ekaterinodar *TsIK* in May, and, in the autumn, there was to be the same trouble with Sorokin in Pyatigorsk and Stavropol. Bolshevik commissars resigned because local commanders refused to listen to them. There were quarrels between Bolsheviks and Left S.R.s, between *inogorodni* and Red Cossacks; within Party committees there were clashes between 'Left Bolsheviks' and 'Moderate Bolsheviks'. Above all, there was the exasperation and resistance provoked by the bands of Red partisans, Ukrainians and (especially) Black Sea sailors who swarmed over the countryside looting, raping, killing and conducting 'devils' weddings'. At Ekaterinodar the printers refused to print the official newspaper; a Bolshevik commissar in Armavir arrested and executed a group of Georgian Party activists on their way to Party work in Tiflis.

In the subsequent post-mortem Trotsky held that 'never

perhaps has *partizanshchina* cost the workers and peasants so dearly as in the North Caucasus. Thus the main cause of our failures in the South was not so much the organizational defects of the Army of the Southern Front as the treacherous—in every sense of the word—role of *partizanshchina*.' Lenin complained of lack of resoluteness: the local Party leadership 'was not iron but jelly (*kisel*).' Borisenko, the historian of the early Soviet régimes in the South-East, admits the weakness of the leadership, the shortcomings of *partizanshchina* and the troubles caused by 'petty bourgeois revolutionaries' (i.e., the Left S.R.s). But he submits that the reason why 'the proletarian revolution in the North Caucasus was unable to bring to its final ultimate conclusion the bourgeois-democratic revolution' was not so much any 'regroupment of class forces' in the spring and summer of 1918; it was because the Brest-Litovsk Treaty had 'cut off Central Russia from close contact with the North Caucasus and at the same time had provided a strong base for the counter-revolution.' In other words, the main cause of the Bolsheviks' defeat in the area was the impact of the German Army to their north and west.

(xvi)

On May 11th there assembled in Novocherkassk a hastily-convened Cossack council of 130 delegates from those parts of the province—less than half of the whole—where the Reds had been ejected. The *Krug Spaseniya Dona* (the Council of the Salvation of the Don) was admittedly provisional: its task was to appoint a régime to complete the liberation of the province and take charge until such time as a full *Krug* could be elected. The 130 delegates were all Cossacks, and the absence of articulate intellectuals earned it the nickname of 'the dumb *Krug*'. Their first measures were to send a mission to Rostov to establish contact with the Germans, and to take a decision that the Don military forces should not be subordinated to Denikin and the Volunteer Army Staff. On May 14th, General Krasnov, the senior Don Cossack officer present, addressed the Council. He took the line that Russia had collapsed but the Don was in being. Until such time as Russia was re-established the Don must assume complete control of its own affairs and avoid involvement in Great Russian politics. To suggest that the Cossacks should start a war with the Germans was nonsense: as and when opportunity occurred the German withdrawal must be negotiated peacefully. Meanwhile one must come to some working arrangement with the Hetmanite Ukraine and the Volunteer Army. On May 16th the *Krug* proceeded to elect a new Ataman; Krasnov was elected by 107 votes in favour, 13 against and 10 abstentions. However, he refused to accept office unless and until the *Krug* confirmed a series of basic laws annulling all measures and regulations adopted since February, 1917, and endowing the Ataman with dictatorial powers. He was asked if he would reconsider such drastic conditions, and replied he was open to persuasion on two points—on the Don National Flag (provided it was not red and had no star of Israel or Masonic symbol), and on the Don National Anthem (provided it was not the *Internationale*). The *Krug* capitulated and on May 18th Krasnov assumed charge.

It is admitted by Denikin, who throughout disapproved of the new Ataman's policy, that the very existence of the Don régime depended on some measure of German goodwill. The original delegation sent by the *Krug* to Rostov had not got very far. The German Chief of Staff had explained that he was not concerned with politics. His orders had been to take Rostov so as to protect the Ukraine from the Bolsheviks. He had as yet no instructions to occupy Novocherkassk. He was not prepared to discuss whether or not Rostov was part of the Don: frontier questions would have to be negotiated with the Ukrainian Government in Kiev. During the interview he inquired as to the status of the Don, and was informed that the Don was part of Russia but its inhabitants did not recognize the Soviet Government. The discussion was not unfriendly, and touched, albeit inconclusively, on the possibility of German-Cossack co-operation against bands of Red Guards.

Krasnov proceeded to transfer the negotiations to a higher level. On the day of his accession he sent off a personal letter to the German Kaiser asking for recognition of the independent Don Republic, and enclosing a copy of the basic laws to make clear the nature of his régime. He emphasized that the Don was not at war with Germany, requested German help in getting arms, and suggested trade exchanges via the Ukraine. He also addressed a letter to Hetman Skoropadsky and sent off a suitable mission to act as his representatives in Kiev. The letter to the Kaiser was routed via the German High Command, with a copy for General Eichhorn. Officers of Eichhorn's staff arrived in Novocherkassk on May 21st, and a provisional agreement was quickly reached. The Germans did not plan any further advance; Taganrog and Rostov were left over for future negotiation; German troops in other parts of the Don territory who had come in at the request of local Cossacks for help against the Reds would remain till order was restored; no German mission would be stationed in Novocherkassk. In mid-June a further emissary arrived from Eichhorn to confirm German recognition of the Don régime. Subsequent negotiations brought agreement on the rate of exchange (one German mark to be the equivalent of 75 kopeks) and the terms of the barter of arms against grain (one rifle and thirty cartridges to be paid for by one pood of wheat). In the event of joint operations against the Bolsheviks all booty captured was to be divided equally between the two armies.

In late May came the Czech Legion's revolt at Chelyabinsk. By early June the movement had spread to the Volga and the newly formed People's Government at Samara was proclaiming its hostility to both Germans and Bolsheviks. Accurate news took time to reach the outside world, and the air was thick with rumour. In mid-June a story was current that the Czechs had taken Saratov, Tsaritsyn and Astrakhan and were establishing a new Eastern front. Krasnov was required by the Germans to clarify his attitude. He replied that he did not believe the story: his own advanced units were within forty miles of Tsaritsyn and would have had information of any Czech approach. But should there come to be hostilities between Czechs and Germans the Don would remain neutral and no Czech troops would be allowed to enter Don territory. The Germans asked for an assurance in writing, which Krasnov, overriding the misgivings of some of his supporters, eventually gave them. As it happened the Czech-Samara offensive was directed northwards, and the complications that would have arisen from an anti-Bolshevik and anti-German drive along the lower Volga never materialized. Throughout the summer Krasnov continued to consolidate his régime, his success, as he rightly maintains, being due to his good relations with Kiev and with the German command, and to the efficient working, under German control, of the railways linking the Don with the west.

(xvii)

When Krasnov assumed office in mid-May the Don was in a state of chaos. A number of settlements were still in Bolshevik hands. Sporadic fighting was continuing. Novocherkassk had no public services and no police. The new Ataman was determined not to follow in the footsteps of Kaledin and Nazarov. Liberalism, as he saw it, had been tried and had disastrously failed; it was time to turn to discipline and strong government. At heart a monarchist, Krasnov understood that monarchy was not a cause for which the Cossacks were prepared to fight, and so, as counter to the emotional appeal of the Revolution, he deliberately called upon the old traditional Cossack spirit of the *Vsevelikoe Voisko Donskoe*. Nationalism, chauvinism even, he notes in his memoirs, is the antidote to Bolshevism; it had been the decline of patriotic fervour that had opened the way to class hatred in Russia. Progressive intellectuals who thought otherwise had no place in the Don. As for the *inogorodni*, they must relearn how to adapt their lives to Cossack hegemony.

Once he had reached a working arrangement with the Germans, Krasnov's main concern was the Don Army; indeed, 57 per cent of his Government's budget was devoted to military purposes. At the time of the capture of Novocherkassk the only regular units were six infantry and two cavalry regiments. Apart from these there were merely volunteer detachments from individual *stanitsas*. Officers, for the most part, were members of the *stanitsas*. Numbers varied from band to band and also from day to day, as volunteers came and went. Few *frontovniks* volunteered, so the fighting men were mostly middle-aged or youths. Uniform was motley; the men wore what they had, and sewed a white strip on their caps to distinguish them from the Reds. Most detachments had a machine-gun or two, and some larger ones a field gun, but arms, and especially ammunition, were short. Transport and supply were primitive. As a rule operations took place in the neighbourhood of the *stanitsa*, and in the evenings, when the firing died down, the men's families would come up to the line and bring them food. After an engagement any Red prisoners taken were tried by an improvised court martial, and if found to be Cossacks were usually executed. The problem for Krasnov and Denisov (now appointed Army Commander) was to 'introduce order without impairing the popular spirit'.

By the end of May the local detachments had been organized into fourteen groups, all under the direct command of the Ataman. A fortnight later they had been amalgamated into six groups, and direct telephone or telegraph communications had been established with all the local headquarters. There were certain instances in June of Cossacks refusing to serve away from their home *stanitsas*, or refusing to allow stores and supplies to be transferred to other areas. These were dealt with sternly and the trouble was scotched. Little by little the old-time discipline was restored. A partial mobilization was successfully carried through. Volunteer groups were integrated into regiments. Intensive training schools were started for officers. Arrangements for supplies and arms began to work satisfactorily. By late summer the Don Field Army amounted to 40,000 combatants, with artillery, tele-communications, a few planes, armoured trains and a river flotilla. A further 20,000 men were under training. Krasnov did not over-estimate the willingness of his Cossacks to fight at a distance from their homes. At most he envisaged a force of 30,000 men to co-operate in any drive on Moscow that Denikin might ultimately organize: the main task of the Don Army was to garrison and defend the Don.

In his second letter to Kaiser Wilhelm, dated July 11th, 1918, Krasnov announced that he had entered into a close alliance with the Astrakhan and Kuban Cossack *Voiskos*, and proposed to organize an independent Federal State in south-eastern Russia. This state was to observe neutrality in the World War, and would welcome German recognition and German aid in the rounding off of its northern frontier by the capture of Voronezh and Tsaritsyn. A draft constitution for the new Dono-Caucasian Federation had already been prepared.

This had long been a pet scheme of Krasnov's, but prospects of fruition were never as rosy as the letter to the Kaiser would imply. Talks and meetings had started in Novocherkassk in late May and continued intermittently throughout the summer. They were attended on occasion by members of the Kuban Government (still with Denikin's headquarters) and by self-appointed representatives from a number of areas and groups from the Ukraine to Astrakhan and the Caucasus. Most of them were refugees, and the talks were coloured by the un-realities and irresponsibilities of refugee politics. Krasnov could point to the apparent solidarity of his achievement in the Don. Against him was the idea of an undivided Russia, so strongly held by Denikin. Against him too were the endemic jealousies of the parties concerned, the opposition to the reactionary nature of the Don régime, and the lurking suspicion that the Western Allies might, after all, win the war, in which case schemes based on German support would be bound to collapse. Krasnov inveighed against the folly of building hopes on the West. The Allies, he maintained, had bled Russia white for their own ends and could offer nothing but empty promises. At one moment Filimonov, the Kuban Ataman, was almost converted to Krasnov's view. But Denikin, then preparing for his second Kuban expedition, informed him flatly that he had no intention of freeing the Kuban in order to make it a German satellite. If Filimonov persisted he would abandon the idea of capturing Ekaterinodar and instead take the Volunteer Army north against Tsaritsyn. Krasnov was well aware that Denikin was against him. In his work in the Don, he notes, he had to reckon with four different sets of opponents: intellectuals and politicians (for whom he had no jobs to offer), foreign powers (whether German or Western), Denikin and the Bolsheviks. The last were the least dangerous as they were open enemies.

(xviii)

At the time of the election of Krasnov as Ataman the Volunteer Army, as we have seen, was taking up quarters to rest and refit a few miles south-east of Novocherkassk. Krasnov paid a visit to Denikin's headquarters on May 28th. The conversations were not cordial. Denikin began by complaining that his troops sent to co-operate with Don Cossacks against the Reds at Bataisk found themselves fighting side by side with German units; he insisted there should be no contact whatever between Germans and the Volunteer Army. Krasnov replied it was now too late to change his dispositions. At one stage he truculently reminded Denikin that he was no longer, as when they had last met, a mere brigade commander: he was leader of a state with five million inhabitants. Denikin demanded a single command. Krasnov said that depended on the plan of campaign: if the V.A. would attack Tsaritsyn he would place any Cossacks available for that operation under Denikin's command. He maintained that now, when the troops were still flushed with victory, was the moment for an offensive, and that a move to the North would give the V.A. a firm Russian base, out of reach of Kuban intrigues and politics. Denikin objected that to go north would involve him with the Germans. Krasnov guaranteed that the Germans would not move east of the present demarcation. Denikin, however, supported by Alekseev, categorically refused to go north. He was committed to the liberation of Ekaterinodar. His Kuban recruits would not fight away from their homes. In any case the V.A. were exhausted by their hard campaign, and needed at least a month to rest and refit. In the end a provisional agreement was reached as between two allies against the Bolsheviks. Denikin should, in due course, undertake his Kuban expedition; once Ekaterinodar had been liberated a joint offensive against Tsaritsyn could be reconsidered. For the moment the question of unified command could be shelved. The V.A. should be considered as responsible for the defence of the southern frontiers of the Don, and as such accorded arms and money (a first instalment of six million roubles was mentioned) by the Don Government. Their wounded should be allotted hospitals and medical care in Novocherkassk.

Meanwhile the Volunteer Army was presenting Denikin and Alekseev with a number of problems. When the troops had recovered from their exhaustion they became restless. The volunteers had enrolled for four months and for many of them that period had expired. A number had wives and families in Rostov and Novocherkassk, and it was essential to grant leave (Denikin was gratified at the high proportion that came back again when leave had expired). The old bickering and jealousy broke out again among the officers. Demands were voiced for a clear statement of what they were fighting for. Denikin and Alekseev drew up a new directive. It laid down that the task of the V.A. was to build up a disciplined army (animated by the spirit of an undivided Russia), to liquidate the Bolsheviks and establish an ordered legal state, to defer consideration of forms of government until after liberation, to favour no political party, to work with all who 'believed in Russia' and finally to entertain no relations whatever with the Germans. The directive was considered in the Army to be too vague, too neutral, too apt to leave the door open for demagogy. Denikin and Alekseev called and addressed a meeting of all officers down to and including platoon commanders in the attempt to restore harmony and morale.

Occasional couriers from the anti-Bolshevik underground in Moscow could now once more make their way to the Army's headquarters. Their reports on the position in Soviet Russia were conflicting, as were their suggestions for future action. The Right Centre urged agreement with the Germans and a drive on Voronezh and Moscow; the National Centre and apparently the French Military Mission wanted the establishment of a new front along the Volga. Savinkov was pushing ahead with his League for the Defence of the Fatherland and Freedom without regard for anybody. There seemed no prospect of unity or coherence among the politicians and social activists. Denikin and Alekseev agreed they should, as far as possible, keep the Volunteer Army outside politics, and they refused to entertain a proposal from Rodzianko to create a Council of the available members of all four Dumas.

There was the chronic question of arms and finance, a serious handicap in the inevitable competition with the Don for volunteers. Drozdovsky, who elected to join the V.A., brought with him some reserves of ammunition. Raids were organized against Bolshevik centres to the south and these brought in some supplies, some Cossack volunteers, and even an armoured train, whose former name of *Death to the Cadets and the Bourgeois* was changed to *General Kornilov*. But this was not nearly enough. With regard to funds, the V.A. was now costing a million roubles a week, and in the month from mid-May to mid-June Alekseev's total receipts from private sources amounted to 55,000 roubles. It was a fact that, in the last resort, the V.A. was entirely dependent on the Don Government and thus, indirectly, on the Germans.

To Denikin and Alekseev and to some (but not all) of their officers the idea of agreement with the Germans was 'a shame and a treachery'. Such an attitude, at a time when the Germans were continuing to advance on the crucial front in France, seemed to many to be romantic nonsense. Paul Milyukov writes of the 'unrealistic mentality' which made it 'impossible to combine in common action with other groups who had freed themselves from the Bolsheviks; and confined the Volunteer Army's activities to just that limited territory where the Volunteer Army's Great Russian aims could not be implemented.' Krasnov was sarcastic: 'The Volunteer Army,' he remarked, 'is pure and undefiled. And I, Ataman of the Don, accept with my dirty hands German shells and ammunition, wash them in the waters of the quiet Don and hand them over clean to the Volunteer Army.' Denisov pointed out that as the Germans were here on the Don, the Don Cossacks had to come to terms with them; they were not 'wandering musicians' like the Volunteer Army. Relations between members of the two armies grew steadily worse, and there was continuous brawling in the cafés and restaurants of Novocherkassk. Volunteer Army officers talked of the *vseveseloe* (all gay) instead of *vsevelikoe* (all great) *Donskoe Voisko*; and compared the Don to a prostitute who sells herself for money. Denisov said that in that case the V.A. were ponces living off the earnings of prostitution.

Anti-German oppositionists in Novocherkassk drifted off to Denikin's headquarters—there was nowhere else for them to go to. Here they issued anti-German statements and articles. When this came to German knowledge representations were made to Krasnov; when these had no result the Germans closed down the Volunteer Army's recruiting offices in Kiev, which had hitherto been functioning openly, and sponsored the formation of two rival and pro-German volunteer forces with the high-sounding titles of the Southern Army and the Astrakhan Corps. In addition the Germans made a show of preventing further arms and ammunition reaching the Volunteer Army via the Don, though these measures were not seriously enforced.

There could be no relief from friction and embarrassment while the Volunteer Army remained in its present quarters. But by the end of June, 1918, the Army was rested, re-equipped and reinforced. There were three infantry divisions, respectively under Markov, Borovsky and Drozdovsky, a cavalry division under Erdely, and a Kuban Cossack brigade under Pokrovsky. It was an army of nearly 9,000 combatants and 21 guns that set off south again on its way to sixteen months of hard-fought victories and to ultimate and absolute defeat.

The main sources for Chapter I are:

Antonov-Ovseenko, V. A., *Zapiski o Grazhdanskoi Voine* (Moscow, 1933).
Borisenko, *Sovietskie Respubliki na Severnom Kavkaze v 1918 Gody* (Rostov, 1930).
Bunyan, *Intervention, Civil War and Communism* (Baltimore, 1936).
Bunyan and Fisher, *The Bolshevik Revolution* (Stanford, 1934).
Denikin, *Ocherki Russkoi Smuty* (Paris–Berlin, 1921–26).
Denisov, S. V., *Zapiski* (Constantinople, 1921).
Krasnov, P. N., in *Arkhiv Russkoi Revolyutsii*, Vol. V.
Lukomsky, in *Arkhiv Russkoi Revolyutsii*, Vol. V.

Other works consulted include:

Lokerman, A., 74 *Dnya Sovietskoi Vlasti* (Rostov, 1918).
Milyukov, P., *Russlands Zusammenbruch* (Berlin, 1926).
Power, Rhoda, *Under Cossack and Bolshevik* (London, 1919).
Trotsky, *Kak Vooruzhalas Revolyutsiya* (Moscow, 1924).
Zeman, Z. A. B., *Germany and the Revolution in Russia* (Oxford, 1958).

CHAPTER II

The Volga and Urals

(i)

Alarge number of Czechs and Slovaks were living in Russia in 1914. Apart from the few Slovak peasant colonies in the Southern Ukraine they were mostly small businessmen, clerks, skilled workers and craftsmen. They were hard-working and competent. Few in those days were politically-minded, but the emotion engendered by the outbreak of war gave rise to a move for a Czechoslovak unit to fight alongside the Russian brother Slavs against the Central Powers. The Tsarist authorities were chary, even in war-time, of encouraging armed nationalist movements in multi-racial empires. But permission was given to form a brigade or *druzhina* under Russian command.

By early 1917 the position was very different. The Provisional Government had none of the inhibitions of its predecessor, and there was a huge field for recruitment in the many thousands of Czech and Slovak war prisoners and deserters (it was often hard to tell which was which) in camps all over Russia. In Paris the Czechoslovak National Council was on the eve of recognition by the Western Allies, and both Beneš and Masaryk were aware of the immense political advantage that would accrue to the movement by the possession of an armed force. Masaryk came to Russia in the spring of 1917. In May a Czechoslovak congress in Kiev elected him as their political leader. A local National Council was formed to be counterpart of that in Paris. Meanwhile the Legion grew rapidly. It took part, not without credit, in the ill-fated Kerensky offensive of July. By the autumn it attained the status of an independent corps; and later, in agreement with the French, it was officially declared part of the Czech Army in France (where Czecho-slovak units were already in being), politically subordinated to Masaryk and the National Council but in all military aspects under the French High Command.

The Legion then numbered some 30,000 men, and more and more recruits were coming in. There were still senior Russian officers in posts of command, two of whom, Kappel and Voitsekhovsky, were to attain prominence in the Civil War. But Czech and Slovak military leaders were also becoming prominent, among them Syrovy, in 1914 a bank clerk in Warsaw and due to become Commander-in-Chief; Čeček, a former Austro-Hungarian second-lieutenant; and Gajda, ex-Austrian hospital orderly, who deserted to the Serbs in 1915 and subsequently made his way from Salonica to Odessa. The rank and file had now been caught up in the fervour of 1917. They felt themselves both nationalists and revolutionaries (of the pattern of the Russian Socialist-Revolutionaries) and speeches, committees and elections loomed large in their military life. But, far more than any Russian formation, they retained their cohesion and solidarity; it was indeed a condition of survival in the confusion of the Russia of that time.

Masaryk noted later: 'Naturally not all of our 40,000 volunteers were of equal character and worth. Naturally, too, not all of them had been prompted to join us by patriotic enthusiasm. Upon them the effects of life in most of the Russian prisoners' camps had been very harmful . . . to many of our men service in our Legion meant release. This was certainly the case in the post-revolutionary period of 1917 and particu-larly in 1918. The Legion offered greater personal safety and better treatment.' One trait was marked from the very beginning—Czechs are practical people, and the Legionaries had contacts and know-how, and the experience of getting things done in Russian conditions. The quality of their subsidiary

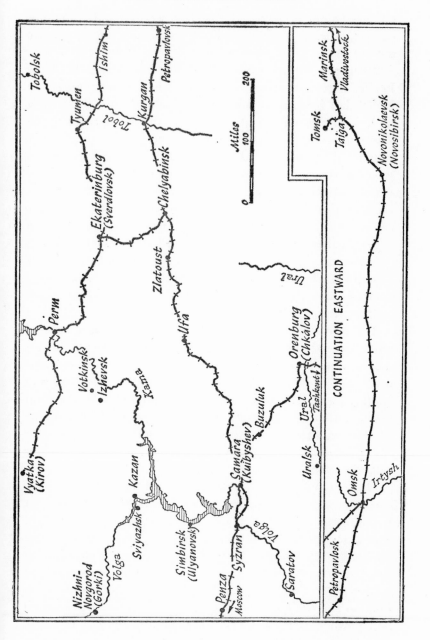

services (supplies, transport, medical services and communications) quickly stood out against the chaos and incompetence
around them.

When the Bolshevik *coup d'état* took place the bulk of the
Legion were near Kiev. Masaryk proclaimed their neutrality
in Russian internal affairs and went ahead with the project
he had already formed of transferring the whole corps to the
Western Front in France. Before leaving Moscow (in early
March) he agreed with the Bolshevik leadership that the Legion
should proceed by rail to Vladivostock and there embark on
Allied shipping; and arrangements were made with Siberian
Co-operative representatives for the supply of provisions on the
route across the continent. Brest-Litovsk brought a note of
urgency: there was a clash between a Czech detachment and
the advancing German troops of occupation. But by the end of
March the whole Legion was clear of the Ukraine, and a more
detailed agreement reached with the Bolsheviks for their
further transportation.

This provided that the Czechs were to travel 'not as fighting
units, but as groups of free citizens who carry with them a
specified number of weapons for defence against counter-
revolutionary attacks.' Penza was fixed as the assembly- and
starting-point. The Czech units would hand over to the local
Soviet authorities all arms above a quota of 168 rifles and one
machine-gun per echelon or trainload and would entrain for
their 5,000-mile journey to Vladivostock. The first echelon was
duly dispatched on March 27th.

On March 31st, the Germans launched their great offensive
on the Western Front in France. In early April the British War
Office, exploring every possibility of reopening the Eastern
Front, suggested that the Legionaries remain in Russia. But
for the French the need for man-power on the Western Front
was paramount, and Beneš saw good political reasons for
following the French lead. However, discussions continued in
London and Paris, and on May 2nd the Supreme War Council
laid down that those Czech echelons already east of Omsk
should continue on their way to Vladivostock, but those west of

Omsk should be rerouted via Archangel. The head of the French Military Mission in Moscow was told to take the matter up with the Soviet authorities, and the agreement of Trotsky was secured.

Meanwhile the movement of the Legion was proceeding, albeit slowly and with ever-increasing friction and mutual suspicion. One obvious cause was the poor state of the Russian railways, and the general inefficiency and frequent truculence of the local Soviets along the line. The Czechs on their side took such chances as came their way to avoid the agreed surrender of arms and indeed before long came to feel they had ample ground for doubting Bolshevik good faith. It has been suggested that these six weeks provide an early instance of double-think on the part of the Soviet Government and the Bolshevik Party. The Government assured the Allied Missions of its readiness to facilitate the Czech departure. But the Party aimed at winning over the rank and file to help meet the régime's desperate need of disciplined troops and skilled technicians, and at the same time sensed a danger to the Revolution if a corps continued to exist where anti-Bolshevik Russian officers held senior posts of command. A Soviet document which later fell into Czech hands shows Stalin as early as late March recommending Siberian Soviets to 'disarm the Czechoslovaks'. The trouble was, of course, that few Soviets had sufficient troops at their disposal to disarm by force a single echelon.

The Party naturally made use of the Czech Communists. There had been very few of them at the time of the seizure of power, but by the end of February Czechoslovak Party organizations had come into being at Petrograd, Moscow and Kiev. The Kiev centre, in receipt of funds and newsprint from the capitals, started a vigorous propaganda campaign to win over the Czech soldiers. When the Legion left the Ukraine the main effort was transferred to Penza. On April 3rd the Czech Communist, Strombach, was writing to Moscow: 'After agitation and recruitment and after we grant our permission, the trains which have gone through our processing (with the remaining scrap officers and servants of capitalism) will be allowed to go further . . . Slow transportation and continuous interruptions diminish enthusiasm for France and the people are becoming convinced that it is nonsense to go there . . . Send us as many newspapers as possible . . . Do not spare money on this. The field for agitation here is really great. We have to permeate the people with internationalism. And, above all, send us more literature. We need more authority. Arrange that the Penza Soviet is ordered to yield to us unconditionally . . .'

The response to this agitation was, in fact, meagre. In all 218 Czech soldiers left the Legion to join the Red Army. However, the agitation continued and at the same time steps were taken towards building up a political centre under Communist control that should take the place of the National Council as the supreme authority for Czechoslovak affairs in Russia. Pressure was put on the Council members: two of them came over to the Bolsheviks. On May 11th the remainder were ejected from the National Council's premises in Moscow. Three days later came the incident at Chelyabinsk in the Urals.

The drive to recruit inmates of P.O.W. camps for the Red Army, to be known as 'Internationalists', had been going on since January. It had met with most success among the Hungarian prisoners, and this, in view of Slovak bitterness against Hungarians, became another factor to add to the Legion's suspicions. On May 14th a Czech echelon proceeding eastwards drew up at a siding in Chelyabinsk station alongside a trainload of Hungarian volunteers coming west. A quarrel broke out; a Hungarian threw a crowbar which injured a Czech, whose companions then lynched the Hungarian. The Chelyabinsk Soviet summoned a Czech delegation to take part in an inquiry. On arrival at the Soviet building they were arrested. The Czech troops then left the station, occupied the town centre and enforced the delegation's release. The local Bolshevik Commissar in his report to Moscow explained that 'we wanted to disarm them [i.e., the Czechs] but we were not strong enough'. The Czechs returned to the station and their train went on its way, but the incident seems to have persuaded

Trotsky, the People's Commissar for War, that the time had come for drastic action.

With the Legion strung out over thousands of miles of railway, special steps had to be taken to ensure unity and co-ordination. Delegates from the various units would frequently come together for consultation; and a particularly important series of meetings and a general Congress were arranged to be held at Chelyabinsk between May 18th and 25th. Points to be discussed included a recommendation drawn up at the First Division's conference on April 13th, to the effect that no more arms be surrendered, that discreet control should be secured over locomotives and fuel in the main railway centres and that hostages be exchanged with the Soviets to ensure smooth transport. But of more urgent importance was the belated receipt, via the French Military Mission and with the backing of the National Council members in Moscow, of the Supreme Allied Commanders' order that units still west of Omsk should be rerouted via Archangel. To the assembled Congress this splitting up of the Legion entailed too great a risk to be accepted; and it was unanimously decided—the French Military Mission representatives strongly protesting— that the order should not be obeyed. On the same day, May 20th, it was agreed to set up a Provisional Executive Committee consisting of the four National Council members present at Chelyabinsk, four nominees of the Congress and three military experts.

Trotsky's decision to disarm the Legion seems to have been taken within three or four days of the incident at Chelyabinsk. Appropriate orders were sent out to Soviets and Party organizations on the 20th and 21st, and one Czech echelon containing Air Force personnel was, in fact, disarmed on May 22nd. On the same day, however, the Congress dispatched a circular telegram proclaiming 'sympathy with the Russian revolutionary people in their struggle to consolidate the revolution'; but 'since the Soviet Government has no power to guarantee free and secure transportation . . . arms will not be surrendered until we receive a guarantee of free departure.'

On the 23rd the Congress received a telegram dated the 21st, signed by Maxa and Čermak of the National Council in Moscow ordering the unconditional surrender of all arms to the local Soviets. Major Guinet of the French Mission urged compliance with the order. But the Congress suspected that these signatures had been obtained under duress—both men, in fact, were now under arrest. A further circular telegram was sent off expressing the hope of a peaceful settlement but reiterating the refusal to surrender arms. A delegation was selected to make its way to Vologda and explain the situation to the French representatives. The Congress declared the National Council suspended and its authority transferred to the Provisional Executive Committee. A special resolution empowered the latter body to assure transportation 'by the Legion's own means and in its own way'. On May 25th Trotsky sent out a telegraphic order: 'All Soviets are hereby ordered to disarm the Czechoslovaks immediately. Every armed Czechoslovak found on the railway to be shot on the spot; every troop train in which even one armed man is found shall be unloaded and its soldiers interned in P.O.W. camps . . .' Some Soviets, including Penza, wired back for reinforcements. Trotsky replied that military orders were not to be discussed but obeyed.

The first clashes took place on May 25th, at Marinsk, where a Czech detachment disarmed a trainload of Red Guards and Internationalists, and at Marinovka, near Omsk, where the Reds attempted to ambush a Czech echelon. Thereafter things moved rapidly. Chelyabinsk and Novonikolaevsk were occupied by the Czechs on May 26th, Penza on May 28th, Petropavlovsk and Tomsk on the 31st, and Omsk after some fighting on June 7th. It is significant of Bolshevik weakness in the East that the total of Czech troops available for these operations was barely 20,000. Before the end of June Vladivostock was also taken, and the whole of the vast stretch of the Trans-Siberian Railway was in Czech hands except for a gap round Irkutsk which was not to be closed for some weeks. The orders originally issued by the Provisional Executive Committee were that armed action was to be undertaken solely for the purpose of the

Legion's further transport; once resistance was broken there should be no interference in Russian domestic affairs. These orders were not always obeyed. Gajda, who in late May was in command at Novonikolaevsk, established contact with underground officers' associations and other opposition groups; and was certainly instrumental in establishing an anti-Bolshevik government at Omsk. But so tenuous was the Bolshevik hold on the main Siberian centres that, as often as not, once the Czechs had seized the railway station the authority of the local city Soviet collapsed.

(ii)

In December, 1917, a few weeks after the Bolshevik *coup d'état* and a few days before the opening of the Constituent Assembly, the Socialist Revolutionaries, at their Fourth Party Congress, passed a resolution to the effect that 'the Party must concentrate on the maintenance of all the rights of the Constituent Assembly, and must organize forces sufficient, in case of need, to take up the struggle against criminal attacks on the supreme will of the people, whatever may be the source of these attacks and whatever may be the slogans behind which they are disguised.' The Constituent Assembly was forcibly dispersed and soon afterwards the S.R. Central Committee, now in effect an underground body, moved to Moscow. There seemed no prospect, in the immediate future, of the Assembly being able to function in either capital, and the Committee scoured the horizon for some area where its members might assemble in security from Bolshevik attack. There were negotiations with the Don Cossacks. But there were suspicions that some Cossack leaders might use the Assembly as a screen for undemocratic aims. The Ukraine was then considered and rejected on account of the general chaos there and the rapid advance of the German Army. The choice finally fell on the Volga-Ural region, where the overwhelming majority of the votes for the Constituent Assembly had been cast for the Socialist Revolutionary candidates. The Committee was also influenced by what has been described as the ' "mystical" conviction that the Bolshevik dictatorship maintained itself only by force and that the people were eagerly awaiting the arrival of "a saviour". Hence arose the idea that any spark might set off the blaze.' It was hoped that the blaze might start along the Volga.

Bolshevik rule in Samara and its neighbourhood was still precarious. Elections to the Provincial Soviet had given a majority to the Maximalists, Anarchists and Left Wing S.R.s; and increasing friction with the Bolshevik Town Soviet had culminated in an armed clash, with the non-Bolsheviks occupying most of Samara for several hours. The trickle of hungry refugees from Moscow had given a depressing picture of the realities of Soviet rule. In the rural areas the Revolution was hanging fire: landlords were coming to terms with their peasants and encouraging them to tell the Soviet not to interfere. When the Bolshevist authorities started requisitioning horses for the campaign against the Orenburg Cossacks the reaction of the peasants was so violent that the order had to be revoked. And then the Samara railway workers began to demand a cease fire.

There were plenty of sparks, but the setting off of a blaze was quite another matter, as soon became apparent to the S.R. conspiratorial emissaries. These were the three local S.R. members of the Constituent Assembly—Klimushkin, Brushvit and Fortunatov, shortly to be joined by two colleagues, Volsky (from Tver) and Nesterov (from Minsk). Klimushkin writes in his memoirs: 'Our chief purpose at that time was to bring about conditions favourable to the overthrow of Bolshevik rule . . . At first our work was very difficult. The army was demoralized and so, too, was the working class. The workers refused to see that the ruin of industry and the bribes by which the Bolsheviks were attracting them were bound to lead ultimately to the ruin of the workers and to famine . . . We started intense propaganda. But we soon realized that the workers were difficult to organize. They had fallen into a marked degree of demoralization and were split into a number of camps fighting among themselves. We turned to the soldiers, especially to the officers, but they constituted a small force and very few believed in the possibility of overthrowing the Bolsheviks . . . As the cities gave us little encouragement we gradually turned our attention to the villages . . . We sent our friends to the villages to organize the peasants. The work, though steadily progressing, was very slow and it was clear that without some external stimulus no hope could be entertained for a *coup d'état* in the near future.'

The stimulus from outside was provided by the Czechoslovak Legion. In the course of their action along the railway line the Czechs seized Penza on May 28th. Brushvit at once proceeded there to persuade the Czechs to come to Samara. It seems that the Czech attitude was at first reserved. They expressed little confidence in the S.R. conspirators and advised them to show their significance by seizing the city themselves. That, of course, they were quite unable to do. But they did organize some peasant disturbances, and their supporters occupied a factory and a bridge over the Volga in the neighbourhood of Samara. What perhaps carried greater weight was the exact account they were able to give the Czechs of Bolshevik military dispositions and of the poverty of Bolshevik military resources. An agreed decision to seize Samara was taken on June 1st or 2nd. The Czechs accordingly set out from Penza. In Samara the officers' associations with whom the S.R.s were in touch staged acts of sabotage and stormed one of the local prisons, releasing 500 prisoners. A mass meeting of railwaymen (mostly Mensheviks) made a declaration of neutrality. The Bolsheviks, conscious of their weakness, sent some Czech Communists to try and win over the Czech rank and file. They made no impression and the Czechs continued their advance. On June 6th they drove back a Bolshevik force defending the outer approaches. The final assault took place on the night of June 7th–8th and did not meet with serious resistance. According to a Soviet historian: 'The circumstances of the Czech entry into Samara across the railway bridge are still not entirely clear. Hitherto it has been the opinion that the Czechs fought their way through with an armoured train in support. Comrade Khataevich in his memoir categorically denies this: "I declare that they came over the bridge without firing a shot and that there was no armoured train. Whether the Ufa detachment who were in trenches defending that sector went to sleep or whether they just surrendered I do not know. But the Czechs appeared across the bridge quite unexpected by the defenders." '

The American Vice-Consul reported: 'The Czechs were familiar with the plan of the city, for within two hours they had their guards in every place where the Bolsheviks had been and were busy cleaning them up . . . Large numbers of Bolsheviks were captured and marched around the city on their way to the prison. The Czechs went about their task of restoring order with intelligence; within three hours men were removing the broken wires and repairing the telephone lines, and within twelve hours the streets were clear . . . There was an enthusiastic burst of national spirit, the Russian flag appeared all over the business district and before the day was over dozens of former officers were on the streets in their old uniforms, and some of the prominent women of the city went about with Czech soldiers, who held out their hats and the women solicited contributions for food for the men. Every hat I saw was running over with roubles, peasants and workmen with merchants alike giving liberally, a clever way to rouse enthusiasm.' But Klimushkin, perhaps with hind-sight, strikes a more sombre note: 'In spite of the universal jubilation we were actually supported only by very few.'

(iii)

It had been agreed during the discussions at Penza that the new régime to assume power at Samara should be composed of members of the Constituent Assembly. It was desired that it should have as broad a base as possible. To quote Klimushkin: 'We entered into negotiations with the Social Democrats (Mensheviks) and the Cadets . . . but neither party was willing to support us. The Social Democrats argued that Bolshevism would liquidate itself, while the Cadets maintained that unless the Czechs remained at Samara our whole enterprise would be a leap in the dark . . . It was in this way that the whole burden of the *coup* fell upon the shoulders of the Socialist Revolutionaries.'

On June 8th, the day of the seizure of Samara, the new authority issued its Order No. 1. 'In the name of the Constituent Assembly we hereby declare the Bolshevik Government in the city of Samara and in the Samara *Guberniya* has been removed. All commissars are dismissed from their posts. All organs of local self-government abolished by the Soviet Government are reinstated to full powers. . . . Pending the formation of governmental institutions by an All-Russian Government, authority, both civil and military, in the city and in the *Guberniya* passes to a committee composed of members of the Constituent Assembly, elected from Samara *Guberniya* . . . All restrictions on freedom and repressive measures introduced by the Bolsheviks are declared void. Freedom of speech, of the press and of assembly is reinstated.' It was to be the only proclamation to be issued as from the Samara members. From June 9th the word Samara is omitted, and the Committee assumed the representation of the Assembly as a whole.

Its first and very serious preoccupation concerned defence against a Bolshevik attack. *Komuch* (the abbreviation used for the Committee of Members of the Constituent Assembly) itself had only a few squads of volunteers. The Czechs were undecided. It was impossible as yet to know what was happening to their fellows along the Trans-Siberian Railway. At first their inclination was to continue eastward. But finally, following a plea from the French Military Mission representatives, they agreed to remain long enough to enable *Komuch* to organize an army of its own. Meanwhile, *Komuch* Order No. 2 called on citizens to volunteer for not less than three months' service. Pay was to be 15 roubles per month, with an allowance of 100 roubles a month for married men. A supreme military staff of three was appointed—Fortunatov, Bogolyubov (who had been a Military Commissar under the Provisional Government) and Colonel Galkin, the Committee's link with the underground officers' group. To these were added Lebedev, another Socialist Revolutionary. In the event Fortunatov spent his time at the front in command of a small detachment he had raised himself, and Bogolyubov from the start and Lebedev after a very few weeks became completely immersed in politics, so that before long Galkin was virtually in sole authority.

For many Socialist Revolutionaries it was a matter of deep reluctance to engage in civil war against a Left-wing party; and most of the innumerable proclamations and exhortations of the time make out the Germans rather than the Bolsheviks to be the main enemy. But as in S.R. eyes the Bolsheviks had become the allies and instruments of the Germans, there was no serious opposition to the call to arms against the 'traitors to Russia, to Freedom and to the Revolution'. Many S.R. leaders sincerely believed that the struggle against the Bolsheviks was merely a stage in the struggle against the Germans.

Days passed and the expected Bolshevik counter-attack did not materialize. The Czechs stayed on. Some sort of local army began to come into being. And then came news which appeared to be of decisive importance. On June 20th the French Ministry of War had notified General Lavergne, in charge of the French Military Mission, that the Czechs should hold their positions along the Trans-Siberian Railway in view of the possibility of Allied intervention. Nine days later Major Guinet, liaison officer to the Czechs, notified Czech H.Q. that 'I have received from the French Ambassador a cyphered telegram informing me of the intervention of the Allies in Russia'. The Czech civilian and military leaders in Russia conferred, and on July 7th Čeček, commanding the Czech forces in the Volga area, issued an order: 'Notify all brothers that in conformity with the decision of . . . our National Council and with the concurrence of the Allies, our Corps has been made a vanguard of the Allied Forces. The instructions issued by the staff of the Army Corps aim at the establishment of an anti-German front in Russia in conjunction with the whole Russian nation and our Allies.'

A few days later it was agreed with *Komuch* that Čeček should be Commander-in-Chief of all Czech and Russian forces in the area, and plans for future operations were discussed. Ufa had been occupied on July 7th: an S.R. colonel in Bolshevik service had kept the Czechs informed of the Red dispositions and had defected with most of his troops at the critical moment. With the remaining main centres in the area already in Czech hands there was no threat to Samara from the East. Four possible lines of advance seemed open to the united forces. These were: (1) upstream along the Volga to Simbirsk, Kazan and so towards Moscow; (2) due west along the railway—Syzran, Penza, Moscow; (3) downstream along the Volga, to Khvalinsk, Saratov and Astrakhan; and (4) the southern route across the steppe via Nikolaevsk and Uralsk. The plan as finally agreed was to advance up the Volga as far as Simbirsk (where there was an important depot) and there form a defensive bastion; to form another defensive bastion on the steppe to the South— Dutov and his Cossacks had by now retaken Orenburg and would look after this sector; and to make the main thrust down the Volga towards Saratov. The Bolsheviks had had a good deal of trouble in that area and in the neighbouring Tambov province; it was hoped the arrival of an army of liberation would encourage the peasants to revolt. There was also the incentive (though hardly one to appeal to *Komuch*) of effecting a junction with the anti-Bolshevik forces in the South.

July was a difficult month for the Bolsheviks. Czech and People's Army units captured Stavropol, Novodevichie (with much of the Red river fleet) and Syzran. On the 10th, Muraviev, the Soviet C.-in-C. on the Volga front, broke up the local Soviet at Simbirsk, denounced the Treaty of Brest-Litovsk and proclaimed an armistice with the Czechs and war against the Germans. He was liquidated by loyal Bolshevik elements, and the Red front, such as it was, was restored; but on the 22nd, Kappel, now in Samara service, with 283 men captured

Simbirsk. There was a surge of optimism in Samara, heightened by the universal confidence in immediate and effective Allied intervention. Lebedev notes in his diary: 'The Allies (through their representatives) promised to send a landing force to Archangel and to Siberia via Vladivostock . . . All our calculations rested on this. Briefly, our plan was as follows: insurrection in the Volga region, capture of Kazan, Simbirsk, Samara, Saratov; mobilization beyond this line; landing of an Allied force at Archangel; and movement towards Vologda to join with the Volga front . . . Under such conditions not only anti-Bolsheviks but even those sympathizing with the Soviets would have had to choose between an alliance with Germany against all the Russian democratic parties and an alliance with us against Imperial Germany which had seized half of European Russia.'

The seizure of Kazan, it should be noted, did not form part of the agreed plan. In a subsequent entry (dated Simbirsk, July 26th) Lebedev writes: 'A French aviator arrived. He had made his way through Kazan. He came from Lavergne with the news that the Allies were already approaching Vologda. I am sending him by aeroplane to Čeček . . . Delegates . . . have come from Kazan where everything is ready for the insurrection. . . . The delegates implore us to come to their aid, saying that the people of Kazan will revolt in any event. Having secured Čeček's consent I sent them back today with an affirmative reply which gave the approximate date of our entry into Kazan . . . We must push on and on as long as the Bolsheviks are in a state of panic.'

It seems to be quite untrue that Čeček's consent was secured. What happened was that on the evening of July 26th, shortly after the capture of Simbirsk, a meeting took place there with Lebedev, Fortunatov, Kappel and the local Czech commander. They agreed, Kappel dissenting, to press on to Kazan. Lebedev and Fortunatov contacted Samara on the direct line and asked for authority to advance: Samara ordered them to remain at· Simbirsk. A few days later Samara received a telegram: 'We are at the gates of Kazan.' The city was captured by a mixed

Czech-Russian force on August 7th. As had been feared it
proved impossible to hold for long, and this diversion to the
north held up the reinforcement of the southern sector, where
an outstanding Red partisan commander—Chapaev—was
able to halt the advance on Saratov. Čeček wished Lebedev
and Fortunatov to be court martialled. 'But one cannot court-
martial a victor.'

It is unprofitable to attempt to judge how far the dissipation
of effort involved by the move on Kazan contributed to the
military failure of *Komuch*. But it is certain that the move, like
the Czech move on Ekaterinburg (captured on July 25th) was
undertaken in the firm belief of speedy and effective Allied
support. Local Allied liaison officers may well have gone further
in their advice and encouragement than was warranted by their
instructions. The fact remains that Czechs and Russians
believed the Allies were coming, in force, to the Volga. As time
went on and Allied aid was not forthcoming the troops lost
heart and the will to fight; and the Samara empire began to
crumble away.

(iv)

I. I. Maisky has provided what is perhaps our most vivid
account of this period, albeit written in the process of working
his passage to Bolshevik favour. At that time a Menshevik, he
describes the meetings of the Menshevik Central Committee
under Martov and Dan in Moscow in the spring of 1918, and
the hesitations and perplexities that followed the news of the
Czech revolt. 'The majority of the Central Committee wished,
possibly unconsciously, to take up an attitude that would
absolve them from the necessity to act.' They were caught up
between hatred of Bolshevism and hatred of the possible
triumph of Reaction. A delegation of railway workers called to
ask for a ruling on transport for Bolsheviks or Czechs in the
course of the fighting. Martov laid down that railway personnel
should be neutral; on being pressed further he suggested that

this neutrality should be friendly to the Czechs and hostile to the Bolsheviks. There were sharp exchanges between Maisky and Dan on the subject of the Constituent Assembly. Maisky was not content to have *Komuch* written off as 'just another Socialist Revolutionary adventure'; he pressed for the dispatch of a proper delegation to Samara. The upshot of long and inconclusive arguments was that for the time being individual Mensheviks might do as they thought best; and Maisky decided to leave for the Volga.

He left Moscow on July 31st, and tells of his astonishment, after the hunger of the capital, at the good white bread being sold by old peasant women at wayside stations as the train neared the Volga. In Kazan he had anxious moments avoiding the *Cheka* while making arrangements for the journey onwards to liberated territory. He was still in Kazan when the city fell, and stresses his disgust at the mass executions of suspected Bolsheviks rounded up by the Czech security squads. He called on the local Menshevik party headquarters and was told: 'We have already sent a deputation, but the Czech Command maintain that the soldiers must have some outlet for their exasperation, otherwise they will mutiny.' He attended a meeting of the Kazan branch of the Menshevik Party, where it was decided to give full support to *Komuch*; and on the evening of August 8th he embarked on the S.S. *Amur* and set off down the Volga to Samara along with Zenzinov (of the S.R. Central Committee), various other notables, S.R. security squads and the complete Academy of the General Staff (evacuated from Petrograd). The Academy's Director, General Professor Andogsky, was in a mellow mood, and full of praise for Socialist Revolutionary strategic talent. The capture of Kazan, he maintained, was one of the greatest feats of military history.

They arrived at Samara on the morning of the 10th. After the drab austerities of Moscow the gay and crowded streets and well-stocked market seemed like a scene from the Arabian Nights. The town was *en fête* for the victory of Kazan. Maisky was taken from reception to reception. He especially notes the venerable E. E. Lazarev, an S.R. member of the Constituent Assembly and now head of the Department of Public Enlightenment, 'who delighted in speeches and functions' and was 'having a veritable gala of passion and rhetoric'. Speeches, songs and rejoicings went on far into the night. Maisky, exhausted, left the local cabaret at 2 a.m. An hour later he was awakened by a senior S.R. member who shared his hotel bedroom and who asked him: 'Do you want to be a Minister?' Maisky said: 'I want to go to sleep.' 'I am not joking,' his friend assured him. 'I have been asked to sound you out about joining the Government.'

The fact was that *Komuch* realized the handicap of its exclusively S.R. composition and was anxious to broaden its base. They had been rebuffed by the Cadets. The local Mensheviks had been very cautious. But in early August a conference of eleven provincial Menshevik organizations had voted (by a majority) general support for *Komuch* and had appointed a Regional Committee to cover the whole area of the *Komuch* Government. This and the arrival of Maisky encouraged a new bid for Menshevik participation. The post in view was head of the Department of Labour: Menshevik strength among the Samara workers made the appointment particularly desirable. Maisky had misgivings as to the reaction of his colleagues on the Central Committee in Moscow. But the Central Committee had recently agreed to the independence of local Party organizations physically cut off by the Civil War. The competent authority in this instance was therefore the new Regional Committee. Maisky proposed to this committee that he should accept, provided that *Komuch* agreed in advance to a programme of social welfare measures. This was approved by the Committee, and the programme accepted by *Komuch*. Maisky thus became Head of the Department of Labour. When the news reached Moscow, the Menshevik Central Committee expelled him for lack of discipline. But the Regional Committee maintained none the less that their decision had been correct.

(v)

Those in power at Samara were very conscious that they were only the trustees of the Constituent Assembly, and they did their best to secure the arrival of at least a majority of that body. S.R. and other underground organizations helped to arrange the journeys, and by late July some sixty members of the Assembly were gathered in Samara. Six weeks later there were 101 of them—eighty Socialist Revolutionaries, one Left-wing Cadet, eighteen Moslem national representatives (mostly with S.R. affinities) and two Cossacks. These 101 members constituted *Komuch*, the supreme authority, under a small presidium of which Volsky was chairman and Gendelman vice-chairman. It was felt that to appoint ministers or a Council of Ministers would be to encroach upon the prerogative of the full Assembly. Accordingly the various branches of administration were allotted to Heads of Departments (for the most part not members of the Constituent Assembly). These Heads of Departments, together with Volsky and Gendelman, formed the Council of Heads of Departments (*Soviet Upravlyayushchikh Vedomstva*) which operated, more or less, as a cabinet.

It was a government of amateurs, many of them idealists, most of them highly articulate and nearly all quite inexperienced in the art of getting things done. The bulk of the *Komuch* members had little or nothing to occupy their time, so they would interfere with the day-to-day working of the various government offices, and attend, and take part in, meetings of the Council of Heads of Departments, causing much irritation to that body. In conditions of peace it is possible that the *Komuch* Government might have achieved some degree of viability. But its life was one of almost continuous crisis, with violent expansions and contractions of territory, and it never had the chance to settle down. It was, of course, a *Komuch* axiom that major decisions must await the reestablishment of the Constituent Assembly. But on one issue their course was clear. The Assembly, at its only session, had declared the ownership of all land to be vested in the state; it merely remained to implement this decision. On June 25th Order No. 51 re-established the Land Committees set up by the Provisional Government, and Order No. 83 of July 6th laid down that it was for them to decide on the provisional use of the land. No details are available of what they actually achieved. Maisky maintains that in no instance was land taken away from landlords who had succeeded in retaining it. This seems possible: such landlords would have come to a private arrangement with the local peasants. Order No. 124 of July 22nd prescribed (as the German General Eichhorn had done in the Ukraine) that whoever had sown the fields should have the right to the crops. This probably did little more than regularize what was happening in any case. There seems to have been no urgent agrarian problem. In any case everyone was busy with the harvest, and had no time to bother much about politics. It was only when *Komuch* tried to gear the peasants into active participation in the civil war that they ran into trouble.

With regard to the workers, Klimushkin has recorded: 'Our *coup* was not actively supported by the workers except for a small group. An important part of the workers was outside our influence, showing neither active resistance nor active support.' *Komuch* policy was therefore designed to promote the benevolent neutrality of Samara labour, or, at least, to prevent their becoming active enemies. Order No. 3 issued on the assumption of power and forbidding arbitrary arrests must have been partly intended to save non-Bolshevik workers from the general round-up. Order No. 4, issued a few hours later, laid down that factory management and organizations should continue for the time being as under the Bolsheviks. The Soviet of Workers' Deputies was dissolved but not abolished: a Workers' Conference was called to arrange for elections to a new Soviet, which duly assembled in early August. Order No. 88 forbade lockouts. Order No. 89 laid down that Bolshevik legislation designed for the protection of labour was for the time being to remain valid. There seemed a fair prospect of good relations between the government and labour. At a workers' conference in mid-June a resolution expressing confidence in *Komuch* was carried by 341 votes against 156 with 21 abstentions. A minority resolution calling for immediate peace with the Bolsheviks was defeated by the same margin.

But good relations with the bourgeoisie were also necessary if the Samara economy was not to break down. Order No. 16 of June 12th denationalized the banks. Order No. 19 of June 14th called for a meeting of labour, employers and official representatives to discuss the restoration of the rights of industrial proprietors. Order No. 93 of July 12th set up a mixed commission to undertake the denationalization of industrial enterprises. A declaration of July 24th, while affirming Trades Union rights, also specified the powers of employers. And Volsky, the President of *Komuch*, declared categorically: 'There can be no question of any kind of socialistic experiments. At the present time the capitalistic system cannot be destroyed.'

Relief at the overthrow of the Bolsheviks aroused, of course, considerable bourgeois enthusiasm in the first flush of 'liberation'. Brushvit raised a substantial loan in Samara, as did Lebedev later in Simbirsk and Kazan. But bourgeois enthusiasm soon waned. S.R. revolutionary rhetoric and the flying of the red flag over government offices may not, in fact, have meant very much, but it did antagonize the middle classes. So did the continued existence of a body bearing the name of 'The Soviet of Workers' Deputies'. To Right-wingers in general it was all to the good that the Bolsheviks had gone. The next stage was to await the collapse of the 'Semi-Bolsheviks'. Neklyutin, a leading Samara factory owner, was extremely frank. 'We will not interfere with you,' he told Klimushkin, 'but we see no sense in weakening ourselves by taking part in your struggle.'

Military organization was quite outside the sphere of the middle-aged intellectuals who made up *Komuch*, and it was natural that Colonel Galkin should take over the Department of Defence and staff it with his officer friends. Galkin, though a poor organizer, was a strong personality and effectively scotched any attempt at interference by politicians. Once when he was away from Samara the *Komuch* appointed a few Socialist

Revolutionaries to posts of command; on his return he insisted on these appointments being cancelled. There were muddles over the reception and equipment of recruits, and disorders in the Samara barracks; *Komuch* pressed for a commission of inquiry but Galkin refused to allow it. He became more and more secretive over the position at the front, maintaining that military secrets must not be discussed with talkative politicians. Eventually information available to members of the Government was reduced to what they could pick up from personal friends on the staff.

Throughout its existence the Samara Government was dependent on Czech military support. The appeal for volunteers resulted only in a few officers' battalions and partisan detachments. On June 20th *Komuch* called up two young classes. Nearly half of the peasants concerned refused to present themselves, and a leading Socialist Revolutionary was sent round the country on a mission of persuasion and enlightenment; he was shot dead at a village meeting and it was impossible to arrest the perpetrator. According to Maisky, in the end the call-up produced some 15,000 men. Klimushkin gives a higher figure, but in any case there was neither the time nor the organization to turn these youths into battle-worthy troops. The Czechs did their best to help by sponsoring volunteer battalions of Russian rank and file under Czech officers, but these units never became a serious factor.

There was, of course, a very different atmosphere in the industrial towns on the Kama, where, on hearing of the fall of Kazan, the workers of Izhevsk and then of Votkinsk rose and removed the Bolshevik authorities. With a sprinkling of ex-officers and N.C.O.s to help them they formed themselves into units of high military value, and drove back a number of Bolshevik counter-attacks. They established a local government styled 'The Kama Committee of Members of the Constituent Assembly' which acknowledged the authority of *Komuch* but which in point of fact was independent. Similarly, although their troops fought alongside the People's Army they never came under Samara command.

In Colonel Kappel, who left Czech service to take over the First Samara Volunteer Detachment, *Komuch* secured a senior officer of quite outstanding quality. But Kappel was essentially a field commander, with little taste for organization or politics. Otherwise the officer material available was as mixed as Alekseev and Denikin had found on the Don. And by early August the Samara authorities were faced with a new problem: serving officers in increasing numbers were being tempted away by the more favourable and more congenial conditions under the rival government at Omsk.

In Samara, as elsewhere, the security organization came under the military. It was inevitably staffed by Right-wing nominees of Galkin, who successfully obstructed any attempt by the government to have any say in its activities. *Komuch* accordingly proceeded to set up, in early August, a service of its own under the S.R. Rogovsky. The Czechs, of course, had their *razvedka*, and three unco-ordinated security organizations were thus functioning side by side. It is significant that none of them was able to ferret out the clandestine underground that the Bolsheviks were building up as early as July.

(vi)

The capture of Kazan marked the peak of Samara's fortunes. Even before its loss to the Reds on September 10th a marked decline had set in. There was the increasing disillusion and unwillingness of the Czech troops and the inability to build up a proper army to replace them. There was the continued failure to arouse any positive popular support for *Komuch*: in the Samara municipal elections in August less than one-sixth of the electorate and less than one-half of the actual voters came out for the combined S.R.-Menshevik list. The Right became more truculent. On the Left the influence of the Bolshevik underground increasingly made itself felt: one of the first acts of the newly elected Soviet of Workers' Deputies was to pass, on August 30th, a resolution embodying political demands (arms for the workers, abolition of martial law, release of political prisoners, etc.) that would have meant the immediate collapse of the régime. The unceasing spate of brave words from the *Komuch* leaders could no longer hide the muddles, the ineffective compromises and the weaknesses that were later to lead Maisky to record his conviction that ' "democracy" has no future in Russia.'

And then there was the trouble with Omsk. Omsk, of course, was only one of the governments to come into being when the Czech revolt had swept away Bolshevik power to the east of the Volga. Most of the others were of national minorities. These last caused no embarrassment to *Komuch*. Satisfaction of the aspirations of the subject races was part of S.R. policy. Assent was at once given to Bashkir and Kirgiz (Kazakh) claims for autonomy, and official notepaper was printed at Samara with the heading R.F.D.R. (for 'Russian Federal Democratic Republic'). To the north-east of the *Komuch* territory a Regional Government of the Urals was in power at Ekaterinburg. It was composed of bourgeois moderates, and while some of its members drew up paper plans for a vast territory stretching from the White Sea to the Caspian, its actual rôle was that of a passive buffer between Samara and Omsk. It was the Omsk Government, now tending more and more to the Right, that was the serious rival to *Komuch*.

The enticement of Samara officers to Siberia was only one of the issues between the 'semi-Bolsheviks' of the Volga and the 'reactionaries' of Siberia. Samara's appeals to Omsk for military aid went unheeded. Omsk had just started creating a Siberian Army and had no desire to risk its young battalions on behalf of a régime which it disliked and in whose future it had no faith. General Boldyrev, at one time Siberian C.-in-C., later noted: 'Because of the political tendencies by which the Siberian Government was now dominated every failure of Samara, even the decline of the fighting capacity of the Constituent army was seen as an advantage to Omsk.' Samara asked for a loan; Omsk refused to consider one unless the State Gold Reserve captured at Kazan were transferred to its territory. The quarrel over goods on the railway was more serious. At the time of the Czech *coup* a number of trains were moving along the line from Vladivostock with goods consigned to the Bolsheviks. As and when they reached Samara the *Komuch* authorities took over the goods. But Omsk set up a Requisitioning Office in Chelyabinsk, stopped the trains and allotted the goods to various Siberian authorities and firms. In retaliation Samara stopped the dispatch of oil and manufactured goods eastwards. There came about what amounted to a mutual blockade.

Bad feeling was accentuated by the existence in Siberia of an articulate S.R. element who had some claims to be the 'legal' source of authority. The Siberian Regional Duma at Tomsk, elected under arrangements made in the time of the Provisional Government, had been suppressed by the Tomsk Soviet in January, 1918. After its suppression a group of its members met clandestinely and appointed themselves 'The Provisional Government of Autonomous Siberia', after which most of them escaped to Manchuria. This government, as such, never had any power or authority. But it was on its behalf and on that of the Regional Duma that the 'Western Siberian Commissariat' assumed charge of the area when the Bolsheviks were thrown out of Omsk with the help of the Czechs; and the Siberian Provisional Government which took over from the Commissariat on June 30th was, in fact, composed of those members of the former paper government who had remained on Russian soil. The Siberian Regional Duma resumed its activities on the liberation of Tomsk. The Tomsk Duma retained its S.R. complexion. The Omsk Government, under military and bourgeois influence, moved more and more to the Right and its Left-wing members resigned or were squeezed out. The Tomsk Duma became the natural ally of *Komuch* against Omsk. Incidents multiplied. One Markov, an S.R. who lost his post at Omsk, decamped to Samara, where he was put in charge of a specially created 'Office for Siberian Affairs'. The official Samara representative to Siberia was accredited not to Omsk but to the Regional Duma.

The position was becoming farcical, and the Allied Missions

and the Czechs urged both sides to find some agreement. A meeting between the two parties at Chelyabinsk on July 15th resulted only in agreement to meet again in August. On this occasion the Czechoslovak National Council presented a memorandum to the participants: '. . . Three months have passed since the Czechoslovak Army rose against the Bolshevik usurpers. At first we had to defend our own freedom, but very soon we decided to . . . come to the rescue of the Russian people . . . We hoped that the Russians themselves would re-establish their military and political organization. Unfortunately the work of reconstruction is progressing very slowly . . . The attempts to form a volunteer army in Siberia and within the territory of the Samara Committee have proved unsatisfactory. Thus far the partial mobilization undertaken by the Samara Committee among the Cossacks and Bashkirs has had little influence on conditions at the front. All this is happening at a time when the Czechoslovak . . . forces are gradually diminishing, while those of the Bolsheviks are steadily increasing . . . Three months of constant fighting have brought the Czechoslovaks to physical exhaustion . . . and they naturally ask themselves the question: What will happen in the future? . . . Why is it that after three months so little is being done by the Russians to form organizations of their own? Instead of a national government being established we witness strife among the different parts of Russia . . . The political situation imperatively calls for the formation of a central government . . .'

At the second Chelyabinsk conference approval in principle was secured for the formation of a Central Government, and it was decided to hold a conference of all interested parties at Ufa in early September for the purpose of bringing this about. The Conference met on the eve of the fall of Kazan.

The Ufa Conference is in one respect unique. Never before or since has so large and so heterogeneous an assembly of anti-Bolshevik Russian groups succeeded in reaching complete agreement. An All-Russian Provisional Government was set up 'as sole trustee of sovereign authority over all the territories of the Russian State' by the unanimous decision of plenipotentiary representatives of the Committee of Members of the All Russian Constituent Assembly; of the Siberian Provisional Government; of the Regional Government of the Urals; of the Cossack *Voiskos* of Orenburg, the Urals, Siberia, Irkutsk, Semirechie, Enisei and Astrakhan; of the Governments of the Bashkirs, Alash-Orda and Turkestan; of the National Administration of the Turco-Tartars of the Interior of Russia and of Siberia; of the Estonian Provisional Government; of representatives of the Congress of Cities and *Zemstvos* of Siberia, the Urals and the Volga Region; of representatives of political parties and organizations—the Socialist Revolutionaries, the Russian Social Democratic Labour Party, the Popular Socialists, the Party of the People's Freedom (Cadets); the All-Russian Social Democratic Organization (*Edinstvo*) and the League for the Regeneration of Russia.

In the spate of rhetoric that marked the first four general sessions of the Conference the crucial issue became apparent: in whom was the supreme authority to be vested. The majority of speakers followed the S.R.s in stressing the supremacy of the Constituent Assembly. A Cadet representative expressed the view that in the absence of any individual fitted to be a dictator, a small directorate should be entrusted with supreme power and should not be responsible to any outside organ. The delegates from Samara and Omsk respectively argued on these two lines. But their speeches were moderate in tone; and it became possible for a conciliating commission to work out a formula acceptable to all.

This provided for a Directorate of five persons who would constitute an All Russian Provisional Government. 'Until the convocation of the All Russian Constituent Assembly the All Russian Provisional Government will be the sole trustee of sovereign authority . . . All functions of sovereignty which . . . have been exercised provisionally by the different regional governments will be turned over to the All Russian Provisional Government when claimed by it . . . The determination of the jurisdiction of regional governments . . . will be left to the discretion of the All-Russian Provisional Government.' The new Government was to act as sole trustee until January 1st, 1919, and then hand over to the Constituent Assembly, provided that by that date 250 members had been collected on free territory: otherwise the transfer date would be February 1st, but only if a quorum of 170 members had by then been assembled. Meanwhile members of the Constituent Assembly already in free Russia were to be recognized as forming a 'constitutional organ' under the title of 'Congress of Members of the Constituent Assembly'. Of far more practical importance was the composition of the new Directorate. After considerable lobbying and negotiation five names were agreed. Three were appointed *in absentia*, and as it was uncertain when or whether they would succeed in reaching the liberated territories in the East, there was more lobbying and negotiation over choosing their deputies. In the event, the Directorate consisted of General Boldyrev, of the League for the Regeneration of Russia; Vologodsky, the Omsk Prime Minister; Vinogradov, a Cadet; and the Right-wing S.R.s Avksentiev and Zenzinov from Samara.

The compromise reached at Ufa was largely enforced by outside developments. News of the loss of Kazan and reports of a Red thrust towards Samara impelled a sense of urgency. A Cossack delegate remarked: 'While we are arguing the Bolsheviks will capture Ufa together with the whole Conference.' Evidence that the *Komuch* military front was crumbling considerably weakened the position of the Samara delegates. They still held the huge State Gold Reserve, which had been transferred in time from Kazan to Samara, and which now, with the threat to Samara, was being moved again eastwards; but a gold reserve with no safe place to store it was hardly a bargaining counter.

The Omsk delegates also had their cares. The Conference coincided with an acute crisis in their relations with the Regional Duma, and the possibility that the Czech garrisons at Omsk and Tomsk might intervene on the side of the Duma made it important to reach a compromise at Ufa. It is true they did not give away very much. They paid lip service to the

Constituent Assembly in its present composition. But there was little likelihood of assembling one hundred and seventy members by February 1st, let alone two hundred and fifty a month earlier. Events were moving, and time was on the side of the Siberians.

(vii)

The successful end of the Ufa Conference was marked by a series of banquets and junketings, but the *Komuch* delegates were called away by bad news from Samara. On their arrival there they found the position had indeed deteriorated. News from the front was vague, but the Red Army was reported to be imbued with a new fighting spirit which Galkin's head-quarters could only attribute to the arrival of German troops. In any case the Czechs were pulling back and the Volga peasants refusing to fight. Of the Samara Rifle Division stationed in the city, 2,945 men deserted during September. The officer commanding the Italian Battalion which formed part of the heterogeneous local force issued a communiqué to 'bring to the notice of the Samara public that the sole motive of his departure from Samara is in order to reinforce his battalion with other Italian soldiers, so that the battalion, thus reinforced, shall be in a position to fight gallantly against the common enemy'.

The town was full of rumours. The Government had fewer friends than ever, and street boys threw stones at ministerial cars. There was a revolt of the workers at the Ivashchenko factory. The Security Services, Russian and Czech, were working at full pressure. (Maisky came back one evening to his bedroom to find all his things had been removed by the Czech *razvedka*.) There was feverish activity in Government depart-ments. The powers of the Department of State Security were drastically increased. A special court was set up with the right to impose the death penalty for mutiny, attacks on the armed forces, espionage, attempts to rescue prisoners and the dissemination of false news. The Soviet of Workers' Deputies was suppressed. There were urgent calls along the direct telegraph line to the All Russian Provisional Government at Ufa: but the new Directorate had no offices, no staff, and no contact with any existing administrative organization. General Boldyrev, the new Commander-in-Chief, could get no information from the front. *Komuch* asked for the nomination of a Governor-General to assume sole charge. When no reply came from Ufa, *Komuch* appointed a triumvirate under General Tregubov to organize evacuation and to hold up the enemy until evacuation had been completed. There were desperate calls for volunteers. Volsky, Gendelman and other Committee members were enrolled in a 'Constituent Assembly Volunteer Detachment'. The S.R. Party formed a unit including a number of girls. The Mensheviks endeavoured to do the same, but met with no response. One of the last decrees of the Government was for the mobilization of all males, but by that time the administration was so disorganized that no attempt could be made to put it into force. People came forward with all sorts of schemes and demands for government funds with which to set them going. Later, Right-wing elements at Omsk made great play of the fifteen million odd roubles paid out without proper authority by the Samara Treasury and never accounted for.

A rumour went round that Trotsky had promised the Red Army three uninhibited days of loot and rape on the capture of the city. There was panic among the bourgeoisie, and the routes eastward were cluttered with refugees. On October 3rd the telegraph to Ufa was interrupted. On the 4th, members of the Government and senior administrative officials were instructed to entrain. It transpired that General Tregubov and his staff had already left. The special Government train was packed with a crowd of refugees, and the notables had to fight for their places. All night they waited for a locomotive. Next morning, from the siding where their train was standing, they could see Czech soldiers pulling out of the last line of trenches defending Samara. A small delegation, including Maisky, went off to plead, ineffectively, with the station master and the

Czech and Russian station commandants for a locomotive. They went on through the empty streets to Czech Military Headquarters. On their way they called at the *Komuch* government building. It was strewn with litter and deserted except for the main conference room where Volsky and some of his fellow-volunteers sat round a table with bottles, cigarette ends and dirty glasses. Volsky, red in the face, stood up and announced: 'I drink to the corpse of Samara.' At Czech Headquarters the Czech Commanding Officer asked them what had happened to their People's Army. The delegation went back to their siding. Late that night a locomotive arrived and they started on their halting journey eastwards. A few hours later the Red forces entered Samara.

(viii)

Victor Chernov, the most prominent and controversial of the S.R. leaders and Chairman of the Constituent Assembly during its only session, arrived in Samara during the Ufa conference. He had left Moscow at the beginning of June and gone to Saratov which both he and the S.R. Central Committee then imagined to be on the eve of liberation. The *Cheka* got on his tracks and he had to go into hiding. Technical and personal complications had held him up further, and when he finally reached Samara in mid-September he had been cut off for eight months from all but underground politics and for nearly four months from any politics at all. He arrived with the ideas that had been accepted (largely at his own persuasion) by the S.R. Central Committee in the spring: that the Bolsheviks were the pawns and allies of Imperial Germany, that Allied military aid might be accepted against the German-Bolshevik alliance, but that in the liberation of Russia from Bolshevik tyranny no section of the Socialist Revolutionaries should count on any force other than the force of the Russian people.

Chernov's conception of civil war was one of popular risings. Peasant revolt would follow peasant revolt with snowball effect till Bolshevik rule was swept away in the avalanche. Civil war, he maintained, is 75 per cent propaganda. He poured scorn on professional soldiers with their hackneyed ideas of fronts and formations and lines of communication. He was keenly alive to the danger of reaction, to the prospect that there might arise 'against the Left-wing Red dictatorship an equally despotic but Right-wing White dictatorship'. In the struggle between these two 'the Socialist Revolutionary Party, if it is to fulfil its historic role, must emerge as a Third Force and fight a determined war for Democracy on two fronts'.

He arrived in Samara with a sense of personal mission. He seems to have felt that his party's failures in 1917 might have been averted had he shown more assertiveness. He reproached himself with having been too 'completely satisfied with literary and oratorical successes'. He had 'sacrificed to the fetish of unachievable Party unity the energetic defence of the very programme which the Party had formally adopted at his initiative.' He was determined that nothing of the sort should happen again.

His arrival caused embarrassment to the Right-wing S.R. leaders. To the military and to the bourgeoisie he was 'the comrade from the undertaker's office, engaged in the burial of Russia'; his presence at Ufa would jeopardize the chances of agreement which the reverses at the front were showing to be so necessary. Accordingly, while he was received with respect, allotted the best room in the Hotel National and given an official reception with a banquet and speeches, he was discreetly prevented from going on to Ufa. His impressions of Samara were most unfavourable. 'I was horrified,' he told his wife later, 'by the progress made by the monarchists and by the weakness of the moderate ones among us in consenting to a coalition with all the anti-democratic forces.' He was constantly on the direct line to Ufa, protesting at the concessions to the Siberians. He told his colleagues they had 'pulled down the bulwark of democracy with their own hands'. When the *Komuch* delegates (except Zenzinov who stayed on in Ufa) came back to Samara there were long and bitter arguments.

At this point Chernov scored an important success. In early September there had been on *Komuch* territory a bare quorum of the S.R. Central Committee, and it was by a majority of one vote only that this quorum approved the Ufa agreement. After the Conference one Right-wing Central Committee member resigned, and the arrival of Chernov himself and three other like-minded members ensured, henceforth, the preponderance of the Chernov faction. They considered themselves bound, more or less, by the agreement concluded at Ufa by their colleagues. But they felt free to interpret and to play their part in implementing the agreement in the light of their democratic ideals.

(ix)

By the late autumn the anti-Bolshevik front was disintegrating, and if the Reds had been in a position to exploit their opportunity they might well have swept on to Siberia. The Samara Army, except for a few scattered detachments, had ceased to exist. The Siberians were not yet ready. Czech regiments were refusing to go into the line, and a Czech colonel committed suicide out of shame at the behaviour of his unit. Stefanik, the Czech Minister of War (Czechoslovakia had now been recognized by the Allies), came out from Paris on a visit, and reported his grave concern to Beneš. The French General, Janin, who arrived with him to assume command of all non-Russian troops in Eastern Russia and Siberia, found the Legion in a state of '*désarroi moral*'. As a fighting force the corps was rapidly becoming useless. With Austria-Hungary dropping out of the war and the November armistice imminent the men were eager to go home. But London and Paris, now hoping for a Bolshevik collapse, put pressure on Beneš to agree to their staying on in Siberia. During the late autumn and winter they were successively withdrawn from the front and set to guard the railway line between Tomsk and Irkutsk.

Meanwhile it was for the politicians to implement the

directives of the Ufa conference. By mid-October the former *Komuch* territory had shrunk to an enclave round Ufa and Orenburg, or rather round Ufa, as Orenburg in effect had all along been run by Ataman Dutov and his Cossacks. Ufa was too small to carry so elaborate a body as the Council of Heads of Departments, and so four of the Council's members were deputed to administer it until such time as the All Russian Provisional Government made other arrangements. This Government, that is, the Directorate, had first to choose their capital. Reports from Omsk were disquieting: reaction was gaining ground there and a prominent S.R. had been murdered by drunken Cossack officers. To move to Omsk involved the risk of the new Government becoming prisoners of the Right-wing military or of grimmer possibilities. On September 29th Avksentiev and Zenzinov, the S.R. members of the Directorate, called a meeting of S.R.s still in Ufa to advise them. Some still favoured Omsk, others Ufa or even Samara. Avksentiev suggested Ekaterinburg as a compromise. The next three days were full of uncertainties. There were rumours of the choice of Ekaterinburg, then of Ufa. Finally it was announced that Ekaterinburg was the definite choice, and delegates set off there to arrange for quarters and offices. This with great difficulty they managed to do, only to receive a telegram that the Directorate had changed their minds again and were on their way to Omsk.

This decision was probably inevitable. The Directorate had no staff, no apparatus, no machinery of government. Had they installed themselves in a provincial town like Ekaterinburg or Chelyabinsk they would have remained a little group of middle-aged gentlemen sitting in a vacuum. If they, as a government, wanted to govern, if they wanted to exert any influence at all upon events, they must go where the tools of government existed. That could only be Omsk. Before departure from Ufa they told their supporters they intended to suppress the forces of reaction. But they were aware of the risks. A friend called on their train in Chelyabinsk station. 'It has to be like this,' Avksentiev explained to him. 'We must cram ourselves into the wolf's mouth. Either he will swallow us or we will choke him.' The friend replied that it would certainly be the former. Zenzinov later wrote: 'The Bolsheviks called all their opponents counter-revolutionaries and believed that they would all bring to life a reactionary programme. Any deviation of ours to the right of strictly democratic ideas would amount to confirmation of the Bolsheviks' accusations and would justify their activities. Therefore we particularly feared any strengthening of the Siberian influences, and yet circumstances were such that we were being drawn into the centre of these influences. Accordingly it was with great anxiety that we travelled to Omsk.'

Their reception at Omsk was frigid. No quarters were ready for them, and their first week was spent in their railway carriages on a siding. Later on they were allotted a school building near the station as offices, and managed to find some sort of living accommodation in the town. The general atmosphere in Omsk bore out their suspicions. Right-wingers were openly talking of a military dictatorship. 'Monarchical circles,' in Zenzinov's gentle phrase, 'were allowing themselves to behave in a manner which could not be tolerated in a state where all citizens should be able freely to enjoy their rights.' The Directorate seemed to be in a sort of vacuum, while the effective masters of Omsk were the local Administrative Council, under the influence of the Right-wing Ivan Mihailov and the Right-wing generals. 'The Administrative Council,' Zenzinov noted in his diary, 'have decided to keep all real power in their hands and to treat us as a decoration,' each member being '"a one-fifth of an His Royal Highness".' But General Boldyrev, who was by no means a reactionary, noted: 'The most vulnerable spot of the Directorate was its detachment from the masses. A child of the intelligentsia, it was absorbed too much in high-sounding principles . . . It had no contact with actual life. It remained cut off from the real life of the peasant, the worker, and even the petty artisan; cut off from these problems . . . which on the other side of the Civil War front were solved so radically.'

(x)

There remained the Congress of Members of the Constituent Assembly, recognized by the Ufa State Conference as an integral organ of the All Russian Provisional Government. The composition of the Congress was largely that of *Komuch*: but the spirit that animated its activities was a different one. The great majority of *Komuch* members were S.R.s, but members of other parties could and did belong to it. No non-S.R. ever played any part whatever in the Congress. And then the balance of power within the Party, and the policy of the Party, had changed abruptly. The bare majority that had approved the Ufa agreement was now a minority. The Congress was dominated by the S.R. Central Committee and the Central Committee was now dominated by Chernov.

The evacuation train from Samara carrying Chernov and his friends did not reach Ufa till after the departure of the Directorate for Omsk. The first decision to be taken was where the Congress should be installed, and for the next few days the rooms and corridors of the Grand Siberian Hotel were buzzing with lobbying and discussion. Ufa presented the advantages of a congenial atmosphere; the local government, such as it was, was sympathetic. On the other hand, now that Samara had fallen the Red Army might soon be approaching. In favour of Omsk was the consideration that there the Congress could support, and if need be spur on, the S.R. members of the Directorate. Against this the cautious argued that this meant putting all the democratic eggs into one basket: the Omsk reactionaries might suppress both the Directorate and the Congress in one *coup*; whereas if the Congress were away from Omsk there would still remain one bastion of democracy. However, the verdict was in favour of Omsk. Special trains were got ready and the members were about to depart when a telegram arrived from Fomin and Bykhovsky (two S.R. leaders who had gone on to Omsk) strongly advising the Congress not to proceed there.

A special session was hurriedly convoked. Attempts were made to contact Fomin at Omsk on the direct wire, but he could not be located. Finally it was agreed to proceed as far as Chelyabinsk, telegraph Fomin to meet them there, and make the decision after seeing him. The Congress entrained on October 12th, and reached Chelyabinsk on the evening of the 15th. Maisky, who travelled up with them, was present at the meeting in the ill-lit *coupé* when Fomin and Bykhovsky made their report. It was of unrelieved gloom. Omsk, they reported, was a hotbed of reaction. There were no workers' meetings, no Socialist Revolutionary newspapers. The bourgeoisie and the intellectuals were bitterly opposed to the Constituent Assembly. One heard well-dressed people saying it would be a good thing if Chernov and Volsky were murdered. The volcano might erupt at any moment. There was no discipline and no public security. Drunkenness was incessant. There was no hope of accommodation. Finally the Directorate members themselves would prefer that the Congress should not come to Omsk.

Deliberations in the *coupé* continued far into the night. There was now no question of the Congress going on to Omsk; but the report seemed to show that the Directorate had failed to take any steps to assert themselves or to bring the reactionaries under control, and it was decided to send a delegation to Omsk to see what the Directorate was doing. Arkhangelsky, Pavlov and Moiseenko were nominated and left for Omsk at once together with Rogovsky, head of the Samara Department of State Security, who was proceeding to the new capital with his security force of two hundred men. Moiseenko had with him over two million roubles of the Congress's funds. Surprise was felt afterwards that he should take so large a sum to Omsk. But with the Congress still homeless he had nowhere to store it— and there were Rogovsky's men to look after him.

As to the Congress itself, it was decided to move to Ekaterinburg. Chelyabinsk was ruled out as too small, too dirty and too provincial; furthermore it was packed with military. On the morning of the 16th an official session approved the decisions taken. But they had to wait two more days in Chelyabinsk before locomotives were allotted, and did not arrive at Ekaterinburg till the morning of the 19th. Here there were three authorities, the Czech military, the Regional Government of the Urals, now on the last lap of its existence, and representatives, both civil and military, of Omsk. None of them showed much readiness to help the newcomers. They were unable to find accommodation, and Brushvit went to Czech Headquarters to make a personal appeal to Gajda. Thanks to Gajda's intervention the members were eventually housed, two or three in a room, in the main hotels as rooms in them fell vacant. Through Gajda they obtained the use of a dilapidated Diocesan School on the outskirts of the town. While the place was being repaired they arranged with the headmistress of a girls' school to use her school for meetings. But the headmistress had to cancel the arrangement because her girls' parents did not approve of the Constituent Assembly.

(xi)

The policy of Zenzinov and Avksentiev, the S.R. members of the Directorate at Omsk, was to make the best working compromise they could with the Siberians and wait for Boldyrev, in whom they had confidence, to obtain effective control over the hotheads in the army. To the Congress at Ekaterinburg, holding endless meetings in their hotel bedrooms, this seemed mere weakness. News from Omsk was bad. Moiseenko was found murdered in the street; his assailant was never arrested and the two million roubles which he had left in his *coupé* on the train were confiscated by the Omsk authorities. Rumours came through of concessions to the Right in the negotiations over the composition of the new All Russian cabinet. A message was passed to Avksentiev and Zenzinov to make full use of the 3,000 Czech soldiers at Omsk, but a reply came back that it was 'impossible for the Directorate to consolidate its power with the help of foreign bayonets'. We are told that when they heard of this the Congress members 'wrung their hands'.

It is quite untrue that the S.R. members of the Directorate gave way to their party colleagues in the Congress. Their great handicap was the general belief at Omsk that they were under their Central Committee's orders. They were thus held to be the Omsk agents of Chernov; and by the end of October Chernov was widely rumoured to be 'negotiating a peace with the Bolsheviks'. In point of fact, Zenzinov and Avksentiev were increasingly (and justifiably) apprehensive about the goings-on at Ekaterinburg. We have a letter dated early November from Avksentiev to a friend of his who was one of the few moderates left there. 'The position of democracy is very difficult and responsible. It is essential that sessions in the Congress should give evidence of great caution and political wisdom. But the more that the influence of certain persons is brought to bear I notice the reverse to be the case. In such circumstances a split [in the S.R. Party] is inevitable sooner or later, and better sooner than later. We learn nothing, and it seems we are capable once more of losing our opportunity, or anyhow of worsening our chances.'

A Congress document that was to achieve some notoriety was the so-called 'Chernov Manifesto' of October 24th. The term 'manifesto' is misleading. It was an internal party document circulated for the guidance of S.R. Party organizations. Its initiator was Chernov himself, and his original draft was, he tells us, toned down far more than he liked to meet the misgivings of his more timid Central Committee colleagues. The final version, however, was uncompromising enough. It starts off with a warning that democracy in Russia 'is dangerously threatened by counter-revolutionary elements who have allied themselves [with it] for the purpose of ruining it.' It goes on strongly to criticize the weakness of the S.R. negotiators at Ufa, who 'suffered from lack of unity and discipline', and gives a long list of the failures and concessions of the Directorate since its appointment. However, the Socialist Revolutionary Party was still 'prepared to give the Provisional Government all possible assistance in defending democratic freedom and Russian independence'. But at the same time, 'whether or not the Provisional Government in its present composition has the power and will to act in the direction here indicated . . . the tactics of the S.R. Party should be to rally its forces . . . around the Constituent Assembly and the Congress of Members of the Constituent Assembly, which is a preliminary to the former . . . In anticipation of possible political crises resulting from counter-revolutionary schemes, all party forces must be mobilized immediately, given military training and armed, in order to be able to withstand at any moment the attacks of counter-revolutionists who organize civil war in the rear of the anti-Bolshevik front . . .' The document seems to have been fairly widely distributed, but not, apparently, to the S.R. members of the Directorate. We have the evidence of Zenzinov, a palpably honest witness, that no copy was sent to him. Inevitably it began to leak. Zenzinov first heard of it when an Omsk government telegraph agency brought him extracts. He felt it was 'at least tactless' and gave instructions that it should not be released for publication. He consulted Avksentiev, who agreed with him. But it was obviously impossible for the matter to remain a secret. Rumours spread wider and became more definite. Extracts were published in an Omsk newspaper. Zenzinov contacted Gendelman at Ekaterinburg on the direct line and asked him to inform the Central Committee that both he and Avksentiev considered such circulars to be most unwise and improper. It is unlikely that either he or Gendelman (who agreed with him throughout) imagined that this message would have much result. On November 5th the matter came up officially at a meeting of the Directorate where, for the first time, Zenzinov saw the complete text. General Boldyrev was angry over the possible repercussions of S.R. agitation (General Knox of the British Military Mission had been pressing him hard about keeping politics out of the Army) and asked how Zenzinov would react to a proposal to arrest the S.R. Central Committee. Zenzinov took the line that if the judicial authorities considered the circular to be criminal then not only the

Central Committee but the whole S.R. Party should be arrested—on condition that Right-wing law-breakers should be arrested also. The usual pattern of Directorate meetings was a line-up between Avksentiev and Zenzinov on the one side and Boldyrev and Vologodsky on the other, with Vinogradov, the Left Cadet, taking a middle position. On this occasion Vinogradov agreed with the S.R.s. The matter was referred to the Ministry of Justice who (surprisingly) ruled that there was no case for criminal proceedings. There, for the time being, the matter rested. But it was raised again a few days later on the eve of Boldyrev's departure for the front, where, among other problems, he had to enforce the handing over to his command of what was left of the Ufa People's Army. He asked his colleagues if they agreed to his taking strong measures, and if necessary shooting any person tampering with the Army's loyalty or endeavouring to form private party armies. All his four colleagues assented.

(xii)

Meanwhile in the hotel bedrooms at Ekaterinburg the psychological temperature continued to rise. There were local frustrations. The Diocesan School was still not ready for the Congress sessions. And the telegraph was in the hands of the Omsk administration, and Siberian officers insisted on reading the tapes of the Central Committee's tele-conversations. It became increasingly hard to get connection on trunk lines, and the S.R. leaders sat waiting for days on end in the Ekaterinburg telegraph office. There were sinister rumours. A friendly Czech officer reported a plot to murder Chernov, and a group of his intimates formed a bodyguard to keep continuous watch in the passage of the Hotel Palais Royal outside his door. There came news of the inclusion in the new All-Russian cabinet of Kolchak and the notorious Rightist Ivan Mihailov, and of the steps to wind up the rump *Komuch* administration in Ufa and take over what was left of the Samara People's Army. The inevitable clash with Reaction was coming nearer and nearer. Congress hotheads came out in favour of denouncing the Ufa agreement and declaring open war against the Right with the help of the Czechs. But it was felt that it was better to wait, to give time to the Reaction to make the first move and then to counter-attack by seizing Ekaterinburg with Czech aid and expelling the Siberians.

Armed Czech aid thus seemed to be essential, however the crisis was to develop. But certain members of the Congress began to harbour misgivings about the Czechs: their attitude to the S.R. Central Committee had recently been non-committal if not cool. It was feared that the Entente repre-sentatives were influencing the Czechs. General Knox and some of his French colleagues had been openly anti-Congress. And so with the Czechs doubtful and the Entente unfriendly, and with the obvious imminence of a German collapse on the Western Front and all that that implied, one or two began to wonder whether it would not be wise to attempt to come to terms with the Bolsheviks. However, as a final gesture, a decision was taken in mid-November to stage a large public meeting in the now nearly repaired Diocesan School on the 23rd. The foreign consuls and local workers' representatives were among those to be invited. All the oratorical big guns of the Congress were to come into action. The meeting was to make clear to Russia and to the world that the Congress of Members of the Constituent Assembly stood as the champion of Freedom and Democracy.

On the evening of November 17th some Congress Members had received an unusually optimistic message from Zenzinov in Omsk. It therefore came as a bombshell when on the following day a Czech officer called at the Palais Royal to say that during the previous night a *coup d'état* had taken place in Omsk and the S.R. members of the Directorate were under arrest. An excited little gathering in Chernov's bedroom awaited further news. When it came, it was that Admiral Kolchak had assumed power. The Central Committee and the Bureau of the Congress were summoned to meet that same

evening to work out plans for the supreme struggle with
Reaction; and Brushvit and Fomin were dispatched to make
urgent contact with the Czechs.

They returned to say that the Czech leaders had all left for a
conference in Chelyabinsk. But the Central Committee and
Bureau members, duly assembled in Chernov's bedroom,
decided that the Congress should assume supreme authority in
free Russia. One of those present asked what force there was to
back this authority. He was told there were the Czechs; furthermore, on the following morning Congress members would tour
the Ekaterinburg factories and barracks and rally the workers
and soldiers. The first essential was resolution: sufficient
resolution itself engenders force. The meeting proceeded to
elect an Executive Committee under Chernov and Volsky. A
proclamation was drafted. A full session of the Congress was
called for the following morning, and was duly held at 11 a.m.
on November 19th. It was the first and last occasion on which
the Diocesan School was used. The decisions taken on the
previous night were approved and the Congress of Members of
the Constituent Assembly announced their assumption of
supreme authority.

The Executive Committee had their proclamation printed
and a few copies pasted up in Ekaterinburg. It had little impact
outside. Disapproval of the Omsk *coup d'état* was expressed in a
number of quarters. Apart from Ufa, resolutions of protest
were passed by municipal and local councils in Irkutsk,
Chelyabinsk and other centres. General Boldyrev exchanged
sharp words with Admiral Kolchak on the direct telegraph
line. But no one seems to have imagined that the Executive
Committee had any role to play. In the town itself nothing
came of the project to rally the factory workers and soldiers.
Of the two Congress members who have left accounts,
Svyatitsky (who went over to the Bolsheviks) says that Siberian
officers were inciting their men against the Congress, so that
the visits were called off as too dangerous. Nikolaev (who
escaped abroad) says that eight hundred factory workers were
willing to come out and fight, but Congress, to avoid bloodshed,

advised them to stay at work. About midday it was decided
to abandon the Diocesan School—it was too tempting a target
for attacks by reactionary rabble—and the Executive Committee went back to the Hotel Palais Royal.

Besides Chernov and Volsky about a dozen Congress
members were staying at this hotel, with a few S.R., non-
Congress members and Chernov's bodyguard of six. They
occupied ten bedrooms on the second floor, one of the dining-
rooms and the corridor leading to Chernov's bedroom. The
other forty rooms of the hotel were filled with merchants,
speculators, bourgeois families from Perm awaiting the liberation of that city and 'ladies of an unknown profession'. It was in
Chernov's room that the Executive Committee resumed its
deliberations.

At about 3 p.m. a Czech security officer gave warning of
reports of an impending attack on the Congress. He was asked
to provide an armed guard but this he was unable to do. Later
came stories of Siberian officers assembling in the Café
d'Orange and in the Grand Hotel. There were scuffles in the
street and the crowd became excited.

The Executive Committee sent a new appeal to their Czech
officer friend for an armed guard. He suggested that Chernov
and his colleagues should leave through the back door and hide
in the town. But this, for the supreme All-Russian authority,
would have been undignified. By seven o'clock the Palais Royal
was surrounded by Siberians. Then two bombs exploded,
wounding a couple of soldiers. (By whom and how they were
exploded was never satisfactorily cleared up.) Troops rushed
through the main entrance and up the stairs. Svyatitsky
records: 'We would have preferred to defend ourselves to the
last—we had sufficient resolution for this. But we decided that
resistance by the twenty or thirty more or less armed men in the
hotel would be reckless, and a needless shedding of blood.' So
there was no resistance, though the leading officer fired his
revolver, wounding an S.R. who later died in hospital. The
rooms were searched, and papers and money confiscated, but
the intruders failed to find Chernov. In the end they arrested

some twenty S.R.s and marched them through the streets towards the Siberian Divisional Headquarters. *En route* they passed a group of Czechs and the prisoners shouted, 'We are members of the Constituent Assembly.' There was a long wait at Divisional Headquarters and then word came that they were to be returned to the Palais Royal. Gajda, apparently, had given orders to this effect when he heard what had happened. Back at the hotel they found a Czech armed guard.

In the small hours the Congress members were called out of bed by a peremptory order from General Gajda. 'In view of the seditious behaviour of the Congress of Members of the Constituent Assembly ... causing anxiety to the general public, and demoralization among the troops,' they were all, except Chernov, to leave Ekaterinburg forthwith for Chelyabinsk. Once more a hurried meeting was held. All were ready to make the move: to remain in Ekaterinburg was obviously impossible. But the tone and wording of the order were more than ominous; any vestige of hope that the Czechs would take up arms against reaction seemed now ruled out. And it was, of course, unthinkable to leave Chernov behind at the mercy of the Siberians. There were frenzied appeals to Gajda, and in the end he relented and agreed that Chernov might leave with the others. To avoid risk of hostile demonstrations and disturbances it was laid down that the departure should take place in the hours of darkness. The following midnight all the cabs in Ekaterinburg were mustered at the Hotel Palais Royal, and drove off in procession (one hundred and one of them, each with one Congress member or official and one Czech soldier as escort) by a roundabout route to the station. There occurred a final humiliation. There were no passenger coaches in the special train provided. It was composed entirely of *teplushkas*, freight wagons fitted with wood-burning stoves.

The action of the Congress had, of course, left no choice to the new Kolchak Government but to order its suppression and the arrest of its members. This put Gajda in a difficult position; he had already ambitions of a high military command in Russian service and could not afford to quarrel with Omsk.

On the other hand, to hand the S.R.s over would (as events were to show) expose them to the risk of being murdered. He decided, therefore, to pack them off to Chelyabinsk, which was at that moment more or less a Czech enclave. Most of the Czech National Council were there; so were Czech Military Headquarters under General Syrovy. The troops in the town were nearly all Czechs. When the party arrived there Syrovy proposed they should establish themselves in Shchadrinsk, a small town within comparatively easy reach of Chelyabinsk. He promised them a Czech guard. But this would have meant the renunciation of active participation in politics and might have turned out to be a form of internment. The members pressed strongly for transport to Ufa. After some discussion the Czechs agreed and the Congress set off on its last journey as a corporate body.

Back in Ufa again most of the members put up at the Hotel Volga. A few days passed in impotent and feverish discussion. Late on the evening of December 2nd an emergency meeting was called at the hotel: a special troop train had arrived in Ufa station from Omsk—obviously a task force come to suppress the Congress. Well-disposed Czech officers advised going into hiding in the town. According to the local Czech Military Headquarters orders had come in from Syrovy to observe strict neutrality. A final appeal was made to Voitsekhovsky, commanding the Czech troops in Ufa. When asked: 'What measures will be taken in view of the threat to the members of the Constituent Assembly?' he replied: 'None.' The emergency meeting decided on resistance to the end. A messenger was sent out to rally such People's Army troops as were still in Ufa—the rump of a Czech-Russian battalion, Fortunatov's detachment (now reduced to a hundred men) and some Constituent Assembly Volunteers. They might, it was hoped, defend at least the Hotel Volga. Time passed and there was no sign of them; it emerged later that the messenger had been intercepted. One by one Congress members slipped out of the meeting and went into hiding in the town. At dawn a detachment of Siberians arrived at the hotel and arrested the thirteen who

were left. Chernov and Volsky were again among those who
eluded arrest.

(xiii)

For Chernov this was the end of his final period of overt
political activity on Russian soil, which had lasted eleven
weeks. In hiding with their devoted Ufa friends, the S.R.
leaders went busily ahead with plans for their war on two fronts.
The first priority, of course, was the liquidation of Kolchak. All
means were to be devoted to this end, including the traditional
S.R. weapon of terror. There was a scheme for a march on
Omsk by the People's Army, who, on deposing Kolchak, would
turn about and restart the war against the Bolsheviks. An
alternative idea was that the People's Army should disperse,
each man returning with his rifle to his village, ready to rally
to the colours again as soon as the banner of the Constituent
Assembly once more was hoisted. The gulf between the S.R.
leadership and any conception of practical possibilities remained absolute to the end.

There were conspiratorial negotiations with the Bashkirs. A
terrorist operation was organized for the assassination of
Ataman Dutov in Orenburg, but it misfired and the participants were arrested. The Red armies meanwhile were pressing
steadily on towards both Orenburg and Ufa. The Bashkirs
decided to come to terms with the Bolsheviks. The irrepressible
Chernov conceived a plan of making his way illegally across
Red Russia to the Ukraine: the German military collapse, he
reckoned, would entail the fall of Skoropadsky in Kiev, and
that would give the Constituent Assembly the opportunity to
impose its authority. He and his colleagues still at large were
chivvied by White security squads from hiding-place to hiding-
place, from Ufa to Orenburg and back again and across the
Bashkir steppe. As the Red armies drew closer the idea of
establishing contact with the Bolsheviks was once more mooted.
Volsky and some of the others saw promise in a direct approach.

They should, they suggested, await the arrival of the Reds in Ufa and then negotiate for a Coalition Government of All Russia to be composed of Bolsheviks, Left S.R.s, Mensheviks and Right S.R.s. But Chernov objected that there could be no equal negotiations between a victorious Red Army and a handful of refugees. One must first establish a basis for agreement. A certain Volnov, a friend of Maxim Gorky, was available as intermediary: he was to be passed across the front, make his way to Moscow, and there inform Gorky of the S.R. willingness to make peace on condition of the restoration of all freedoms and the recall of the Constituent Assembly. If and when, and only if and when, a satisfactory reply to this feeler was received were the S.R. leaders to come out of hiding.

This proposal, Chernov tells us, was accepted. Volnov went off on his mission. A very few days later Ufa was captured by the Reds. Chernov escaped to Orenburg, where he lived in hiding, first from the Whites and later, when the Reds arrived, from the Bolsheviks. S.R. underground communications between Ufa and Orenburg broke down. There was no news of Volnov (who in point of fact took some months to reach Moscow). Chernov had no inkling that his Ufa colleagues had changed their minds again and approached the Bolsheviks till he read in an Orenburg Bolshevik paper a proclamation of theirs appealing to lovers of liberty to stop fighting the Bolsheviks and actively to attack Kolchak and 'the Allied imperialists on his side'. The official Kremlin announcement of the talks with the S.R. leaders was issued on January 13th, 1920. It laid down specifically that 'there could be no discussion of the convening of a Constituent Assembly and that there could be no change in the constitution of the Russian Soviet Republic'. The announcement meant, in effect, that the Socialist Revolutionary Party in Russia was as dead as the Constituent Assembly.

The main sources for Chapter II are:

Boldyrev, V. G., *Direktoriya, Kolchak, Interventy* (Novonikolaevsk, 1925).

Bunyan, J., *Intervention, Civil War and Communism* (Baltimore, 1936).

Chernov, V., *Mes Tribulations en Russie Soviétique* (Paris, 1921).

Chernov, V., *Pered Burei* (New York, 1953).

Fic, M. V., *The Origin of a Conflict between the Bolsheviks and the Czechoslovak Legion* (Chicago, 1958).

Gins, G. K., *Sibir, Soyuzniki i Kolchak* (Peking, 1921).

Klante, M., *Von der Wolga zum Amur* (Berlin, 1931).

Klimushkin, in *Grazhdanskaya Voina na Volge* (Prague, 1930).

Krol, L. A., *Za Tri Goda* (Vladivostock, 1922).

Lelevich, G., in *Proletarskaya Revolyutsiya* (May, 1926).

Maisky, I., *Demokraticheskaya Kontr-Revolyutsiya* (Moscow-Leningrad, 1923).

Nikolaev in *Sovremmeniye Zapiski*, No. 45 (Paris).

Pichon, Col., in *Le Monde Slave* (Paris, Feb., 1925).

Popov, F., *Chekho-Slovatski Myatezh* (Moscow-Samara, 1932).

Serebrennikov in *Sibirski Arkhiv* (Prague).

Svyatitsky in *Kolchakovshchina* (Ekaterinburg, 1924).

Varneck and Fisher, *The Testimony of Kolchak* (Stanford, 1935).

Zenzinov, V., *Iz Zhizni Revolyutsyonera* (Paris, 1920).

Other works consulted include:

Beneš, E., *Souvenirs de Guerre et de Révolution* (Paris, 1930).

Budberg in *Arkhiv Russkoi Revolyutsii*, Vol. XIII.

Janin, Gen., *Ma Mission en Sibérie* (Paris, 1933).

Masaryk, T. G., *The Making of a State* (London, 1927).

Zenzinov, V., *Gosudarstvennyi Perevorot Admirala Kolchaka* (Paris, 1919).

CHAPTER III

The Beginnings of the Red Army

(i)

One obstacle to face the Bolsheviks in the creation of the Red Army was their heritage of nineteenth-century revolutionary thought and feeling with regard to military matters. The French armies of 1793 were both revolutionary and effective fighting armies: that they were so was in great part due to the influence of the *Commissaires* and the *Représentants en Mission*. But as time went on it was the military element that prevailed, and the revolutionary spirit faded away; and subsequent generations of Left-wing thinkers took little account of the purely military lessons of the French Revolution. Throughout the century, when established governments called out troops to disperse recalcitrant workers and when regular officers were mostly monarchists or extreme conservatives, it became natural to regard regular armies as the arch-enemy of Socialism, and to forget that only in those armies were preserved qualities of discipline and technique that might be essential for the survival of a socialist régime in times of crisis.

Babœuf held that regular armies should be abolished, that the common people should be armed, should elect their leaders and be empowered to change or dismiss them. These ideas, later developed and refurbished by Jaurès, remained the basic doctrine of those Left-wingers who felt that revolution would leave a need for any form of military organization. Marx had little to say on the subject. He was keenly interested in the Paris Commune, whose failure he attributes to lack of the offensive spirit. Here he was wrong—it was organization rather than the will to fight that the *Communards* lacked. Engels, on the other hand, had taken part in the minor skirmishes of the end of the German revolution of 1848 and liked to be thought a military expert. His contribution was to emphasize the importance of the economic, political and social factors in warfare, but he had little practical guidance to offer future revolutionaries. He foretold the emergence of new, proletarian, military techniques, but he did not say what these were.

Lenin began to read Clausewitz in 1915 and was considerably impressed. But from early March, 1917, in his preoccupation with the completion of the Russian Revolution, his exhortations ran on traditional revolutionary lines. He urged in his *Letters from Afar* the arming of the poorest and most exploited sections of the community, so that 'they themselves may take into their own hands all the organs of state power, that they themselves may constitute these organs'. He laid down no plans for this proletarian militia: 'when the workers, and all the people as a real mass, take up this task in a practical way they will work it out and secure it a hundred times better than any theoretician can propose.' He looked forward to 'a comradely discipline practised with enthusiasm'.

On Lenin's return to Petrograd in the spring of 1917, the Bolsheviks, as far as military matters were concerned, began to work on two quite different tasks—the undermining of the old Imperial Army and the building up of a proletarian militia completely loyal to the Party leadership. By midsummer the number of Red Guards recruited from the Petrograd factory workers had reached some ten thousand, to be more than doubled in September when the call went out to save the Revolution from Kornilov. Meanwhile, Party cells were organized in an ever-increasing number of army units, and propaganda was directed at the rank and file with increasing intensity and success. At a conference of delegates of the Party's Military Organization held in Petrograd in June a resolution was passed calling for the building up of a 'material revolutionary bulwark of the Revolution' out of 'army revolutionary democratic elements'. It would appear that in Party thinking of the time the role of the old army was to supply recruits and arms for the new proletarian militias.

The Red Guards, of course, played an important, perhaps decisive, role in the Bolshevik seizure of power. But their limitations soon became apparent. The counter-offensive against Petrograd by Krasnov and his small force of half-hearted Cossacks was a very unformidable affair, but the Red Guards sent out to meet it made little better showing than the Cossacks. The issue was decided by the arrival of a detachment of Red sailors under Dybenko. The sailors would, indeed, fight when in the mood, but they were so undisciplined that right from the start they were an embarrassment to the Party leadership. The leadership could count on the Latvian Rifle Regiments and a few other units—some thirty thousand men spread out over the vast empire. The old imperial army was disintegrating. There was still no sign of the outbreak of the world revolution. The German forces retained their cohesion and their discipline: fraternization at the front meant, in effect, that the Germans had every opportunity for reconnoitring the Russian dispositions. Realization of the weakness within and of the threat from without provoked heated arguments in the top Party circles. As Lenin was to admit to the Eighth Party Congress in March, 1919, 'the task of building up the Red Army had in no way been prepared, even in theory.'

An immediate task was the suppression of the anti-Bolshevik régimes that had emerged in the Ukraine and the Don; and a very heterogeneous force of Red Guards, old army details and volunteers was scraped together for this purpose. Meanwhile, an All Russian Collegium for Worker and Peasant Military Organization was set up and made plans for a Worker and Peasant Army. In late January *Sovnarkom* issued a decree for the recruitment of an army of volunteers 'from the class-conscious organized elements of the toiling masses'. Recruiting began, but the response was meagre. At the same time,

independently, the Bolshevik Command at General Headquarters in Mogilev issued instructions for the formation of
military forces by provincial and local Soviets. A few courses
were started for the training of officers for the new army. And
an energetic propaganda drive was started in prisoner-of-war
camps to induce the inmates to volunteer for service in the
Red Army.[1]

The drawn-out negotiations at Brest-Litovsk broke down,
and on February 22nd the Germans resumed their advance.
The crisis had come, and the slogan was put out: 'The Socialist
Fatherland is in danger.' There was some response by the
Petrograd workers; only 5,500 had volunteered up to February
25th, but the number had tripled by early March. Even so it
was not impressive. The rush of offers to serve by former army
officers and action by peasant partisan bands along the line of
the German advance seemed to show that other motives
counted for more than revolutionary zeal. In any case the
Germans met with no effective resistance, and the acceptance
of their peace terms became inevitable. In the bitter controversy round Lenin's stand for peace a comrade from Moscow
claimed, in all sincerity, that the Moscow workers were eager
to fight and sixty thousand of them had volunteered for active
service; it transpired that the actual figure was under three
thousand. Lenin bluntly maintained that the means for waging
war did not exist, and (later in the Seventh Party Congress)
added a further cogent reason. 'To declare war now on
Germany,' he said, 'means to give in to the provocation of the
Russian bourgeoisie . . . this is the best way to overthrow us
now.' He was right. The Party, at the beginning of 1918,
numbered some 115,000 for the whole of Russia; and the poor
response to the appeal for volunteers revealed how few there
were prepared to risk their lives for the Revolution. The
casualties among these few in a hopeless war with Germany

[1] Reports of the formation of these 'Internationalist' units caused
considerable flurry in the Allied capitals. But not more than about 50,000
men (mostly Hungarians) seem to have been recruited, and they played
an active role only in two of the minor theatres—in Transcaspia and against
Semenov on the Manchurian frontier.

might well have proved fatal to the precarious régime. The fiasco of the Ukrainian Reds' resistance after Brest-Litovsk merely proved how right Lenin had been, and doubtless predisposed him to support the successive measures that Trotsky was to introduce.

One result of the crisis of late February was the establishment, on March 1st, of the Supreme Military Soviet. On March 13th —the day after the transfer of the government to Moscow— Trotsky became its chairman and People's Commissar for War. Trotsky knew that the great asset of the régime was the fanatical devotion of the hard core of Party members: this devotion must be geared to military tasks and fertilized by the technical military know-how of former professional army officers. Above all there must be discipline, centralization, control; a sharp reversal of the trends of 1917; a final end to the old romantic thinking on the business of war. But the new army must be a class army. Every specialist—i.e., former officer—'must have a commissar on his right and a commissar on his left, each with a revolver'. No class enemies might benefit from military instruction; their place was in unarmed labour units well away from the front. The Revolution must remain paramount.

Throughout March and April came a spate of appeals, proclamations and orders. Regulations were issued defining the tasks of provincial and local Military Commissariats, each of which should be headed by a triumvirate of one military specialist and two Party stalwarts. On April 6th an order defined the functions of the Commissars for Military Affairs, who were to be 'irreproachable revolutionaries, capable of remaining the embodiment of the revolution under the most difficult circumstances'. They were to 'see to it that the Army does not become a thing apart from the entire Soviet system and that the various military establishments do not become foci of conspiracies or instruments against workers and peasants'. On April 22nd a decree provided for the compulsory military education of workers and peasants. On April 29th elections to posts of command were finally forbidden.

In spite of Trotsky's powerful personality, progress at first was slow. There was no administrative machine to implement the new measures. The People's Commissariat for Military Affairs—heir of the former Ministry of War—was being merged with the Collegium for Worker and Peasant Military Organization. This would in any case have led to confusion, and the transfer of the capital from Petrograd to Moscow brought chaos. Meanwhile, in the provinces, local Soviets were acting independently on the authority of the instructions of January 26th from General Headquarters. Soviet military power, such as it was in early 1918, consisted largely of a hotch-potch of weak and unco-ordinated little private armies, some of which (as in the expedition against the Orenburg Cossacks) were engaged in what amounted to little private wars. In the East, where the first major campaigns of the Civil War were to be fought, the pattern was especially variegated. In Perm there were companies of Red Guards, in Ekaterinburg there were regiments; in Ufa the fighting men (*boeviki*) were grouped in bands (*druzhiny*) under an old Party stalwart of 1905 who refused to believe that any further organization was necessary. At Omsk, on the other hand, there existed at the same time three supreme authorities—the *Ispolkom* (Executive Committee) of the Omsk Soviet, the Revolutionary Military Staff and the West Siberian Military Operational Staff; while everything pertaining to the seventeen steamers on the river Irtysh came under the Steamship Flotilla Staff. There was no co-ordination between these bodies, no arrangements for supplies or intelligence, and no control over individual units.

A Party activist who was there at the time has recorded that many provincial Bolsheviks were essentially pacifists, and that the others had varying and conflicting ideas about what ought to be done in the way of military matters. The large Left S.R. and Maximalist elements in so many of the local Soviets were even less inclined to take orders from the centre. Communications from Moscow were slow and precarious. When they arrived they were apt to be ignored. Even when a local Military Commissariat was set up on the lines laid down by the centre it was, as often as not, unable to impose its authority on its own units. It was bad enough, from the standpoint of military efficiency, that commanders should be elected by the rank and file, as were also the committees who were supposed to control the commanders. But it quite often happened that 'anyone who wished was a commander or could call himself a commander, but not even he knew what he commanded or where it was'. As to the men, they had joined up as volunteers in the first flush of revolutionary enthusiasm and remained volunteers at heart; that is to say, when the enthusiasm cooled off and the hardships and irksomeness of military life became apparent they had no compunction in deserting. As Trotsky was to put it: 'It was only natural that the army attracted, along with idealist young workers, a large number of low-class vagabonds, who were then wandering around.' And again, at the All Russian Congress of Military Commissars in Moscow in June, 1918, 'Have our hopes been justified? To the extent of 30 per cent. Certainly there are many heroic, selfless fighters in the Red Army, but also unsatisfactory elements, rowdies, ne'er-do-wells, social rejects.'

(ii)

The revolt of the Czechoslovak Legion in late May inevitably brought drastic counter-measures. On May 29th universal liability for military service was proclaimed. A Revolutionary Military Soviet for the Eastern Front was set up on June 2nd. During that month the age limits for service were fixed at eighteen to forty years; there were call-ups in the Volga and Urals areas, and of Moscow and Petrograd workers. The sense of crisis was increased by the initial Red fiascos. Losses from enemy fire were negligible—except when Red detachments, through ignorance or carelessness, blundered into Czech machine-gun traps. Losses from flight or desertion were enormous.

Some at least of the men on the spot became convinced of the need for discipline and organization that Trotsky in Moscow had been demanding for the past ten weeks. In early June there were meetings of the 3rd and 7th Ural Regiments which passed unanimous resolutions to the effect that (1) Committees of the rank and file should be abolished forthwith; (2) Meetings might be held only on the demand of the Military Commissars; (3) Field Courts (Revolutionary Military Tribunals) should act so that 'deserters and traitors see that they meet their deserts in deed and not just in word'; (4) Proper attention must be paid to supplies, and (5) Commanders (down to and including platoon commanders) must be men of some military experience. This unanimity may not have been difficult to obtain. The spate of desertions had acted as an effective purge, and those remaining in the regiment were too ashamed of their performance to come out in opposition to the resolutions proposed by the stalwarts.

A stream of instructions came through to the Volga and the Urals and attempts were made by the local Party leaders to carry them out. Following the order for the call-up of workers and non-*kulak* peasants, the Ural Regional Staff 'with ex-Colonel Strogov of the Inspectorate and Comrade Svinkk worked out a mobilization plan in great detail but were unable to bring it into effect'. They had no personnel to set about the registration of recruits or the issue of call-up notices; far less to look after any men who presented themselves. Furthermore, efforts 'to bring unity and order into the Eastern Front' were apt to fall down because of the intransigence of the local commanders. These last were by now convinced of the need to establish discipline in their own units, but not yet prepared to take orders from anyone else. And often they lacked the staff to look after their own commands. Comrade Yakovlev in charge of the important Orenburg-Ural sector had only a Chief of Staff and an adjutant to help him: otherwise he had only his personal bodyguard. He did not know where all his units were. Worse still, the Chief of Staff was an anarchist who (till he was arrested) 'agitated against the Soviet régime'. The first real step forward was made on local Party initiative. In early June, the Ural Regional Committee of the Party called a conference of the local Party organs, the Left S.R.s, the Soviets, the Military Commissars, the Military Inspectorate, and what was left of the Central Siberian Military Commissariat. The conference decided to cut through the welter of unco-ordinated and often barely existent authorities and to subordinate all military activities to a Collegium of the North Ural Siberian Front, the Collegium to consist of Comrade Berzin (as Commanding Officer), General Nadezhny (as Military Specialist) and Comrade Anuchin (as Military Commissar). The new Collegium reported to Moscow and asked for instructions. No reply was forthcoming, but when, a few days later, belated notification came through of the establishment of the Revolutionary Military Soviet of the Eastern Front, Berzin was able to get into touch, on the direct telegraph line, with Muraviev, the new Eastern Front commander. He learned that the forces available were to be grouped into four armies—Berzin (Northern Urals), Kharchenko (Simbirsk, Syzran, Samara), Yakovlev (Ufa, Orenburg) and Raevsky (Saratov, Uralsk). General Headquarters was to be at Kazan. A new flow of orders came in. All partisan and volunteer units must now be incorporated into proper regiments, and these regiments into divisions. Subordinate units must stop trying to communicate directly with Moscow: all communications must pass through the regular hierarchy of command (Order 100). All troops must be cleared out of railway trains and all rolling-stock sent back to the rear. Except on special orders from above, use of railways must be confined to staffs of higher formations, senior supply authorities and armoured train detachments. All units must provide themselves with and exclusively make use of road transport. In particular no unit could be allowed to make use of a train to get away from the front line to the rear (Order 147).

Berzin and his fellow-activists, working at high pressure, felt that they were making progress, and encouraging reports were sent to G.H.Q. at Kazan and to Moscow. More military specialists had arrived from the rear and been posted; volunteer and partisan units had been incorporated into regular formations, and all had their Political Commissars; the *Cheka* had established its network of internal informers and was functioning successfully; agents were being dispatched to enemy territory; special sections had been set up at provincial and district levels to take care of military supplies; repair shops for mechanical transport had started to work; progress had been made with the requisitioning of horses (mainly in districts of suspected anti-Soviet disaffection); the Political Section of the front under Comrade Feierabend had rallied all the local Party members and most of the local Left S.R.s; they had already issued thousands of leaflets and appeals and were forming special sections to work on prisoners of war and on the Czech rank and file; popular feeling throughout the area was, it was bravely hoped, on the side of the Reds.

But in July this optimism suffered severe blows. From the South came news of Red defeats and then the shock and confusion of Muraviev's mutiny. In the North, the Czechs took Ekaterinburg more or less as they pleased; and Bykov, the local Party boss (and protagonist in the murder of the Imperial family) could only report: 'Like the honourable captain of a sinking ship, the Soviet marches out [of Ekaterinburg] with one of the last detachments.'

It was difficult, at Berzin's headquarters, to obtain information as to what was happening. There were reports that Tukhachevsky was now in command; then a circular telegram announced that Vatsetis had taken over charge of the whole Eastern Front. Berzin got through to Vatsetis at Kazan on the direct line and warned him he had reason to believe that the G.H.Q. staff there were unreliable. Vatsetis replied that that might well be true; he had not selected them, but he had no good staff officers available—could Berzin lend him any? Very shortly afterwards a small Czech-Samara force attacked Kazan and the defences collapsed, the defection of the G.H.Q. staff being one cause of the disaster. Vatsetis managed to escape with an A.D.C. and a few soldiers. He later reported: 'The fighting in Kazan demonstrated the complete incapacity of the workers' detachments. Local Party comrades in high posts displayed the greatest energy, but their efforts were wasted in the chaos of unpreparedness. The soldiers proved utterly lacking in discipline. The whole burden of defence fell upon . . . the Latvian Rifles . . . As regards Russian units they proved incapable of fighting in mass because of lack of preparation and discipline.' Latsis (at that time chairman of the Kazan *Cheka*) wrote afterwards: 'It seemed to us that Kazan should not have been surrendered, that the surrender of Kazan was opening all the approaches to Moscow, that our army defeated at Kazan would roll further to Nizhni-Novgorod and that in this way the enemy would surround us in a closed circle from the east and from the north.'

(iii)

It was thus at a moment of serious crisis that Trotsky arrived in person in the front-line area in the special train that became his permanent headquarters. He himself writes: 'After the fall of Simbirsk it was decided that I should go to the Volga, where we were facing the greatest danger. I began to get a special train ready—in those days not so simple a matter. Everything was missing or, to be more exact, no one knew where to find anything . . . I left Moscow on August 7th, still ignorant of the fall of Kazan the day before.' His train halted at Sviyazhsk, the last station of any size west of the Volga on the line to Kazan, and a main assembly point of the Red troops in the area. Trotsky continues: 'The army at Sviyazhsk was made up of detachments which had retreated from Simbirsk and Kazan and of assisting units rushed in from all directions. Each unit lived its own distinct life, sharing in common only a readiness to retreat . . . the soil itself seemed to be infected with panic. The fresh Red detachments, arriving in vigorous mood, were immediately engulfed by the inertia of defeat . . . Despite all this the Revolution was saved. What was needed for that? Very little. The front ranks of the masses had to realize the mortal danger in the situation. The first requirement for success was to hide nothing, our weakness least of all; not to trifle with the masses but to call everything by its right name. The Revolution was still very irresponsible.'

Elsewhere Trotsky put it otherwise: 'By means of a combination of exhortation, organization and reprisals the metamorphosis was effected in the course of a few weeks. A wobbly fluid mass became a real army.' On yet another occasion he described the conditions of the reconditioning of the Red Army as (1) the liquidation of *partizanshchina*, (2) the punitive work of field tribunals, (3) intensification of political work, and (4) the urgent rallying, in the rear, of Communists to go to the front and stay there. Of these at that particular stage, it was perhaps the punitive work that was the most effective. As one of those with him at the time suggested: 'Comrade Trotsky's harsh methods were most expedient and necessary for that period of undisciplined and irregular warfare. Persuasion counted for nothing and there was no time for it.'

The month at Sviyazhsk had its dangerous moments. On one occasion if Kappel, commanding a White raiding party behind the Red lines, had been better informed of the defencelessness of Sviyazhsk he could have captured the whole headquarters, together with the Commissar for War. On another, when Trotsky set out at night on a Red Flotilla gunboat and the ship's engine failed, the Czech artillery in Kazan unaccountably failed to open fire. Either event might have had an appreciable influence on the course of the Civil War. There were instances of collapse of morale among even the most trusted Red units. The 4th Latvian Regiment refused to go into action; the chairman and one member of the regimental Party committee were handed over to the tribunal. Worse still, a battalion of the much-vaunted Petrograd workers bolted on board a steamer and ordered the crew to steam back to Nizhni-Novgorod. An improvised gunboat manned by twenty loyalists held up the steamer, and at Trotsky's insistence a specially appointed field tribunal passed death sentences on the commanding officer, the battalion commissar and one man in every ten of the rank and file.

These drastic measures could be undertaken because of the

presence at Sviyazhsk of a number of Party leaders of extreme devotion and a ruthlessness equal to Trotsky's. Vatsetis paid only a brief visit for consultation with Trotsky, and then went off to Vyatka to work on similar lines. But Larissa Reisner (who, to quote Trotsky, 'flashed across the revolutionary sky like a burning meteor') took a prominent part in the operations round Kazan; more important still was I. N. Smirnov, 'the conscience of Sviyazhsk' as Reisner called him, who went on to play a leading role in the victorious advance of the Fifth Red Army across Siberia. And perhaps the most decisive contribution of all was that of the young Party members who acted as transmission belt between the Party leadership and the military rank and file. Trotsky was one of the first to grasp the importance of their presence. Much of his speech of July 29th to *TsIK* and to the Moscow Soviet was taken up with demands for Party members to go to the front and 'stay with the troops to the end'. When he left Moscow he took fifty of them on his train. 'Most of the youth of the Party did not know how to handle arms, but they had the will to win and that was the most important thing. They put backbone into the soft body of the Army.' And again, 'They simply outdid themselves, stepping into the breach and fairly melting away before my eyes through the recklessness of their heroism and sheer inexperience.'

Thus it was that Trotsky completed his task at Sviyazhsk. On his arrival there the atmosphere was well illustrated by a remark of Commissar Markin of the Red Volga Flotilla: 'When it is a question of retiring the ship's engines all work splendidly; when it is going up to battle stations the machinery goes wrong at once.' By the time Trotsky was recalled to Moscow, following the attempt on Lenin in late August, the atmosphere had changed. There was still a great deal to be done. But the Red Army was, for the moment, just good enough to beat the Whites in front of them.

Trotsky's speeches and writings both during the War and after throw light on the building of the Red Army and on Trotsky himself. Here are a few examples.

On his methods: 'We were constructing an army all over again, and under fire at that. This was true not only at Sviyazhsk, where the train recorded its first month, but on all the fronts. Out of bands of irregulars, of refugees escaping from the Whites, of peasants mobilized in the neighbouring districts, of detachments of workers sent by the industrial centres—out of these we formed at the front companies, battalions, new regiments, sometimes entire divisions. Even after defeats and retreats the flabby, panicky mob would be transformed in two or three weeks into an efficient fighting force. What was needed for this? At once much and little. It needed good commanders; a few dozen experienced fighters, a dozen or so of Communists ready to make any sacrifice; boots for the barefooted, a bath-house, an energetic propaganda campaign, food, underwear, tobacco and matches. . . . The train took care of all this . . . the shovelful of coal necessary at a particular moment to prevent the fire going out.'

On military theory: 'We must now devote our whole attention to improving our material and to making it more efficient rather than to fantastic schemes of reorganization. Every army unit must receive its rations regularly, foodstuffs must not be allowed to rot and meals must be properly cooked. We must teach our soldiers personal cleanliness and see that they exterminate vermin. They must learn their drill properly and perform it as much as possible in the open air. They must be taught to make their political speeches short and sensible, to clean their rifles and to grease their boots. They must learn to shoot and must help their officers in strict observance of regulations for keeping in touch with other units in the field, reconnaissance work, reports and sentry duty. They must learn and teach the art of adaptation to local conditions, they must learn to wind their puttees properly so as to prevent sores on their legs, and once again they must learn to grease their boots. This is our programme for next year in general and next spring in particular, and if anyone wishes to take advantage of some solemn occasion to describe this practical programme as "military doctrine" he is welcome to do so.'

On the vexed question of supplies: 'The most important thing is system. That is absolutely true . . . But the point is that we did not want to perish before we could build up a smoothly running system.' There were the inevitable delays and bottlenecks. 'The road taken by a cartridge, a pair of boots or a shirt from the time they leave Comrade Rykov (in charge of the central administration of supplies) to the time they reach a rifleman in the firing line is far too long.' On the other hand, 'The military always demand more than they ought to get, and demand it more drastically than they ought to.' Trotsky's own methods were characteristic: 'After making the round of a division and ascertaining its needs on the spot I would hold a conference in the staff car or the dining-car, inviting as many representatives as possible, including those from the lower commanding grades and from the ranks as well as from the local Party organization, the Soviet administration and the trade unions. In this way I got a picture of the situation that was neither false nor highly-coloured. These conferences always had practical results. No matter how poor the organs of the local administration might be, they always managed to squeeze a little tighter and cut down some of their own needs to contribute something to the Army.'

Trotsky had, of course, a great deal to say about morale and discipline. It is notorious that the White war effort was partially hamstrung by the ingenuity of vast numbers of officers and others in evading front-line service by making themselves 'indispensable' in posts they had found or created in the rear. The same tendency showed itself among the Reds, and Trotsky took strong measures against this 'nauseating ulcer' of 'legalized desertion'. He fulminated against the mildness of sentences passed by the softer-hearted field tribunals. To sentence a man who had twice deserted to imprisonment for the duration of the Civil War was merely to grant the criminal what he had hoped to achieve by his crime. 'The sentence of a court must have an agitational character: must frighten some and raise the faith and cheerfulness of others.' The question of desertion (often merely non-compliance with the call-up in the absence of mobilization machinery) called for special measures. In his order dated October 7th, 1918, Trotsky placed the responsibility upon the village Soviets and Committees of Poor Peasants. Chairmen of both bodies were to be arrested if deserters were found in the village. Any deserter who surrendered and promised loyal service must be pardoned; any who resisted must be shot forthwith. A special standard, of course, must be required from Communists. An order of December 11th, 1918, laid down that 'a soldier who is a Party member has just the same rights as any other soldier—but not a hair's-breadth more. He has only incomparably more duties.' Complaining or arguing by Party members must not be tolerated. Fighting organs were not debating clubs. In the event of retreat on the part of any unit the behaviour of Party members in that unit must be rigorously checked by the Commissar of the division or by the Political Department of the Army (order of March 24th, 1919). In the same month of March, from his train at Vyatka, he fulminated against the retreating Third Army. It had claimed to contain 12,000 Party members—whereas if there had been two thousand, or even one thousand Party members worthy to be Party members there would have been no question of withdrawal. There must be an immediate purge of the Party cells as well as of the officer cadres, and Commissars must do their jobs.

Trotsky's attention also covered civilian affairs in the rear of the Red Armies. The impact of the rough and imperfect Soviet administration inevitably caused friction with the peasantry, and this friction could be dangerous at the time of Red retreats. In the early spring of 1919 the Kazan area seemed ripe for trouble. Trotsky recalls; 'On March 22nd, 1919, I demanded over the direct wire that the Central Committee should come to a decision on the question of an official inquiry by the Central Executive Committee in the Volga region and of the appointment of an authoritative commission from the Central Committee and the Central Executive Committee. The commission's task should be to strengthen the faith of the Volga peasantry in the Central Soviet Power, to correct the most conspicuous local irregularities and to punish the guilty representatives of the Soviet Power; to gather complaints and materials to be used as the basis of demonstrative decrees in favour of the middle peasant.'

(iv)

We have a number of accounts from different levels of the new beginnings of the Red Army after Trotsky's stay at Sviyazhsk. One Vavrzhenkevich was appointed on August 18th, 1918, to be Political Commissar of a new regiment to be formed out of what was left of the 1st Kazan Division. He established himself in a village near Sviyazhsk and took charge of the little bands of fugitives arriving there. When he had a total of 300 men Trotsky gave instructions that they should be organized as a regiment, entrained and sent south to Ibresi. Operational orders were vague: they were to act as a link between the Red forces on the Kazan and Simbirsk sectors. Morale was still poor, there was no information about the enemy, and local villagers were unfriendly. First contact was made at the end of the month: the Reds panicked, suffered fifty-one casualties and lost three of their machine-guns. The Whites, however, did not follow up their advantage, and the regiment was pulled together. On the recapture of Kazan the unit took part in the general advance, but there was no fighting until seven weeks later they caught up with a Czech rearguard. Shots were exchanged, the regiment stood fast, reinforcements came up and the Czechs retired. Vavrzhenkevich could now feel that his unit was of some military value.

On a higher level we have the account of Shorin, a former officer who volunteered for service with the Reds and became commander of the Second Red Army. His first assignment was to collect any troops available and send them to recapture Izhevsk and Votkinsk. The expedition failed, the troops fell back in disorder and the building up of the Second Army had to start again from scratch. A new Revolutionary Military

Soviet was formed based on Vyatka. Shorin and Gusev, on behalf of the R.M.S., toured the area to ascertain the location and condition of the troops. It was the usual story of confusion and dejection, with soldiers crowding on to the river steamers to get back to the rear. The front-line commanders and commissars were in a state of nervous exhaustion and no longer up to their task. Reorganization was assisted by the timely arrival of a number of Party members and military specialists from Moscow. Requisitioning parties brought in foodstuffs, clothing, horses and livestock. Moscow sent up some field guns complete with gunners. By the end of the month there was no longer anxiety about rations—in fact, four trains of food grains were sent to Petrograd. Workshops were making boots and repairing rifles. The Army's Political Department was in full activity, and a local newspaper, the *Izvestiya Vtoroi Armii*, was appearing. The Army *Cheka* and the field tribunals were tightening discipline. On September 28th Shorin was officially confirmed in his command.

In early October the Second Army advanced. Small parties of Whites were mopped up and operations mounted to liquidate partisan bands who claimed to be fighting the Whites but who were, in effect, merely raiding and looting the larger villages. The assault on Izhevsk took place in November. There was sharp fighting with heavy casualties. The (Red) 2nd Moslem Regiment panicked and had to be re-formed. But after a three-day battle Izhevsk was taken, and within a week Votkinsk. Further progress eastwards in the bitter cold of the early winter was slowed down by transport difficulties and the exhaustion of the troops. Manpower still remained a problem. Reinforcements were arriving from the rear, of varying quality. But there were not enough of them, and the Army command had to undertake the mobilization of males in the occupied villages. These recruits turned out to have no military knowledge and to be liable to panic; they were on the whole a liability rather than an asset. So special battalions were set up to give them military and political training. All this took time. Shorin complains of the 'thousands of foreign-employed agents' who crossed into the Red lines and spread scare rumours and disaffection. This is most unlikely. The truth was that the men had little interest in the Civil War and wanted to go back to their villages.

The Second Red Army had not yet faced serious opposition. They had made their advance at a time when the Czechs and most of the Samara People's Army had lost the will to fight. The Izhevsk and Votkinsk militias lacked organization and experience. The new Siberian White Army had not yet come into action. When it did, in December, it captured Perm and the left flank of the Second Army was uncovered. Faulty White strategy gave Shorin's Army some respite. But in early March the White offensive in the Central Sector drove back the Fifth Red Army and the Second Army was left in the air and had to pull back. Izhevsk was lost, and Votkinsk (with large stores of supplies). Once more there were panics and large-scale desertions. Confusion was caused by White reconnaissance parties occupying post offices behind the Red lines and tapping out and impersonating direct wire conversations between Red headquarters. By the end of April the Army was back on the Vyatka river and did not advance again until after the Red successes farther south had practically decided the issue of the Civil War on the Eastern Front.

The organizer of these Red victories was Frunze, a record of whose command has been left by his chief of staff, Novitsky. In the late summer of 1918 both Frunze and Novitsky (a former officer) were members of the Regional Military Commissariat at Ivanovo-Vozhnesensk. Their task was to tidy up the chaos prevailing in North Central Russia and raise as many divisions as possible to reinforce the Eastern front. After weeks of meetings, speeches and office work, both became frustrated and applied to Moscow for appointments at the front. Much argument and a personal visit were necessary before Moscow would agree. But towards the end of the year Frunze was appointed officer commanding the Fourth Red Army, with Novitsky as his Chief of Staff, and left for his headquarters at Samara.

On this sector the Reds had recently taken Ufa, Orenburg

and Uralsk, joining up with the Turkestan Red Army. These successes to some extent counterbalanced the loss of Perm. But (as Trotsky had warned the new commander) the state of the Fourth Army was not satisfactory. Discipline was bad. The 30th and 25th Divisions were 'partisan-minded'. Things had come to a head with the murder of a senior military commissar by the crew of a Red armoured train. Then a brigade of the 25th Division (with the approval of its commander) had indulged in extensive looting in Uralsk. Frunze made a tour of the disaffected units, and there were stormy meetings. The officers were truculent and the men inclined to back their officers against the Army command; but gradually, by force of personality, Frunze imposed his will.

February was taken up with minor operations against small Cossack forces in the steppe south of Uralsk and with preparations for a general offensive in the spring. But the Whites struck first. On March 6th General Khanzhin, commanding Kolchak's centre, overran a division of the Fifth Red Army. A few days later it seemed that the Whites had broken through. The Reds fell back towards the Volga. The urgency of the crisis was realized in Moscow and in early April Frunze was appointed to command the whole Southern Sector, comprising the 1st, 4th, 5th and Turkestan Red Armies. There was a hurried conference of senior commanders and commissars. It was impossible to improvise a central staff for the Southern Sector, and so Frunze took with him his Fourth Army staff, arranging for a new staff for that Army. Meanwhile the Whites were pressing ahead. One of Khanzhin's orders of the day (which fell into Red hands) spoke of an early entry into Moscow. General Belov, of the White Southern Group, reported Red disorganization and peasant risings in their rear. Frunze concentrated all available Red troops round Buzuluk. Drastic steps were taken to suppress panic and to prevent premature withdrawal or evacuation. The White advance began to lose momentum, and in a successful action on the river Salmysh a detachment of the 25th Red Division captured documents giving the complete White order of battle. The Red counter-offensive, when it came, was entirely successful. Khanzhin's front was broken; Belov's force cut off and destroyed piecemeal. By August the war in the East had been won. Frunze was appointed to Central Asia and a large proportion of the armies was either sent there with him or transferred to the Southern front. Eventually it was the Fifth Red Army alone that undertook the final drive across Siberia.

(v)

The major problems in the building up of the Red Army may be listed as (1) supply and transport, (2) manpower, (3) command and (4) morale and discipline. Trotsky, as the protagonist of centralization, was doubtless one of the initiators of the central authority for supply, *Tsekomprodarm* (Central Committee for Army Supply), established by *Sovnarkom* on September 14th, 1918. In November a new organization, *Chrezkomsnab*, was set up to look after war industry. In December local organs of *Tsekomprodarm* were established in all sectors, and in the summer of 1919 *Tsekomprodarm* was reorganized into *Glavsnabprodarm*. At first the rear had little to send to the fronts. There were some field guns, and an occasional aeroplane (though air power played a very minor role in the war); the ingenious transfer eastwards of river gunboats along the canals made a real contribution to the operations on the middle Volga and Kama; and there was an occasional consignment of rifles. Otherwise the armies had to look after themselves, and in fact continued to do so. Little was being turned out in the factories of central Russia. During 1918 workers in war industries fell from 152,000 to 47,000, and productivity per man is likely to have fallen still more sharply. Accordingly, when the *Tsekomprodarm* representatives appeared at the various Army headquarters there was, apart from sending food grains back to Moscow (2,400,000 poods of produce were sent back in the autumn of 1919), little for them to do except attempt to take over local sources of supply that were already being run by the military. This naturally led to friction: and for most of the campaign *Tsekomprodarm*–Army relations were very strained.

Trotsky inveighed bitterly at the tendency of military commands, commissariats and Soviets to grab all locally available supplies and hang on to them. But there was not very much that he could do about it. When the Reds were advancing, as in the autumn of 1918 and, in the East, after May, 1919, there was, of course, a good deal to be captured from the Whites. Given the circumstances, there were not many cases of looting. But in the case of military supplies commanders were naturally inclined to look after their own units first, and there was competition between units as to who first could occupy a town or railway station. Strong pressure from above was needed to ensure a fair sharing out.

According to the regulations, an Army's authority over production and supply extended only over 50 versts behind the front; but the military tended to keep hold of their workshops and depots, and, in spite of protests from *Prodarm*, the army-controlled belt grew wider and wider. In the rapid advances of the summer and autumn it became anything up to 1,000 kilometres. Tukhachevsky records: 'An immense part was played in army leadership in the Civil War by questions of local mobilization, local supplies, etc. All this compelled an Army to be not only a mobile entity but also an organizational administrative entity on a very large scale.'

However, in spite of friction and difficulties, the Red Army's operations were not held up by supply problems. There was plenty of food provided it could be moved. Mostly the Red Army lived off local food supplies; but sometimes it was the Army that fed the population. By and large the troops had more ample rations that the scale fixed by *Prodarm*. There was a chronic shortage of matches and cigarette-paper. The military did their best by taking over small factories in the occupied centres: the same thing happened over small arms ammunition although it is probably true to say that the Reds won their war on cartridges captured from the Whites. (In the spring of 1919 the total output of all S.A.A. factories in Soviet Russia amounted to two cartridges per day per Red Army fighting soldier.) In the latter stages of the campaign in the East the supply problem became acute only in September, 1919, after the White counter-offensive on the Tobol. Both armies were mauled, and the Fifth Red Army could only make up its strength by a mass enrolment of local peasants, for whom it had neither arms nor uniforms. Headquarters of the Eastern front had no reserves, and in view of the huge demand from the Southern front, neither *Prodarm* nor *Chrezkomsnab* had anything to offer. Personal telegrams were sent to Lenin and Trotsky appealing for 15,000 rifles. Eight thousand were received and the balance made up by reconditioning unserviceable rifles in workshops extemporized in rail wagons and in a derelict factory in Chelyabinsk. As for uniforms, recruits were told to turn up in their own clothes. Many of them had old army overcoats for which the Red Army paid in Soviet currency. As the Reds advanced they annulled all Omsk roubles, and it became important for the peasants to find some means of getting Soviet roubles in order to buy their necessities. This peasant need of Soviet roubles helped the Reds to buy horses and carts in the villages. These peasant carts and sleighs were an important military factor. The railways functioned, after a fashion. But, in spite of orders from the centre, throughout 1918 and for much of 1919 the working of the railways in the front areas was a matter of local improvisation. The soldiers on the spot regarded rolling-stock in their area as their private property. In the bitter winter and with no other shelter troops used trains as billets, and often had to be turned out by force. Local commanders would threaten to shoot stationmasters who tried to follow directives from above rather than do as local commanders told them. In the end half the railwaymen went down with typhus and many of the others deserted their jobs: search parties were organized to check rearbound trains and pull out retreating railwaymen. The problem was eventually solved, more or less, by the establishment of a network of station commandants and by building up their authority, and by the use of special military detachments for railway work. But it was not till the occupation of Novonikolaevsk at the end of 1919 (when Kolchak's régime had collapsed) that any large proportion of the Red forces moved eastwards by railway: during the summer and autumn, with fighting over a depth of 1,500 kilometres, the Reds had brought up their men and the bulk of their supplies in peasant carts.

(vi)

As to manpower, at the time of the Czech revolt the total number of Soviet troops amounted on paper to some 300,000 men. As we have seen, mobilization was handicapped by lack of organizational machinery. It was comparatively easy to set this up in Moscow and Petrograd where, in addition, moral pressure could be brought to bear on young workers; but in the rural areas the position was very different. Local Soviets had no lists. They could merely issue a notice that a certain age group should report, but they did not know what individuals belonged to what age group. So easy was it to evade the call-up that S. Kamenev, the Red Supreme Commander, suggests that in the first few weeks all the recruits on the Eastern front were in a sense volunteers. But by August 1st, 1918, in spite of the wastage of defection and desertion, the total had increased to 330,000, and by early September to 550,000. By the end of the year it was 800,000.

There was argument over the method of reinforcing the front. In the early months the front commands were hard pressed to put their own affairs in order, let alone absorb a mass of raw recruits. And so Moscow laid down that military commissariats in the rear should form their men into complete units before sending them forward. Later, as the front Armies acquired experience and organization, they became increasingly dissatisfied with this arrangement. They complained of the quality of the units sent up—cases occurred where as many as 30 per cent deserted *en route*—and demanded that reinforcements arrive as drafts, whose advanced training and integration should be the affair of the Armies themselves. For this purpose special holding (*zapasni*) commands were set up in the various army areas.

Of enormous concern was the incidence of desertion, described by Frunze as an 'evil eating up the Army'. Deserters were of two kinds, those who failed to answer the call-up and those, rather less numerous, who disappeared after being enrolled. A number of Soviet writers obediently ascribe desertion to 'the failure of the middle peasant to understand the significance of the struggle'. A simpler explanation would be dislike of military service and ample opportunity to evade it. The following figures for all fronts (albeit as dubious as all Civil War statistics) do at least illustrate the scope of the problem. 1,975,000 men were called up during the year 1919, and a further 500,000 mobilized by the military in the front areas. The figure given for the number of deserters apprehended or voluntarily reporting is 1,750,000. We have no figure for the number that got away.

Trotsky, as we have mentioned, was taking steps against desertion as early as October, 1918. In the spring of 1919 a central organization, *Tsentrokomdesertir* (Central Committee for Deserters), was set up with branches in the provinces and districts. The general principle remained the same, free pardon for those who returned voluntarily and drastic punishment for those who did not. As potential military material deserters were of much the same quality as the bulk of the Red Army rank and file. Trotsky declared in early 1919, 'Give me three thousand deserters. Call them a regiment. I will find a fighting regimental commander, a good commissar, fit officers for battalions, companies and platoons—and these three thousand deserters in the course of four weeks in our revolutionary country will produce a splendid regiment.' There was, of course, much propaganda in this claim. But just as the tightening of the Bolshevik hold on the rear made it more difficult to desert, the improvement of the military and Party machinery in the front areas (where a big role was played by the *zapasni* units) made it possible for the Armies to keep these men and turn them into soldiers. The deserter problem was never solved; but it was sufficiently held in check so as not to hamstring the Red military effort.

Victory, of course, considerably eased the manpower problem. There were mass defections from the Whites. During the Red advance of the summer of 1919 we hear of 3,000 Kolchak soldiers arriving at the 1st *Zapasni Polk* of the Fifth Red Army in Syzran in one batch. When the Fifth Army reached Petropavlovsk, in Western Siberia, White rank and file came over in such huge numbers that it was impossible to absorb them or even, in view of the transport shortage, to send them back to the rear. They were accordingly disarmed and told to make their own way home.

Improved morale when victory grew certain became apparent in other ways. The Red Armies had their full share of the wastage caused by lightly wounded men being evacuated and finding ways of not returning to the front. Towards the end they were coming back in reasonable quantities and with reasonable speed. The final test of manpower procurement in the East came in the battles over the Tobol in the autumn of 1919. Casualties were heavy—a figure given for Red losses in one fortnight in September is nearly 15,000 men. It was clear that victory would go to the side that first succeeded in making up its strength. There was an intensive recruiting drive in the Fifth Red Army rear, within two weeks some 20,000 men were secured and passed through the *Zapasni Polk* at Chelyabinsk. What is more, very few of them deserted on the journey from the depot to the front.

(vii)

Trotsky's insistence on the use of former professional officers provoked much controversy in Party circles, but in the last six months of 1918 no less than nine decrees and orders were promulgated by *Sovnarkom* and other authorities dealing with the employment of military specialists. By the end of 1918 over 20,000 former officers were serving in the Red Army; by June, 1919, the figure had risen to 27,000, of whom more than 22,000 were combatant officers. Between June, 1918, and August, 1920, some 48,000 officers were enrolled. At the same time urgent steps were taken to secure former N.C.O.s—many of whom were made officers either at once or very shortly after enrolment. 128,000 former N.C.O.s were called up during 1918, and the total by August, 1920, was nearly 215,000. It was, of course, emphasized that as soon as possible the Army should be officered by class-conscious proletarians, and a number of Red Army Officers' Schools were set up. In 1918 these schools turned out 769 infantry officers, 533 artillery, 108 cavalry, 130 engineers, 89 machine-gun and 124 others, a total of 1,753. In 1919, with more schools functioning, some 11,500 cadets were passed out. But the Red Army numbered three million. Throughout the Civil War the availability of former officers to hold posts from company commander upwards was essential for Red Army efficiency.

As to the motives of the officers who enrolled, patriotism certainly played a part when it was a case of war against a national enemy, as with the Germans in February, 1918, or the Poles in 1920. There was resentment against the Japanese in the Far East. But, in spite of the assertions of Soviet writers and of the foreign historians who follow them, there is no evidence that Western intervention, such as it was, caused officers (or indeed other classes) to rally to the Soviet cause. Some officers may have seen the opportunities for making a career in the Soviet service. But it is reasonably certain that the great majority, after the exhaustion and frustration of war and of revolution, responded to the call-up only because it was difficult and dangerous to avoid it, and because it provided the only available means of livelihood for themselves and for their families.

Insight into the mentality of former officers in the Red Armies is afforded by the report to the Kolchak authorities of Colonel Kotomin, who defected to the Whites in the summer of 1919.

The report was eventually captured by the Reds, and extracts published by Trotsky with his comments. With all allowance for what Kotomin thought it proper to report and Trotsky thought it desirable to select, it emerges that only a minority of officers were pro-Soviet, and those mostly front-line officers. Those who had volunteered for service with the Bolsheviks (as opposed to those called up) mostly held front appointments. Furthermore, by the summer of 1919 those front-line officers who intended to go over to the Whites would have had opportunities to do so; and in any case front-line combatant service—in all armies—tends to foster loyalty to the unit rather than to the cause. One officer told Kotomin that 'if he served in an army it was his duty to serve honourably'. Senior officers, from regimental commander upwards and staff officers of corresponding rank were in favour of the maintenance of the Soviet régime.

Kotomin divides the anti-Soviet officers into three classes: those with no political views who merely wanted to earn their living; a few fanatical anti-Bolsheviks who joined in order to work conspiratorially against the régime; and the great majority who would like to see the end of Bolshevism but were unable or too timid to take any steps to that end. Kotomin stresses the extreme effectiveness of Trotsky's order prescribing reprisals against the families of defectors; and the enormous importance of the Political Commissars, who, more than anyone else, were responsible for the fact that army officers gave good value to their Soviet masters.

(viii)

Of all the 180,000 Party members who served in the Red Army up to the beginning of 1920, the key men were the Commissars attached to units from company upwards. Kotomin asserts that the majority of former officers came in the end, chiefly through fear, entirely under the influence of their Commissars. Of the Commissars themselves Kotomin rates 5 per cent as 'ideal

Commissars', that is, men of selfless devotion to the well-being and efficiency of the Red Army; the other 95 per cent were 'egoists and opportunists'. Trotsky makes the point that Kotomin classes as an egoist or opportunist all those who would not have had so good a chance of making a career if the Revolution had not taken place. Furthermore, Kotomin's report was almost certainly coloured by the widespread anti-Semitism among former officers, whereas an appreciable percentage of the Commissars were Jews. No doubt the Commissars were a mixed lot. There were some failures. To make a success of their job they had to be tough, and most of them were very tough indeed. There was friction and rivalry, and they spied on each other as well as spying on the military specialists. But one quality that all possessed was an enormous capacity for hard work; and a token of their success was the confidence they eventually inspired not only among the senior front commanders but also among the rank and file, who at first had tended to regard them merely as harsh martinets to enforce the performance of unpleasant tasks.

Of course, the Political Commissars formed only part of the Party's organization in the Army. It took some time to overcome the spirit of volunteerism and democracy that in the early days was rampant in Party as well as in military life. In July, 1918, the Revolutionary Military Soviet of the Eastern front set up its Political Department, and within a month the Political Department of the First Army was established. By the end of the year all armies had their Political Departments; work on the establishment of Political Departments for divisions was now being taken in hand. But even so, throughout 1918, there was a lack of suitable Party members to man these departments. This meant more responsibility for the Commissars, but in these early days a number of Commissars themselves were not yet imbued with the proper spirit of discipline and centralization. Many of them had been elected by the Party rank and file, and they continued to allow Party cells to pass resolutions on operational and administrative matters. Hence the denunciations, both at the front and in the rear, of 'Army syndicalism' and '*Partizanshchina*'. As late as January, 1919, it was necessary for the Central Committee of the Party in Moscow to issue a sharp reminder that Party cells in the Army must not interfere in military or administrative matters.

Some Party members were too soft. The Red Army of 1918 is depicted in glowing colours by one Yan Grunt, who took part in the (almost unopposed) advance on the Central sector in the late autumn of that year. His picture is one of unbroken comradeship, confidence and hope. Grunt was prosecutor of a Military Revolutionary Tribunal and found he had little to do. The advance was so rapid that he was often unable to overtake the units whose conduct he was to investigate. On one occasion when expressly instructed by Rosengoltz to hang the guilty he came to the conclusion, after inquiry, that no one was particularly to blame. He never knew, he tells us, what Comrade Rosengoltz thought of his decision not to prosecute; but very soon afterwards he was taken off his job as prosecutor and set to work on an army front-line newspaper.

A milestone in Party work in the Red Army was the appeal for Party members for the front issued in the crisis of the White offensive of the spring of 1919. The response was very considerable. The Vitebsk provincial Party organization, to take a typical instance, mobilized and sent off 20 per cent of its members, including two members of the Provincial Committee. This meant that at last there were Party men to fill the vacant posts, and the work of organization, indoctrination, supervision and example could be intensified. There were, of course, still to be delays and failures. On June 20th, 1919, Lenin telegraphed a sharp reminder to the Revolutionary Military Soviet of the Eastern front complaining that in the course of the advance Party workers were finding themselves civilian posts in the newly occupied territories; these people, he insisted, must stay with the front-line troops. As late as the end of September the newly appointed Commissar of the 35th Division discovered (as he had been warned by Tukhachevsky) that the division was politically and, indeed, generally, in very poor shape. But the new Commissar, with the help of his fellow-

Communists, did in fact make the 35th Division battleworthy. And this is typical of the whole Civil War. When things went wrong there was nearly always a Communist or little group of Communists to take charge at the top, with a transmission belt of Party members right down to the firing line, to bring that modicum of discipline and resolution that made the difference between victory and defeat.

———————

The main sources for Chapter III are:

Berzin in *Rabochaya Revolyutsiya* (Ekaterinburg, 1921).

Borba za Ural i Sibir (Moscow-Leningrad, 1926), especially the articles by Vavrzhenkevich, Tukhachevsky and Smirnov.

Bunyan and Fisher, *The Bolshevik Revolution 1917–1918* (Stanford, 1934).

Fedotoff-White, D., *The Growth of the Red Army* (Princeton, 1944).

Grazhdanskaya Voina 1918–1921 gg. (Moscow, 1928–1930), especially the articles by Shorin, Novitsky, Brinkhanov, Volpe, S. Kamenev, Movchin, Efimov and Grunt.

Gusev, S. I., *Grazhdanskaya Voina i Krasnaya Armiya* (Moscow-Leningrad, 1925).

Parfenov, P. S., *Grazhdanskaya Voina v Sibiri* (Moscow, 1924).

Trotsky, *Kak Vooruzhalas Revolyutsiya* (Moscow, 1923–1925).

Trotsky, *Ma Vie* (Paris, 1930).

Wollenberg, F., *The Red Army* (London, 1938).

Other works consulted include:

Antonov-Ovseenko, *Zapiski o Grazhdanskoi Voine* (Moscow, 1933).

Bunyan, J., *Intervention, Civil War and Communism* (Baltimore, 1936).

Frunze, M. V., *Izbrannye Proizvedeniya*, Vol. I (Moscow, 1957).

Krebs, P., *The Political Institutions of the Soviet Army* (A doctoral thesis in the Library of St. Antony's College, Oxford, 1958).

Rabinovich, S. E., *Vserossiiskaya Voennaya Konferentsiya Bolshevikov 1917 Goda* (Moscow, 1931).

CHAPTER IV

Murmansk and Archangel

(i)

Throughout World War I an important route for the shipment of stores to Russia was via the White Sea ports. To relieve the pressure on Archangel (icebound for more than half the year) a single-track line was hurriedly constructed to Murmansk in the Kola Peninsula, and was in operation in 1917. Allied naval units were stationed in northern waters for the protection of these deliveries. In the flurry and uncertainty of a possible breakdown of the Brest-Litovsk negotiations, Trotsky (on March 2nd, 1918) instructed the Murmansk Soviet to co-operate with the Allies: there were no Bolshevik members of this Soviet and the instruction was obeyed wholeheartedly. In Archangel, where the Bolsheviks were establishing control, relations between the Allied naval units and the local authorities were more strained, but no actual break occurred until the late summer.

Meanwhile the Allied war planners, in particular the British, were considering the dispatch of an expeditionary force. Among its tasks would be to check any German moves to the far north, to safeguard the considerable stocks of stores accumulated in Archangel and to form a reception centre for Czechoslovak units coming up from the South. In point of fact, the Germans had no intention of coming north, the Bolsheviks removed the bulk of the stores before ever the British force arrived, and the Czechs refused to route any units via Archangel: but it would be unfair to blame the planners for lack of hindsight. At a conference in London in late March, General Knox, head of the British Military Mission in Russia, suggested a force of 5,000 men; the Mission's representative in Archangel pressed for three times that number. A few days later the Germans launched their great offensive in France, and the Allied leaders were entirely taken up with the military threat in the West. However, H.M.S. *Cochrane*, together with French and American naval units, was sent to Murmansk, a few British marines were put on shore, and plans went ahead for the dispatch of a land force as well.

The ideas then held by the British military are revealed by the briefing of General Maynard, who was appointed to command at Murmansk. Maynard was on sick leave when, in mid-May, he was summoned to the War Office, where a Colonel Steel explained to him that in view of the situation at the front in France the main British problem was that of manpower, and the most promising solution seemed to be the re-establishment of an Eastern front. The authorities had, therefore, decided on a two-fold plan for North Russia. A military mission numbering 560 in all was to be sent to Archangel. It would be composed mainly of officers and N.C.O.s with experience of training and administration, whose task would be to train and equip the Czech troops as they arrived and any Russian detachments that might become available. It was hoped in this way to get together an army of 30,000 men who would proceed south-eastwards to join up with the pro-Allied elements who were believed to exist in Siberia and thus form a new Eastern front. Steel's information was that the Soviet Government was unlikely to raise serious objections.

The second part of the plan, Steel explained, was to dispatch an expeditionary force of 600 men—infantry, machine-gunners and engineers—to Murmansk, where it would join up with the Royal Marines and the French and Serbian details already on the spot. The task of this force would be to defend Murmansk and Pechenga, repel any advance by Germans or pro-German Finns, and raise, equip and train as large a local force as might

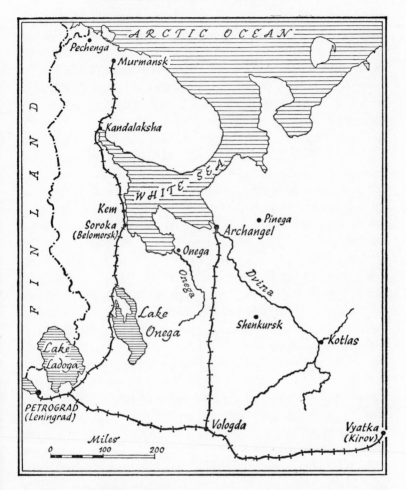

be possible. Steel understood that the Soviet authorities had agreed to the landing of naval parties. General Poole was to be in command of the whole expedition, and Maynard would command the Murmansk force.

Maynard spent the next month persuading a medical board to pass him as fit for active service, and endeavouring without much success to acquire some information about North Russia. He realized that his assignment was likely to involve financial problems and approached the Treasury, but all the Treasury could offer him was a consignment of salt herrings in a Norwegian port. In due course news reached London of the Czech revolt along the Trans-Siberian Railway. It was hard to assess how this would affect the position in North Russia, but in any case the plans went ahead. Maynard embarked with his force on the s.s. *City of Marseilles* at Newcastle on June 18th, and arrived at Murmansk on June 23rd. Here for the first time he met his superior, General Poole. Poole was completely taken up with the problems presented by Archangel. For one thing it had been a hard winter and Archangel was still icebound. Maynard accordingly took stock of the position in and round Murmansk.

At Pechenga was a landing-party from H.M.S. *Cochrane*, numbering 150. Otherwise, apart from the troops in the *City of Marseilles*, there were at Murmansk 150 Royal Marines, 400 Serbs and 150 Russians and Poles. The Russians, nearly all officers, were embodied in a 'Slavo-British Legion'—the first that Maynard had heard of the existence of such a formation. A hundred and eighty miles to the south, at Kandalaksha, were a few French field guns and their gunners, part of a Serb battalion, and some Left-wing Finns whose presence there was due to German support of the Right-wing Finns in Finland. A further hundred and seventy miles to the south, at Kem, were 250 Royal Marines and 250 Serbs. The total force, amounting to some 2,000 men, was thus strung out along three hundred and fifty miles of the single-track Murmansk railway. There were many sick, especially among the French and Serbs, and some of the units were of uncertain fighting quality. Of the strength, disposition and intentions of actual or potential enemies—Germans, White Finns or Bolsheviks—there was no information whatever. But the thaw had turned the terrain to the west of the railway into a vast morass so that there was no risk of an attack in any force from Finland. There was a track leading west from Kandalaksha and another one from Kem, but both were in poor condition. In Murmansk Maynard met the leaders of the local Soviet, General Zvegintsov and Commander Veselago, who owed their original appointment to Bolshevik fears of a German attack. They appeared co-operative, though the railwaymen and dock workers who made up the population were dour and suspicious. The 'town' itself was bleak—an untidy assembly of wooden barracks, with no accommodation for the troops in the *City of Marseilles*, let alone for a headquarters. There was little skilled labour, and no local resources apart from timber. On June 27th, Maynard left for the South along the rickety railway line to inspect his command. He had with him two staff officers and one platoon of infantry.

The timing of this journey turned out to be of crucial importance. The Brest-Litovsk Treaty was working, and the Bolshevik leaders had abandoned any ideas that any of them may have had about co-operation with the West. The good relations established by the Murmansk Soviet now appeared to those leaders to be not only pointless but dangerous; and Moscow accordingly sent off a force of three thousand men to bring the whole area under effective Bolshevik military occupation. Thus it was that Maynard found a train full of Red troops in Kandalaksha station, and subsequently two others at Kem. The Red commander was drunk, and his attitude truculent and unfriendly. It was a situation for which Maynard had had no prior warning and no briefing. But he realized that here was a serious threat not only to the security of his own force but also to the whole northern expedition and that he must act at once. By means of bluff, determination and skilful use of the tiny Allied forces available, all three train-loads were disarmed and sent back to Soroka (some thirty miles beyond Kem). On July 3rd, Maynard came back to Murmansk, where he learned that the Murmansk Soviet had now definitely broken with the Soviet Government.

The following day he went south again, disarming pockets of Red sympathizers. It seemed wiser to extend the zone of occupation to Soroka, so he pushed southwards from Kem across the broken bridges of the railway, and arrived outside Soroka at the same time as a British gunboat, H.M.S. *Attentive*. The Red detachments retired, again destroying the railway bridges behind them. There was no resistance except for a small group of workers who barricaded themselves in a timber yard. The town was searched for arms and explosives, and the Serb battalion was brought down to act as garrison. Maynard himself returned to Murmansk on July 14th, where he found that General Poole had negotiated an agreement with Zvegintsov and Veselago under which the Allies undertook to provide finance for the administration and food for the whole area. There followed a busy period of reorganizing the command, of recruiting for the Slavo-British Legion and the Finnish and Karelian detachments, and of sorting out some of the muddles and misunderstandings that inevitably arose. There was urgent repair work to be done on the railway, and quarters to be built for the troops. There was the perpetual struggle to get London to send food supplies and money. Time and again work at Murmansk was held up by strikes of angry, ill-fed and unpaid workers. 'For month after month,' Maynard notes, 'the Allies failed completely to fulfil their obligations under the Agreement of July 7th.' Nevertheless, for the time being, the Allied hold upon the area had been consolidated.

(ii)

As things turned out, the Murmansk-Archangel venture grew into an uneasy partnership between the British military and anti-Bolshevik Russians. On the Russian side, in the earlier stages the leading roles were played by two men of very different background and character, the veteran revolutionary N. V. Chaikovsky and Captain G. E. Chaplin of the Imperial Russian Navy.

Chaikovsky, a Popular Socialist and a member of the Constituent Assembly, had been convinced, since the dissolution of that body, of the need to build up an All-Russian anti-Bolshevik centre. He believed that the Bolsheviks must be resisted by force of arms. He was ready to welcome Allied intervention with certain provisos, and he demanded a united anti-Bolshevik front. He stated flatly, 'There is no such thing as a third force, and under these conditions a coalition with monarchist elements is unavoidable.' Chaikovsky was one of the first to adhere to the underground League for the Regeneration of Russia (*Soyuz Vozrozhdeniya Rossii*) and encouraged contact between that body and the more Right-wing National Centre for the purpose of joint consultation with Allied representatives. There is no such evidence that Chaikovsky himself took part in any such consultations,[1] and it seems unlikely that he took any active part in the setting up of the local branches of the League in the provinces. His role throughout was to inspire rather than to organize. But he had good contacts with Co-operative leaders and was instrumental in securing grants from the Co-operatives to support the League's activities. He was not informed of the Socialist-Revolutionary underground work in the Volga area, and the Czech revolt at the end of May came as a surprise to him, as indeed to so many others. But the emergence of the Samara Government appeared to offer, at last, a real base for the anti-Bolshevik effort, and in late June he set off for the Volga. By the end of the month he had got as far as Vologda.

Vologda was then the residence of the Allied diplomatic missions, and the centre for much scheming, planning and plotting. Chaikovsky here was met by Maslov and Dedusenko, old personal friends of his, 'non-doctrinaire' S.R.s and in charge of the Vologda headquarters of the northern branch of the League for the Regeneration of Russia. He was informed of the British landing at Murmansk and of the hopes of the seizure of Archangel. He was introduced to the local anti-Bolshevik inter-party committee of Cadets, S.R.s, and Popular Socialists. He met representatives of workers and Co-operatives. Maslov pressed him to stay on and personally participate in the

---

[1] These talks which the Russian conspirators took so seriously were conducted by individual Allied officers usually without the knowledge of their Governments and not infrequently without the knowledge of the head of the mission concerned. Kerensky wrote to Chaikovsky in August that neither Lloyd George nor Clemenceau had heard of the existence of the League for the Regeneration of Russia, let alone its negotiations with the Allied missions.

northern venture: the old man's patent integrity of character and great revolutionary prestige made him an enormous asset to any movement that hoped for Left-wing support. At first Chaikovsky held to his original plan of going to the Volga, but was eventually persuaded. In late July he set off with a false passport to join the anti-Bolshevik underground in Archangel. He was then nearly seventy. It was a courageous decision, for with his tall, thin figure, flowing white beard and piercing blue eyes he was quite impossible to disguise.

Captain G. E. Chaplin, a graduate of the Naval Academy, had served in various appointments during the war, including attachments for some months to British submarines, which gave him a fluent knowledge of English and a number of contacts with British naval officers. The Bolshevik seizure of power found him in a shore job at Petrograd. He at once went underground and began to plot. At one stage he established touch with certain members of the British Naval Mission, though his main work during the winter was the recruitment and dispatch of officers to the Volunteer Army on the Don.

According to Chaplin's own account, which must in parts be taken with reserve, some time in May, 1918, he was summoned to the offices of the British Naval Mission and there informed of a German plot, with Bolshevik agreement, to seize Murmansk and all Russian ships in that area. It was suggested that Chaplin should recruit and infiltrate 'sound elements' into Murmansk and organize the sabotage of any ships taken over by the Germans. Chaplin claims that it was he who suggested that Archangel must also be liberated, and that after various messages between him and General Poole (presumably passed through British naval channels) this suggestion was accepted on condition that he, Chaplin, seized Archangel by his own efforts.

Be all this as it may, it is certain that Chaplin got busy. He had difficulty in recruiting a team. It is possible that most of the officers who really wanted to fight the Bolsheviks had already left Petrograd. Those that remained were of lesser calibre. Their first question was about pay and family allowances. Many had far more respect for the Germans than for the Western Allies. In the end he found some twenty volunteers, and in late May left for Vologda. He arrived there as 'Commander Thomson' of the British Naval Mission, and seems to have had little difficulty in maintaining his cover. He made a number of calls and contacts, dispatched a few selected officers to the North, and in mid-June, still in his British uniform, left for Archangel where he remained on and off until the rising took place six weeks later.

The seizure of Archangel was a purely Russian affair, and the contacts of the Russians involved seem to have been with Allied service officers rather than with the diplomatic missions. Noulens, the French Ambassador, probably knew more about what was going on than he reveals in his memoirs, where he merely refers to a visit of a delegation from the Archangel underground in April and an approach by the League for the Regeneration of Russia in May. The American Ambassador's first intimation seems to have come some time in mid-June from a British officer with a message from General Poole that plans for a landing were well under way and that he (Poole) did not wish the Ambassador to be held in Bolshevik hands as a hostage. There were, in any case, a number of reasons why the embassies should leave Vologda, and on July 24th the diplomats entrained for Archangel. There was trouble over obtaining a locomotive for their train, and they did not start their journey until the 25th, arriving at Archangel on the 27th. Here there was similar trouble over a steamer to take them on—renewing Ambassador Francis' forebodings of being held as a hostage. However, they were embarked on the 29th and landed at Kandalaksha on the 31st.

Meanwhile, Chaplin was planning the military side of the projected *coup*. In late June, when the harbour was at last ice-free, Admiral Kemp (the senior British naval officer) arrived in his yacht and Chaplin went on board to call on him. Messages from General Poole reiterated that no Allied troops were available for the seizure of the town, which must therefore be carried out solely by the' Russians themselves. As the local

Bolsheviks had as yet no qualified men of their own to put in, the military and naval establishments at Archangel were still under old-time officers. These were nervous of the *Cheka*; but Chaplin was able to satisfy himself that when the moment came they would bring their units over to the side of the conspirators or at least keep them neutral. It remained for him to recruit a small striking force: and once again he complains in his memoirs of the cowardice and apathy of so many of those he approached. It is not clear what was the degree of co-ordination between the military and civilian sides of the conspiracy. The only civilian whom Chaplin mentions favourably is N. A. Startsev, chairman of the Archangel branch of the National Centre. Local representatives of the League for the Regeneration of Russia were certainly at work, but apparently it was not till the last week of July that Chaplin met Chaikovsky and learned that he was to head the new anti-Bolshevik government. He knew of him as 'an honest man but one anxious to conserve the gains of the revolution'. He 'reluctantly' gave his agreement to the proposed arrangements: it is possible that he imagined that effective power would be shared between himself and General Poole. At the end of the month, when the Allied diplomats passed through, we are told they impressed upon Chaplin that the new government must be one Left of Centre.

Preparations went on. Zero hour was finally fixed for July 31st, and the *coup d'état* was completely successful. The repeated rumours and scares of an Allied invasion in force had merely lowered Bolshevik morale, and when two small British hydro-planes flew over the town the Red forces, such as they were, disintegrated. The city itself was taken over by the Whites without casualties, though there was some desultory fighting around the docks and the railway station on the western bank of the Dvina. On August 2nd the national flag was hoisted over the town hall and the new regional government came into being. A few hours later General Poole landed at the head of his expeditionary force, and received an enthusiastic welcome.

(iii)

We are given the Bolshevik side of the picture in the accounts of one Metelev, a local Party activist, and of M. S. Kedrov of the *Cheka*, who, in the critical weeks, was the main representative of Bolshevik power in the North. Both emphasize the Party's weakness. The combined total of Party members and candidates in the whole Archangel province did not amount to more than 600. The regional party secretary had died in late 1917, and his successor went off to Petrograd, leaving the post vacant. The Soviet was composed mainly of Left S.R.s and Mensheviks.

Early in 1918 a large Bolshevik inter-departmental commission was formed and sent north, with the Chekist Kedrov in charge. The commission had the dual task of making a reality of Bolshevik rule in Archangel and of removing to the interior the imported war supplies and coal piled up on the quays. Local conditions made progress difficult. Kedrov's first impression was that in Archangel 'there had not been an October Revolution'. The *Gorodskaya Duma* still functioned. Most of the sawmills (the town's most important industry) were still owned and run by their original proprietors. The workers were imbued with a 'peasant mentality', and most of the trade union leaders appeared to Kedrov as anti-Bolshevik. There were groups of Allied soldiers who had come up north in the hope of evacuation. The Allied Consulates were natural centres for intrigue by bourgeois and Right-wing elements, and the Consuls made trouble over the removal of the stores, until agreement on the subject was reached in early May between Trotsky and Bruce Lockhart in Moscow.

At the end of May came news of the Czech revolt. Kedrov suppressed the *Gorodskaya Duma*. He raided the premises of 137 private merchants, and arrangements were made for the distribution of the foodstuffs confiscated to needy workers—one of the main complaints against the Bolsheviks was that no supplies were coming through from the interior. An appeal was issued for the recruitment of Red Guards, but met with no response.

At the end of June, Zvegintsov of the Murmansk Soviet called through on the direct line and informed the Archangel military command of the arrival of the British force: he recommended that the Archangel authorities should negotiate an agreement with the British on the lines of what was being done in Murmansk. Faced with the certainty of crisis the Archangel Bolsheviks held a secret meeting and decided to declare a state of siege. The tempo quickened. Trotsky telegraphed that all foreign troops in the area must be disarmed (if necessary by force) and sent up to Moscow. Certain detachments were in fact disarmed, in spite of consular protests, and a number of arrests were made by the *Cheka*.

In early July was held the Second Provincial Congress of Soviets. The delegates were chiefly concerned with local shortages; peasants could procure no manufactured goods, fishermen no nets, fur-trappers no ammunition or equipment. When warned of the danger of a British landing some were incredulous, others uninterested. In spite of all the pressure the leaders could exercise, Kedrov's proposal for martial law was only passed with 74 votes in favour, 2 against and 73 abstentions. The subsequent mobilization order was a fiasco: in one *volost* (rural district) the voting on a proposal to enforce it was defeated with one vote in favour, 195 against and 9 abstentions. Later in the month an attempt to enforce it in the Shenkursk area provoked a rising (possibly encouraged by Chaplin's agents) which even the dispatch of some hardly spared detachments from Archangel failed to quell. The question of the arming of the Archangel workers was discussed, but it was decided that not more than 400 of them could be trusted with rifles. The only field in which real progress was made was the removal of the stores and coal; a daily trainload left for Vologda, and such ships as were available were loaded and sent up the river to Kotlas. As far as physical defence works were concerned it was decided to fortify the island of Mudyug in the White Sea so as to prevent the approach of hostile shipping. The workers sent over to dig the trenches and emplacements at first refused to stay there because of the mosquitoes, but mosquito netting was requisitioned in the town and the work was completed after a fashion.

During June and July it was natural that the leadership in Moscow should be fully preoccupied with the crisis along the Volga: and to secure attention to their own problems the northern Bolsheviks had to send commissions and delegations to the capital. Both Kedrov and Metelev have left accounts of conversations with Lenin, Trotsky and other leaders. Both wrote their memoirs after the eclipse of Trotsky, and Trotsky's contribution is accordingly soft-pedalled. Lenin insisted that the goodwill of the masses was more important than the retention or temporary loss of any particular town: the workers in Archangel were hungry, the Bolsheviks must therefore seize, by force if need be, one or other of the Allied grain ships in the harbour and thus secure the credit for increasing the ration.

At these Moscow talks it was suggested that the British now in Murmansk intended to drive eastwards overland through Onega, cut the Archangel-Vologda railway and advance to the Dvina: Archangel would thus be completely isolated and incapable of prolonged resistance, and the British would then take Kotlas and press on south-east towards a junction with the Czechs. Proposed counter-measures included a general call-up in all the northern provinces, a thorough clean-up of suspected traitors and spies, the establishment of a proper military head-quarters at Vologda, and the evacuation from Archangel of the key Bolshevik organizations.

On the night of July 28th, Kedrov again arrived in Moscow from the North, went straight to Lenin and was making his report when Trotsky came in with a telegram that the British fleet had put to sea from Murmansk; Kedrov should therefore return at once to take charge of the defence of Archangel. Kedrov insisted he must have a night in bed and some military reinforcements to take back with him. He left Moscow on the 31st in a special train carrying two field guns, some machine-guns and a hastily collected party of infantry.

At Yaroslavl he had news that the British had occupied Onega. At Vologda, on August 1st, he appointed a military commander for the whole region, put the railway under martial law and stopped all passenger traffic. That night, as he continued northwards, came news from Archangel that Mudyug had surrendered; Kedrov wired back that every inch of ground must be defended to the last and that reinforcements were on their way. But then came news that Archangel itself had fallen. (Two block ships should have been sunk in the navigation channel to Archangel harbour, but the operation was bungled and the channel left clear.) Panicky refugees and deserters came swarming south. At Tundre Kedrov's train was held up by two echelons of Latvian Rifles making their hurried way to the rear. Kedrov arrested and shot the ringleaders, and also a number of Party workers who had deserted their posts. Gradually order was restored along that section of the railway, but there could be no question of an effective counter-offensive. Kedrov wired Zinoviev at Petrograd asking for Gittis to be seconded to take over the military command. Zinoviev replied that Gittis could not be spared. On August 8th, Kedrov was back in Moscow. Lenin was disgusted to see him and told him he should be at the front. Kedrov insisted that he must be given the authority and resources to set up a proper military organization, and Lenin instructed Bonch-Bruevich to issue the necessary orders.

Lenin on this occasion still showed anxiety over the British threat to Kotlas. In reality, however, no such threat existed, and claims in the Great Soviet Encyclopaedia that an attempted British advance up the river Dvina was defeated by the local inhabitants and the Red Army are without any foundation. The Allied landing force was far too small to do more than defend the approaches to Archangel, as the Bolsheviks soon became aware. Bruce Lockhart in his memoirs reports Karakhan's satisfaction at the insignificance of the British expedition. The Bolsheviks were able to organize and deploy their Sixth Red Army on the Northern front without any Allied interference.

(iv)

General Poole, on arrival in Archangel, assumed overall command of all armed forces in the area and established his headquarters. Detachments were sent out, respectively up the river and along the railway, to establish defensive positions about a hundred miles south of the town. Chaplin was put in charge of the various Russian units, and endeavoured to get his command into some sort of shape. He was not entirely successful. The Russian forces were a very mixed lot (there had been cases of looting when the city was captured), and there were few officers available who were qualified either for command or for staff duties. On August 8th the diplomatic missions came back from Kandalaksha. They arrived with some misgivings as to how far the soldiers would recognize their importance and authority, and there were difficulties over accommodation and precedence. These, however, were smoothed over, and good relations established between Poole and, at least, the French Ambassador.

'You cannot imagine,' Chaikovsky wrote to his children in those early days, 'my happiness at having fulfilled my sacred task.' The local government, of which he was president, came into being as a result of the conversations at Vologda in which members of the League for the Regeneration of Russia had been the principal participants. It consisted of seven of the northern delegates to the Constituent Assembly and two municipal counsellors, and its political complexion was rather left of centre. Its assumption of office was made easy by the absence of any rivals. Its position was fortunate in that the two really urgent problems—defence and the provision of food for the town population—were being taken care of by the British. The government's main activity was, therefore, the issue of a series of eloquent and high-minded proclamations, the first ten of which had been drafted by Chaikovsky and Maslov back in Vologda. It regarded itself as purely provisional—its task was to restore the democratic order of 1917, and hand over its powers to the All Russian anti-Bolshevik authority that was about to be set up in the East. All its members optimistically believed that a physical junction with the Czech and Samara forces now on the Volga was only a matter of weeks.

Soon there were signs of discontent and friction. To the Russian officers and the Right-wing bourgeoisie the local government, with its emphasis on revolution and its tendency to govern by demagogic exhortation, seemed bent on reviving the worst features of the Kerensky régime. Indeed, there were reports that Kerensky himself was due to arrive, on which Chaplin gave out that if he did he would arrest him. The government and their sympathizers in their turn had reason to complain of the indiscipline and provocative behaviour of monarchist and Right-wing officers who made no secret of their aim to put the clock back. Matters came to a head when Chaplin was confidentially informed by Poole that the Allies were about to recognize the government. Chaplin decided to forestall this, and very possibly with the connivance of some British officer friends proceeded to take action. On September 9th there was arranged a formal parade and reception to welcome a newly arrived American contingent. None of the government members turned up, and Chaplin announced that the government no longer existed: he had arrested them *en bloc* the previous night and removed them to one of the off-shore islands.

This caused a considerable flurry. The American Ambassador described the case as 'the most flagrant usurpation of power I ever knew'. Orders were given for the government at once to be brought back. As the news spread into the town there were strikes and preparations for a big workers' demonstration. All the tramway personnel stopped work, and Ambassador Francis was disturbed to find that the newly arrived U.S. contingent (mostly transport workers) were running the trams. He felt this might be American interference in Russian internal affairs, though the officer commanding the unit explained that no fares were being charged.

There was a vigorous exchange of telegrams between the

Ambassadors and their ministries at home, and, when Chaikovsky and his colleagues were brought back to the mainland, there was some attempt at a post-mortem and hard bargaining as to what should be done next. The result was a compromise. Chaikovsky remained president, but the government was reconstructed, the S.R.s being dropped and the new cabinet consisting of three Cadets and one non-Party man, with a Colonel Durov in command of the Russian forces *vice* Chaplin. Chaplin was neither brought to trial nor expelled from the area: he was sent to the front to serve under his friend, General Finlayson. The Western Allies agreed that in future their representatives should exercise some supervision over Archangel affairs. Francis was satisfied at what he felt to be a victory of democracy over the military, all the more so as Poole was recalled to London shortly afterwards. Noulens took the line that the authority now granted to the diplomats was too vague to be effective, especially with a doyen who was as lacking in knowledge and in judgment as was Francis. His general verdict was that the Russian Socialists had revealed themselves as incapable either of governing or of being governed.

The September affair was in many ways a farcical incident; within twenty-four hours the life of the city went on as if nothing had happened. But it was a reminder to the Left-wing intellectuals and the workers (which they did not forget) that the forces of reaction were willing and were able to act. The not entirely unlikely suspicion that Chaplin had acted with British connivance convinced many Russians that the British intention was, in fact, to interfere in Russian matters. Finally, such unmistakable evidence of the Northern Provisional Government's impotence was an effective bar to its acquiring either authority or prestige.

In any case events quite outside Archangel were to diminish the importance of that government. At Ufa on September 23rd a Directorate was set up as an anti-Bolshevik All Russian supreme authority. The armistice with Germany on November 11th removed the Allied need for a potential second front in the

North. On November 18th a *coup* at Omsk overthrew the Directorate and installed Admiral Kolchak as Supreme Ruler. This provoked the bitter resentment of the anti-Bolshevik Left, but in the eyes of the world there had emerged at last a White régime with more than local authority. Accordingly there was little point in maintaining embassies at Archangel, and the Ambassadors were withdrawn in December. In January, Chaikovsky, the one national figure in the government, left for France.

(v)

On September 30th, 1918, General Ironside landed in Archangel with British reinforcements. He had been hurriedly summoned back to London from the front in France and told he had been appointed Chief of Staff to General Poole. As had been the case with Maynard three months previously, he found it difficult to obtain any satisfactory briefing. Just before leaving he was called to the C.I.G.S., General Henry Wilson, whose last words were 'your business in Russia is to hold the fort until the local Russians can take the field. You are to prepare for a winter campaign. No joke, that.' On landing in Archangel he found that Poole 'appeared to think that the command would be considerably strengthened and would take part in a general advance of all the White Armies on Petrograd and Moscow.' Poole then surprised him by saying that he was about to go back to England on leave, so that he, Ironside, would be temporarily in charge. On October 14th Poole embarked. A month later the War Office telegraphed that Poole would not be returning and that Ironside was appointed C.-in-C. at Archangel. Murmansk became a separate command under General Maynard.

Edmund Ironside, who was to be the dominating personality in the northern area for the next twelve months, was then thirty-seven years of age. He stood six feet four in his socks and was heavily built. He was a competent linguist. He had had a good deal of experience overseas before his service at the front in France; but he was now to be faced with a number of problems of a very different order.

One of his first official calls was on Chaikovsky, whom he describes as 'a placid old gentleman, very tall and thin, but surprisingly active in body . . . The old man was completely and utterly un-military and did not seem to realize that force would be necessary to defeat the Bolsheviks.' It was thus natural that as far as military matters were concerned, Ironside was referred to Durov, the Russian C.O., and Samarin, his second-in-command. It at once became apparent that very little was being done to build up the Russian Army. 'I was told,' Ironside notes, 'the situation was most delicate and nothing must be done in haste. The new army must be a truly democratic one.' There were 1,500 soldiers in the barracks, including a number of ex-p.o.w.s. They were not organized into units. Durov and Samarin explained that the ex-officers available locally were unsuitable. 'They admitted that they had not been through either the officers or the N.C.O.s with a view to seeing if there were any suitable ones among them. Though they agreed that volunteering was totally alien to the Russian mind and they did not expect to get many men that way, they had never put the question of conscription to the Government. They rather haughtily told me that conscription was un-democratic.' Ironside telegraphed to the War Office in London to send out two good senior Russian officers.

On October 29th there was a minor mutiny in the Russian barracks: the men refused to turn out for Ironside's inspection. One of the causes, that subsequently came to light and was corrected, was that owing to an administrative muddle the men were on half rations. Meanwhile there was the mutiny to be quelled. Durov and Samarin were unwilling or unable to take action and it was Ironside in person who restored order. He then called on the head of the government to complain of the inadequacy of the higher command. Chaikovsky was distressed and said: 'If only we could have left the men alone.' However, Durov and Samarin resigned (no doubt in view of

Ironside's attitude) and were replaced temporarily by two other officers appointed on Ironside's insistence. On November 17th General Marushevsky arrived in Archangel to assume command of the Russian forces, and the little local army slowly began to take shape.

Meanwhile things were by no means satisfactory in the Allied force. The Dvina column, 120 miles south-east of Archangel up the river, depended for its artillery on river gunboats under naval command. At the beginning of November, in view of the approaching freeze-up, these were withdrawn by Admiralty orders without any notification having reached Ironside. Their departure soon became known to the Bolsheviks, who brought up improvised gunboats and shelled the Allied positions without fear of retaliation. On Armistice Day the Reds attacked, and fighting continued for three or four days before the position was stabilized. Allied losses were 28 killed and 70 wounded. In late November the port of Archangel was frozen up, and for the next seven months, apart from the occasional entry of an ice-breaker and the tenuous overland route from Murmansk via Onega, the area was isolated.

It was important both for Ironside and for the Ambassadors (as long as they were there) to obtain a clear statement of Allied policy *vis-à-vis* the Bolsheviks following the armistice with the Central Powers; but in spite of repeated requests no such statement was forthcoming. Local policy had to be conducted from day to day. The first practical problem was food supply. The British seem to have handled this with some success: all are agreed that the population, military and civilian, were well fed throughout the whole period. Then the currency problem was tackled. To take the place of the various heavily devalued and wildly fluctuating paper roubles it was decided to introduce new rouble notes based on sterling and exchangeable at the rate of 40 to the £. These were printed in England and brought out by a Mr. Harvey of the British Treasury. On arrival it was found that they bore the imperial crown and were thus unacceptable, so the crowns had to be blocked out (and, according to Noulens, the effigy of the Empress Catherine changed to that of Mrs. Harvey). Efforts were made to revive foreign trade, particularly the timber trade, as large stocks of timber were piled on the docks. Timber was short in the West, and for the rest of their time in Archangel the diplomats were involved in heated arguments over allotments and shipping space.

For the Russians the important political issue of that period was the seizure of power by Admiral Kolchak at Omsk on November 18th. Chaikovsky was horrified; the affair appeared to him as a successful variant of the Chaplin *coup* at Archangel on September 8th. There was no direct Russian channel of communication until the turn of the year, when French W/T equipment (shipped along the north coast and then up the River Ob) was installed at Omsk. But vigorous protests were transmitted through Allied channels. The Ambassadors sympathized with Chaikovsky, and telegraphed to their governments appeals to arrange for the setting up of 'a democratic framework' round Kolchak. Ironside took a different line: 'knowing the inefficiency of the Socialist Revolutionary Government, as I saw it, it is difficult to believe the White armies could ever have defeated the Bolsheviks without some form of Military Dictatorship to direct operations in the field.' This fundamental difference on what Chaikovsky regarded as the supreme issue, and Ironside's continued and unwelcome insistence on matters of practical administration about which the old man knew and cared very little, were certainly among the factors that helped him to decide to leave. His main interest was high policy, and it was becoming obvious—especially since the recall of the Ambassadors—that Archangel was to be a political backwater. Paris, he felt, was now the centre where the main decisions should be taken, and after working out an elaborate seven-point memorandum on Russian problems, he left in early January to join the Russian Political Delegation there.

His departure coincided with the arrival in Archangel of the Russian General E. K. Miller, who was destined to replace him as the leading figure in the Northern Provisional Government.

(vi)

Shortly after assuming command Ironside noted that 'we were a tiny army of not very first-class troops sitting on the edge of Russia's vast territory in which was being fought a bitter civil war.' During the late autumn and winter the number of Russian and other troops (while still insignificant) nearly doubled. Prodded by the British command, the Provisional Government introduced conscription in October. The total of volunteers for the Russian Army in the month of September had been seventy, but in November over two thousand men were enrolled. By the end of March the Russian forces in the Archangel area numbered 14,000, of whom half were regarded as sufficiently trained to serve at the front. There were then about the same number of Allied troops, the great majority of whom were British; and there was, further, the Dyer battalion of the Slavo-British Legion (a formation on which the British command set great hopes) consisting of volunteers for various reasons unacceptable to the Russian authorities, under officers half of whom were Russian and half British.

Murmansk, from the point of view of civil administration, was subordinate to the Provisional Government at Archangel, who had sent over one Ermolov as governor. Militarily, as we have seen, it was a separate command under Maynard. In October and November, 1918, reinforcements arrived from England, and by the turn of the year Maynard had a total of over 14,000 men—7,000 British, 3,000 Frenchmen, Serbs and Italians, and 4,000 Russians, Karelians and Finns. Of these he considered that some 10,000 might be counted as combatant troops. Conscription was introduced somewhat later than in Archangel, but when it came it produced 3,500 men from the area Murmansk-Soroka. Maynard was in favour of a drive to the South in order to tap further reserves of manpower. But it was not an easy command. There was trouble with the Finns and the Karelians. There was Bolshevik-inspired subversive activity, particularly among the railwaymen. In January two

British officers were murdered in Murmansk. There was always a shortage of labour, which meant restiveness among the troops over too many fatigues. Some French units declared they would not go into action. Maynard writes that 'before the undertaking reached its close there were units of nearly every nationality upon which I could not rely with absolute confidence.'

The quality of the Archangel troops was no better—Bolshevik propaganda (by means of line-crossers) was fairly intense throughout: it seems to have made no impression on the Allied forces, and, at this stage, little on the Russians. But war-weariness was universal. Many of the British were of a low medical category—the battalion of the Royal Scots, for instance, were all C3 (fit for garrison duty only). The severity, and above all, the dreary monotony of the long, dark Arctic winter further lowered the morale of men who, now the Armistice had come, thought only of going back to their homes. For the Allied rank and file this was not their war, and the same held good for the Russian conscripts. Ironside, who knew some Russian, made a point of listening to peasant conversations at the halts on his visits to the front. 'The change of ponies went on to a running commentary on the news from the last post, but it was never anything military—always the price of food and drink and the health of friends and relatives. Nobody took any interest in what we were doing. . . . They knew nothing about the Provisional Government in Archangel. . . . They considered the Allies to be in a private quarrel with the Bolsheviks.' Such was the raw material of the Russian forces.

Life in the front line meant, for eight months in the year, complete isolation in cramped and snowbound quarters. Periods of relief in Archangel did not help discipline. There was far too much liquor about, with the Provisional Government's monopoly selling vodka at a shilling a bottle. Conditions gave ample scope to the Russian genius for Black Market operations; 'skolko-ing' became a regular occupation of both officers and men of all nationalities. As Ironside noted, 'every base of an army in war rapidly becomes a sink if it is not cleaned out at frequent intervals.' With the port frozen up there was no means of cleaning it out.

Incidents were continuously taking place in one or other detachment. A Russian unit mutinied on December 11th. In February there was trouble in a battalion of the Yorkshire Regiment: two sergeants refused to take part in any further fighting. They were court-martialled and condemned to death, but the sentences were commuted to life imprisonment on instructions from London. A few days later a French battalion resting in Archangel refused to return to the front. It was by no means certain that the front could be held, and it was a natural precaution for Ironside to prepare, discreetly, an inner line of defences some eighteen miles south of the town.

But the opposing Sixth Red Army under Kuzmin was also in poor shape. The Reds were inferior in strength: figures given by Kuzmin put their numbers at little more than two-thirds of their opponents. They were helped by a few partisan detachments, of which that under a certain Mandelbaum became notorious for its atrocities. The Reds were desperately short of officers—former officers who had fought well against the Germans and Finns were so far proving to be of little use on this northern sector. Little in the way of supplies was forthcoming from Petrograd. Food was inadequate, and losses from frostbite were heavy. The Kronstadt sailors, whose improvised river batteries had so surprised the Allied Dvina column in November, refused to fight on land when the river froze. As so often in the Civil War it was the ruthless determination of a few Bolsheviks that kept the Sixth Red Army in being.

At the turn of the year news reached Archangel of the capture of Perm by Kolchak's northern army. Ironside had received no details of Kolchak's plans, but the possibility of an attempt to advance across the intervening 400 miles to the British positions on the Dvina could not be ruled out. Ironside notes: 'To have received a destitute Czech corps of 70,000 men [*sic*] in our northern region in the depths of winter would have constituted a formidable problem.' There was, then, no question of a corresponding British drive from the North, but the Bolsheviks could not be sure of this, and Kuzmin was instructed to go over to the offensive. On January 1st, 1919, the Reds attacked a small outpost with some initial success, as the French outpost commander did not obey his orders and the British officer in charge of the machine-gun section was drunk. A probe directed at one of the railway outposts was beaten off, but a few days later an Allied post near Onega was overrun. Finally, on January 19th the Reds attacked in some force at Shenkursk. For five days the position was critical: the British and Russians were pushed out of the town of Shenkursk and a number of neighbouring villages. It was not until the 25th that new defensive positions were established and the line stabilized once more. For the next few months there was no fighting of real importance on any of the northern sectors.

(vii)

But a policy decision of some importance was shortly to be taken in London. On March 4th the British War Cabinet decided to press the Allied representatives in Paris to agree to the early evacuation of North Russia. This was not to mean the abandonment of the anti-Bolshevik Russians: two new British brigades, each of 4,000 volunteers, were to be formed and shipped out at the earliest possible date. The scope and nature of their employment would be decided in the light of circumstances. But their stay on Russian soil was to be strictly limited. On April 5th Ironside received a telegram from the War Office to be passed to the troops under his command. 'Whatever may be the plan of action towards Russia decided upon by the League of Nations, we intend to relieve you at the earliest possible moment, and either bring the whole force away or replace you by fresh men. These reliefs are being prepared now . . .' Ironside suppressed this message, which would have had a deplorable effect on local morale. It was not until towards the end of the month, when a senior staff officer arrived with a War Office appreciation dated April 15th, that he obtained a picture of British policy as then determined.

This appreciation emphasized the finality of the decision that all British and non-Russian units must be withdrawn before the closing of the port in the coming winter. There were two possible alternative situations at the time of withdrawal— (1) that the local Russians would be able to carry on by themselves, or (2) that they could not continue independently, in which case all Russian civilians and military who so wished would have to be evacuated along with the British. It was stressed that His Majesty's Government would prefer the former alternative. It was just possible that the Russians might be able to maintain themselves provided that enough British officer and N.C.O. volunteers were available to build up the Slavo-British Legion. It was, however, extremely desirable that, in addition, junction should be effected with Kolchak's armies. The first step to this would be the capture of Kotlas. Ironside's reports (the appreciation continued) had disclosed the lowered morale of the Allied troops and the need for good volunteers for the Slavo-British Legion. His further requirements for the capture of Kotlas were an adequate naval river flotilla; 5,000 good British fighting men; capable British personnel for administration and for lines of communication duties; the certainty that the Siberians were coming; and finally the engagement of the Red Army on other fronts.

This last role might be filled by Denikin in the South. 'On the other hand the Polish forces, torn by fears of Germany and occupied by hostile forces of the Ukraine in the South, cannot be reckoned on to bring any effective pressure to bear on the Bolsheviks . . . Similarly, the lack of Allied policy in regard to Finland and the other Baltic States precludes the timely, effective (and perhaps decisive) action which might otherwise have been undertaken against Petrograd.'

(viii)

British-Russian relations during the whole of the Archangel operation were never really cordial on any level—quite apart from the absence of any common ground between the British military commanders and the 'utterly unmilitary' Russian civilian politicians.

Both Ironside and Maynard possessed high professional competence within the limits of the background and experience of the British regular army of 1914. Unlike Russian officers, they were still unused to being part of a big, highly centralized machine. Their schooling had been in small wars on the North-West Frontier or in Africa, where politics played no part and where the local commander had a high degree of independence and a special sense of responsibility for the little force under him. Civil administration in the areas where these little wars were fought was usually primitive, so the soldiers had to do almost everything by themselves and for themselves. Discipline was strict; emphasis was laid on what was then called 'spit and polish' and later known as 'bull'; but the need to improvise brought with it a certain informality. There was much about the British expeditionary forces in North Russia that seemed strange to Russian eyes.

General Marushevsky, when passing through Murmansk in late 1918, was astonished at the comfort of the railway coach where Maynard had established his command post and headquarters mess. On the other hand, bewilderment was caused by Ironside's habit of touring his huge area in two pony sleighs, accompanied only by one orderly and the two drivers. (On one occasion the C.-in-C. had a little private battle with a Bolshevik line-crossing group.) The general was even seen carrying his own bed. Then there was the fussiness that the British showed over their latrines.

Ironside and Marushevsky never got on well together. Apart from anything else there was the psychological difficulty arising from the fact that Ironside was six feet four in height, and Marushevsky barely five feet one. Ironside's tone in his memoirs is consistently a superior one. He keeps referring to the 'curiously conversational Orders of the Day in which Russian generals so often indulged'. One of Marushevsky's that he quotes with some gusto begins 'from the direction of the Cathedral I heard a disgusting flow of gutter language. Going nearer I met two sailors, and approaching one of them I called his attention to the absolute impermissibility of such filthy language in the street. The second sailor went on, but the one to whom I addressed myself slovenly declared himself as being drunk, and with a broad gesture he blew his nose on the pavement . . . How pitiful all this is and how deeply disgusting.' Ironside also cites later the case of a Russian colonel on the lines of communications who complained that his unit had no baths, and was astonished at the suggestion that he should himself construct a bath-house even though he had no specific authority from headquarters to do so. He was continually struck with the Russian regimental officers' apparent lack of interest in their men's welfare. He quotes two replies to this complaint. 'Are we our men's valets that we should do all this for them?' And 'Have any of your officers been shot by their men?'

Four years of war and revolution had left their mark on the northern provinces. The general atmosphere was one of weariness and muddle. Essential tasks were not being done. The British commanders had no confidence in the Russians being able to do them, and so did them themselves. They ran the supplies; they ran the hospitals; they ran their own security services. Russian suspicions of Machiavellian British plans for the permanent domination of the north were, of course, fantastic. But it was in a way true that the British treated Archangel as a colony, though the British themselves thought they were merely doing what was necessary to ensure the survival of the régime and of the Russian and Allied forces. A significant instance of British 'colonial' mentality was the scheme, that so appealed to Ironside and others, for the Slavo-British Legion. The reasoning was very simple. Russians were obviously potentially good fighting material. Of the Russian officers available a great number were equally obviously of poor quality. The solution must therefore be to form units with British officers and Russian rank and file. When in 1919 one of these battalions murdered its five British officers the British command was genuinely bewildered.

It is easy today to appreciate the resentment caused by the fact that the British troops were immeasurably the better off as regards amenities, equipment and pay, with all the advantages this gave them in the competition for girls, liquor and black market opportunities. And it was perfectly natural, then, for the British expeditionary force, both officers and men, to tend to look on the Russians as poor relations. They were perfectly willing to be friendly, but the Russians found them complacent, patronizing. A few of the less unsensitive British were unhappy at this attitude. But there was no Anglo-Russian fraternization at the front.

Behind all this was a mutual misconception of the respective roles in the Civil War. To the end the Russians were expecting the British to launch a large-scale offensive. The British regarded themselves as merely there till the Russians were ready to attack.

Each side accused the other of unwillingness to fight; each side could find plenty of material to support the allegation, and each was prone to impute sinister motives. It was all very well for Miller, when he assumed command, to fulminate in Orders of the Day when British soldiers were beaten up in brawls in the Archangel bars, or for Ironside to forbid any disparagement of Russian efforts. As time went on relations tended to deteriorate rather than improve.

In the early spring of 1919 the Provisional Government was reorganized, with a shift towards the Right. It was thus possible, on April 30th, to recognize Admiral Kolchak as Supreme Ruler of Russia; and from that date until Kolchak's collapse in the late autumn there was an unceasing and voluminous exchange of telegrams, reports and directives between the various ministries in Omsk and the corresponding authorities in Archangel.

This mass of paper was of little practical importance, but the new set-up strengthened the position of General Miller, who became Governor-General of the northern area, Kolchak's personal representative, and Commander-in-Chief of the Russian troops. It also led to the departure of Marushevsky, who was unwilling to step down to be Miller's Chief of Staff. Ironside somewhat unkindly remarks that Marushevsky 'had lost interest in Archangel and was asking for permission to go to another front'. In point of fact, Marushevsky, who had served with a Finnish Division during the Great War and gone underground in Finland when he broke with the Bolsheviks, was one of the very few Russian generals to realize the importance of Finnish co-operation. He accordingly went to Helsinki and re-established his Finnish contacts; but his self-imposed mission foundered on the refusal of Kolchak and the other Whites to recognize Finnish independence.

Meanwhile, on the northern front the stalemate continued. Throughout the summer there was a steady trickle of hungry and disillusioned Red Army soldiers coming over to the White lines. But Bolshevik propaganda activity continued, and it was presumably with a propaganda motive that the Bolsheviks sent over a captured British officer, Captain Wilson of the Royal Engineers (who had been purposely well-treated in captivity), to discuss a possible exchange of prisoners. In April Miller wrote to Chaikovsky in Paris emphasizing the poor quality of the Allied troops and the need for them to be replaced by volunteers. Chaikovsky visited London and had a long and inconclusive talk over breakfast with Lloyd George. On the 25th fighting flared up again on the Dvina. The 3rd North Russian Rifle Regiment mutinied; seven officers were murdered and 300 of the rank and file crossed over to the Bolsheviks. But the Reds were unable to exploit the incident.

Kolchak's spring offensive was, of course, of great concern to the British command in the North. In late April, when the offensive reached its peak, Ironside was complaining of lack of information as to its progress. As he noted later, 'it seemed a ridiculous thing in modern times that we could not get accurate news from Siberia and had no personal knowledge of what was going on in the front line.'[1]

The first official report to reach Ironside was a War Office telegram of May 22nd to the effect that Kolchak's plans were (a) the capture of Kazan and Vyatka, and the dispatch of a force north-westwards to join up with Archangel; (b) the establishment of a line along the Volga as far south as Samara, with a force dispatched south to the Don; and (c) a general advance to Moscow. Kolchak appeared to lay greater urgency on a junction with the North than with Denikin. The telegram ended: 'We are warned by Knox [of the British Military Mission with Kolchak] that it is part of the Russian character to draw up plans without the means of carrying them out being taken into consideration.' Ironside telegraphed back for definite dates.

There was no inkling in Archangel that at that moment Kolchak's armies were suffering a decisive defeat. Ironside and Miller discussed the advance on Kotlas, and Miller maintained 'the British had only to set the ball rolling by breaking the enemy front, the Russians would certainly do the rest'. Supplies and equipment were unloaded and stored in preparation for the coming Siberians. There was a formal inspection of the Slavo-British Legion (though Ironside was warned by a Russian officer that 'it was often the case that the worst and most dangerous men were those who seemed the best disciplined'). The first of the new volunteer brigades arrived and received an official welcome. The volunteers, mostly too young to have served in the Great War and piqued to have seen no active service, made an excellent impression that was to be justified by their subsequent performance. There was a message from King George V. The Slavo-British Legion were presented with their Colours. All this more than off set the fiasco of a minor (Russian) offensive at Pinega, and all the very real transport

[1] A small patrol of twenty Russians and five British and French N.C.O.s had, in fact, set out in March across the four hundred miles of No-Man's-Land to join up with Kolchak's First (Siberian) Army. They did eventually reach the Siberians, but no news of their arrival seems to have got back to Archangel.

and administrative difficulties brought about every spring by the thaw.

On June 4th the War Office telegraphed: 'Our latest information indicates Admiral Kolchak maintains his intention to capture Vyatka. If this were done it would entail the Bolsheviks abandoning the whole railway as far as Kotlas. However, in view of the reverses he has suffered in S. Russia you must face the possibility of his offensive being delayed in the North or seriously weakened, and must therefore be prepared to modify your plans accordingly. In any case, it is considered that as soon as the necessary means are available a hard blow should be struck at the Bolsheviks and you should make all preparations for doing so.' Ironside replied with a proposal for an offensive designed to break the Red front. If at that time Kolchak were doing well, Miller's Russians would push on to Kotlas; if not, they would take up positions and Ironside would prepare to evacuate. Meanwhile he hoped that if news from Siberia was bad it would not be released to the press.

On June 5th further reinforcements arrived. On the 6th a small (Russian) force failed in an attack on the Reds near Onega. On the seventh the War Office telegraphed that the proposed operation was approved, but that Kolchak was doing badly. The Cabinet was to review the position on June 27th. In his reply Ironside pointed out that after the northern offensive the northern command would pass to the Russians and it would be for them to decide on their ultimate objective.

The next few days were taken up with the embarkation of the greater part of the original British force in the ships that had brought the new brigades. Ironside decided on a limited probe at the Red positions on the Dvina with a mixed Anglo-Russian force. This took place on June 20th. The Russians fought well but a British battalion commander lost his head and the initial advantage was not followed up. However, the Reds lost 500 prisoners and 100 killed.

On July 1st the War Office telegraphed that Kolchak's position was bad, due 'not so much to inferiority in numbers or morale as to incompetence in the higher command'. London had 'no details as to the withdrawal' and could not say whether 'the precarious communication with the Archangel force [*sic*] has been cut'. The message ended by saying there was 'no reason to despair of Kolchak's ultimate recovery'. Ironside, however, thought otherwise. His experience gave him no reason to hope for any recovery on the Eastern front, and he felt it would be pointless to wait for one. His preoccupation was to carry out his instructions to evacuate his force before the winter. There was no object in going for Kotlas. He would break the Bolshevik line, but the sole object of that operation would be to enable Miller and his Russians to establish a strong position. The following day he explained the situation to a tired and disillusioned General Miller.

Three days later a serious mutiny broke out in the Slavo-British Legion, and a number of British and Russian officers were murdered. What remained of the unit was disarmed and turned into a labour force. On July 20th a Russian detachment near Onega murdered their officers and dispersed. But a Bolshevik attack, presumably timed to synchronize with the mutiny, was beaten off by the Poles (the one national contingent on the whole northern front who consistently earned the praise of their commanders). On July 25th the War Office passed on a telegram from General Knox to the effect that Kolchak was decisively and utterly defeated.

(ix)

As late as June 27th Miller was sending urgent messages to Chaikovsky to persuade the British Government to abandon the idea of evacuation and to send out further troops. It was not till his talk with Ironside on July 2nd that he realized the British decision was irrevocable. Both leaders agreed that for the sake of local morale the public announcement should be delayed. Naturally there were rumours. At the reception for King George's birthday in June, Ironside had confidentially foreshadowed a coming junction with Kolchak; at the French reception on July 14th no top generals were present, and their subordinates were evasive. The conclusion to be drawn was obvious; and an ever greater number of Russians became involved in one way or the other in the preparations for the British departure.

There was one serious decision that Miller had to take. The British Government, as Winston Churchill later made clear in Parliament, wished to honour its obligations to the anti-Bolshevik Russians and was prepared to evacuate, together with the British force, any Russians who so wished. Ironside accordingly put to Miller a choice of three courses: (1) complete evacuation of the whole Russian Army, (2) the abandonment of Archangel and the transfer of all Russian forces to the Murmansk area, (3) the Russian Army to be provided with all necessary stores and supplies and left to hold the existing territory. Ironside himself had little confidence in the Russians being able to maintain themselves, but he carefully refrained from any suggestion or move that might influence the decision.

The matter was keenly debated in the *Stavka*, the Russian military headquarters. Telegrams were sent to Omsk, but the harassed Kolchak ruled that the choice must be made on the spot. Officers from combatant units were called back from the front to advise. Opinion was sharply divided. Front-line officers, and regimental officers generally, were in favour of (1) or (2), and were vigorously backed by Marushevsky now returned from Finland. The *Stavka* itself, and in particular a number of generals who had arrived within the last few weeks and had found themselves jobs in Archangel, were in favour of (3). Miller's final decision was to stay and hold the whole area. It was prompted by the reluctance of a patriotic general to take the responsibility of yielding any territory, and by the hopes he set on the success of Denikin's offensive in the South.

The British authorities sent out General Sir Henry Rawlinson with an imposing staff to take command of the evacuation of Archangel and Murmansk. It is not clear from the records available what was the reason for this appointment, nor what was its contribution to the operation's success. Both Ironside and Maynard felt somewhat slighted at not being left in charge to the end. Rawlinson had no knowledge of local conditions and no common language with the local Russian leaders. He is described by Marushevsky, who called on him, as 'receiving us like a Viceroy receiving a delegation of niggers'. Rawlinson's arrival coincided with a limited Anglo-Russian offensive designed to break the Red front. The attack, under Brigadier-General Sadleir-Jackson, was a complete success: the Bolsheviks lost 3,000 prisoners and three gunboats. Maynard successfully carried out a parallel offensive on the Murmansk front. The evacuation preparations could be now conducted without risk of interference by the Reds.

In due course a public announcement was made of the impending withdrawal and of the British offer to take out all civilians who wished to leave Archangel. This at first caused general alarm and indignation. 'Dislike of the Varangians was not equal to the fear of the Bolsheviks.' The British were accused of treachery. One Russian colonel called at the British head-quarters, pulled off his newly awarded D.S.O., and threw it down on Ironside's desk in protest. There was a spate of appeals, petitions and deputations. A delegation of members of the local political parties left for London (where they could find no one to listen to them). But before very long alarm subsided into apathy. The British had expected to take out 18,000 civilians, but in fact only 6,000 applied. These were mostly people with friends or money either in Western Europe or in Denikin's area in South Russia; or else rich businessmen and speculators who could take out with them enough cash to start again elsewhere. There were a great many war brides—the last few weeks saw a boom in weddings.

It was natural that the circumstances of departure should give rise to bad feeling. There were bitter complaints in the press of the poor accommodation allotted to Russian civilians in British troopships. There was an abortive attempt by the Russian authorities to establish their right to decide what Russians should or should not be evacuated. There were one or two British businessmen who owed the Northern Government money and who got away without paying. Deep resentment was caused at the destruction of surplus stores and at the hurried tempo of the British departure, which it was felt showed lack of confidence in the Russian Northern Army and administration.

It was certainly true that, after the experiences of the past twelve months, Ironside felt unable to relax until the last British troopship had left the harbour. On August 29th the North Russian Army staged a successful minor offensive, capturing 1,000 prisoners, and Miller put in a final plea for British participation in an advance on Vologda to synchronize with Yudenich's projected thrust at Petrograd. But Ironside was adamant. The plans for the complicated series of leap-frog withdrawals were meticulously drawn up and put into operation in mid-September. On the night of the 26th/27th September the last British soldier embarked at Archangel. A fortnight later the British were out of Murmansk, and as far as the British were concerned the northern adventure was over. The total British casualties for the whole period had been 106 officers and 877 other ranks, of whom respectively 41 and 286 had been killed.

Ironside was later informed in London by the official war historian that no official history of the Archangel expedition would be undertaken.

(x)

The look and the atmosphere of Archangel changed overnight. A senior Russian officer, on the morning of September 27th, remarked to a friend whom he met in the street: 'Now at last we are back in Russia.' This Russia of the North, with its total population of under half a million, was to last for five months.

For a short time after the British departure news of the advances of the armies of Denikin and Yudenich made it seem that the Whites were about to win the war. There was a prolonged telegraphic squabble between Omsk and Archangel over the powers and forms of the Northern administration: the exchange was still going on when Kolchak's government fell to pieces. There was some political activity. It was a time when pleas for democracy were being raised in all White centres. In Archangel a consultative assembly was called into being, and the cabinet was reorganized again to include one Popular Socialist and two Socialist Revolutionaries. Material conditions throughout the area were good. The British had left an abundance of supplies, and right up to the end prices of food and other necessities were considerably lower than in any other part of Russia. The one really urgent issue was the question of an amnesty for the large number of political detainees, who had been arrested by the haphazard British and Russian security services. Many of them were still being held in deplorable conditions in concentration camps. After much argument a commission was appointed to consider cases individually. The S.R. ministers, who had pressed for a much more sweeping solution, resigned over this issue, and there were some strikes in the factories.

The charge has been levelled by Socialist critics of the Northern Government that the civilians failed to impose their will upon the generals. It is difficult to find evidence that they had much will to impose. The apathy that had marked Archangel during the two revolutions and under the Bolsheviks continued during the White régime. Not untypical is the statement of two leading S.R.s in late 1919 that they did not approve of the military dictatorial aspects of the régime but they did not propose to hamper General Miller in his defence of the region.

There was no strong reactionary element in Archangel except for recent imports, military and civilian. The area had no big landowners. Big business, such as it was, had gone out with the British. Small business was passive. The peasants, too, were passive except round Shenkursk and in those other areas which had come into conflict with the Bolsheviks: it was these peasants who formed partisan detachments and who fought the Reds right up to the end. The potential opposition were the Left-wing parties, S.R.s and Mensheviks, made up of the local intelligentsia (including some old political deportees) and a few workers. Bolshevik cells were very few and deep underground: their activities were confined to helping the skilful and persistent Bolshevik propaganda effort. The one very real political grievance was that against the security services. The psychological background of opposition was war-weariness, minor frustration and ignorance of the realities of Bolshevik rule.

As to the Northern Army, General Miller, Minister of War and Commander-in-Chief, earned general respect for his integrity and conscientiousness. He was by no means a reactionary: he established and maintained friendly contact with some of the local S.R.s. As a soldier his tendency was to stay in his headquarters. Unlike Ironside or Maynard, he was not the type to go round the front and see things for himself. He would spend up to eighteen hours a day in his office meticulously working on matters of detail. The take-over from the British meant, of course, extra staff work, and it may well be due to Miller that the Northern Army's supply service continued to function so well. But all this meant that he was out of touch with his front-line commanders and too accessible to the views of senior members of his staff, and indeed the final disaster showed that much of the operational side of the staff work was very inadequate. Little confidence seems to have been inspired by General Kvintinski, the Chief of Staff; and another element to be criticized were the score or so of middle-aged Tsarist generals who arrived a few weeks before the British departed, and who seldom got anywhere near the front line. In many cases their motive in coming was that they had families to support and could find no other employment.

The regimental officers fell into three groups—local residents who were called up, officers who happened to be in the area when the British arrived and who volunteered for further service, and volunteers brought in from overseas. These last were mostly ex-Skoropadsky officers who had spent the intervening period in internment camps: some were strongly pro-German and were constantly quarrelling with their pro-Entente colleagues. The officers varied in quality. Many showed personal courage and some possessed professional ability. Inevitably there were those whose main preoccupation was to find a safe post in the rear. Inevitably, too, many were psychologically affected by the strains and humiliations of the past six years. This came out in lack of discipline, irresponsibility, savage private attacks on individuals suspected of Bolshevism, peculation of regimental funds and, above all, drunkenness. Much depended on the personality of commanding officers, and standards of behaviour and competence varied enormously from unit to unit. One factor was constant: dislike and contempt on the part of the combatant officers for the lines of communication and headquarters staffs.

The rank and file also were of three categories—local volunteers, the locally mobilized, and Red Army deserters. The few volunteers were nearly all members or ex-members of partisan detachments and were peasants from villages which had suffered from Bolshevik occupation or had been raided by Mandelbaum's Red partisans. They fought with determination and ferocity: to them the Reds were wild beasts to be killed. But their loyalty was to their native villages, not to any general anti-Bolshevik cause. The locally mobilized and the ex-Red Army men were politically passive. It was bad food and hard treatment that had brought the latter over, not any ideological motive. On various occasions, when well led, they fought well against their former comrades. But they had learned by experience that the ultimate way of getting out of a really nasty situation was to shoot one's officers and cross over to the other side.

Mutinies could usually be traced to the existence of a small Bolshevik or pro-Bolshevik cell in the unit concerned, whose members had been able to exploit their fellow-soldiers' grievances—war-weariness, desire to go home, misdeeds of individual officers. The task of the cells was made easier by the mounting tide of Bolshevik successes. It was said of the Northern Army as a whole that the men fought well when there was news of White victories on the other fronts, but if the Whites were being beaten they fought badly. While individual officers were hated there seems to have been little bitterness on the part of the men towards the officer class as a whole. When the Northern Army finally disintegrated there were very few instances of officers being killed. The men left them their arms and told them it was time for them, too, to go home.

(xi)

At the end of the year Kolchak, Denikin and Yudenich had all been decisively defeated; and it was apparent that within a few weeks the Northern territory would stand alone. The value of the Bolshevik rouble rose sharply on the Archangel Black Bourse. Bolshevist propaganda on the futility of continuing the struggle became more effective. Wishful thinking played its part. It was said that the Bolsheviks had mellowed. It was true they had committed crimes, but 'that was all in the past . . . Now they have become more level-headed . . . They are not wild animals . . . they understand that real success is not obtained by blood.' And the widely publicized 'reconciliation' with Moscow of such well-known S.R.s as Volsky gave the impression, at least in the North, of a coming partnership between the Bolsheviks and other socialists.

In the *Stavka* work was proceeding on plans for a large-scale offensive designed to acquire new territory in which fresh man-power could be mobilized. But this planning seemed less and less realistic. Some of the newly arrived generals thought out schemes under which they were to be supplied with foreign currency and dispatched on various missions to the Western capitals. Miller himself once more attempted to secure more active popular support for the government. There were long negotiations with Left Centre groups. A Regional Assembly was convened, but after a wordy session the majority declared itself against participation in the cabinet, as this would imply acceptance of responsibility for the cabinet's past mistakes. In the end a new government was formed out of all the defensist groups, under the ominous title of 'Government of Salvation'.

It was slowly borne in upon the higher command that the one solution might be the transfer of the whole of the army and the administration to Murmansk. Archangel, of course, was frozen up and there were not enough ice-breakers for any appreciable movement by sea. The staff accordingly were set to work to plan the formidable task of overland evacuation via Onega. (When news of the plans leaked out partisan delegations came to plead with Miller against any withdrawal, as that would mean the extermination of their families.) A special emissary was sent over to Murmansk to make arrangements at that end. He seems to have done little beyond quarrelling with the local command and the local Deputy Governor. (It was later unkindly said that his one achievement was to arrange for his own evacuation.) In any case the area had its special difficulties. Feeling now was anti-Government, partly due to the fact that Murmansk had been used as a dumping-ground for political undesirables from Archangel. Dock and railway workers were openly pro-Bolshevik. Karelian partisans were attacking the railway. Above all, it was now apparent that Marushevsky had been right: there was little prospect of viability or stability without active Finnish co-operation. Belatedly a delegation was sent off to Helsinki.

On the night of the 3rd/4th February, 1920, the Bolsheviks attacked on the Dvina front. Three days later there was a mutiny in the 3rd Northern Rifle Regiment, who held a key position there. Thereafter no clear picture of the military position on any sector appears to have reached Archangel, though there was a steady trickle of officers and men making their own way back from the fronts. Messages were exchanged between Miller and Kuzmin (commanding the Red Army) on the possibility of an armistice. Miller informed his government that these exchanges were taking place but did not reveal the texts. In any case both sides were merely playing for time or tactical advantage.

Archangel itself was calm, or rather, apathetic. A number of middle-class residents were buying up gold, valuables and Bolshevik currency and leaving with their families for the neighbouring villages: they intended to come back when the Bolsheviks had taken over and conditions had (as they imagined) reverted to the pattern of 1917.

On February 14th the government debated a proposal by Miller to transfer to Copenhagen and London in the name of Chaikovsky the balance of the local Treasury's foreign currency, amounting to £120,000. No orders for evacuation had yet been given, though numbers of officers and officials were already endeavouring to make their own way to Murmansk. By the 17th, however, it was obvious even to Miller that evacuation was inevitable, and the government had to decide to what authority they should hand over. The municipal council and other local bodies refused to act: it was eventually decided to hand over to the trade unions, and in the small hours of the 18th, details were worked out and agreed with trade union representatives. Later that morning the government held what was to be its last meeting, entirely taken up by discussion of evacuation arrangements. At noon Miller still believed that immediate withdrawal was unnecessary: he was proposing to visit the front. During the afternoon and evening messages came in which showed there was no longer any front; the Red Army might be expected in Archangel in a matter of hours. Evacuation was formally ordered at 3 a.m. on February 19th.

(xii)

The story of the Northern Provisional Government came to its grim and muddled end in the darkness and bitter cold of the extreme northern winter. On February 19th the nearest Red troops were eighty miles from Archangel, and did not, in fact, enter the city till the 22nd. But in spite of the absence of enemy interference the planned evacuation scheme did not even start to function. Sleighs earmarked for the transport overland of military and civilian establishments did not materialize. For some reason unknown only one ice-breaker, the *Minin*, was in harbour, and on the quay a crowd of would-be refugees was struggling to force their way on board. The town was now under the nominal control of the trade union committee. The prisons had been opened and there was some looting. The *Minin* eventually carried 1,100 persons (including Miller and his staff) instead of her normal complement of 120. She tried to coal at Ekonomiya, some miles down the river, but the local commandant was hopelessly drunk and the port in the hands of hostile dock workers. Two other ice-breakers in the harbour were flying the Red flag. On the 21st the *Minin* passed three ice-bound vessels and took in coal from them. One of the ice-breakers from Ekonomiya came out in pursuit, and shots were exchanged. On the 22nd the wind changed and the *Minin* reached open water. The original intention had been to make for Murmansk, but intercepted wireless messages showed that Murmansk had fallen. The *Minin* rounded the cape and came into Norwegian waters on February 25th.

It is typical of the confusion in the *Stavka* that no notification of the evacuation order was sent to Murmansk. The first that General Skobelev, in command at Murmansk, ever heard of it was a message that Miller had already left. The Murmansk front disintegrated overnight. Skobelev collected the 1,500 men that were left of his army and took them across the frontier into Finland. A Revolutionary Committee assumed charge of the town.

Of the troops directly under Archangel, those on the left or Dvina sector started their westward move too late. They reached the railway only to find the troops of the right or railway sector had already left. Much thinned by desertions, the column turned north towards Archangel, and capitulated as soon as the Reds caught up with them. The troops of the railway sector made their way as ordered to Onega and crushed a Red revolt that had broken out there. It was at Onega, according to the evacuation scheme, that they should have been joined by the headquarters staff. It was only now they learned that the headquarters staff and the Commander-in-Chief were on board the *Minin*. The column, 1,500 strong, went on to Soroka on the Murmansk railway, where they found the Red Army established in force. After a council of war they decided to capitulate. Eleven of them, who did not wish to surrender, managed to elude the Reds and reach the Finnish frontier.

In due course the Red Army occupied Archangel and Murmansk, and the *Cheka* set about its task of cleaning up.

———————

The main sources for Chapter IV are:

Chaplin, G. E., in *Beloe Delo*, Vol. IV (Berlin, 1928).
Dobrovolsky, S., in *Arkhiv Russkoi Revolyutsii*, Vol. III.
Ironside (Lord), *Archangel* (London, 1953).
Kedrov, M. S., *Za Sovietski Sever* (Leningrad, 1927).
Kuzmin, in *Grazhdanskaya Voina 1919–1921 gg.* (Moscow, 1928–1930).
Marushevsky, V. V., in *Beloe Delo*, Vols. I, II and III.
Maynard, Sir C., *The Murmansk Venture* (London, 1928).
Melgunov, S. P., *N. V. Chaikovsky v Gody Grazhdanskoi Voiny* (Paris, 1929).
Metelev, in *Proletarskaya Revolyutsiya*, Vol. 2 (29) (Moscow, 1926).
Sokolov, B., in *Arkhiv Russkoi Revolyutsii*, Vol. IX.

Other works consulted include:

Bruce-Lockhart, R., *Memoirs of a British Agent* (London, 1932).
Churchill, Winston S., *The Aftermath* (London, 1929).
The Evacuation of North Russia (Command paper 818, London, 1920).
Francis, D. R., *Russia from the American Embassy* (New York, 1922).
Gorodetsky, S., in *Beloe Delo*, Vol. III.
Kedrov, M. S., *Bez Bolshevistskovo Rukovodstvo* (Leningrad, 1930).
Lloyd-George, D., *My War Diaries*, Vol. II (London, 1936).
Noulens, J., *Mon Ambassade en Russie Soviétique* (Paris, 1933).

CHAPTER V

Kolchak: The Last Phase

(i)

Aleksandr Vasilevich Kolchak was born in Petersburg in 1873, his father being a regular officer who had served in the Crimean War. The Kolchaks had no private means and the family tradition was of service in the armed forces. Aleksandr Vasilevich passed out of the Naval Academy in 1894. At sea he specialized in oceanography and hydrology, and distinguished himself sufficiently to be invited by the explorer Baron Toll to take part in an expedition to Arctic waters. He spent some months in intensive scientific study, and the expedition left for Taimyr and the New Siberia Islands in 1900. In 1902 Toll with three companions set off in search of a rumoured continent, ordering the main party home via the mouth of the Lena. When, the following year, there was still no news of Toll, Kolchak proposed to organize and lead a rescue party to Bennett Island. The scheme was opposed as too foolhardy, but Kolchak got his way, and after a journey of extreme danger and privation he located what must have been Toll's most northerly camp. Toll himself and his three companions were never found.

Kolchak arrived back in Yakutsk on the eve of the Russo-Japanese War. The expedition had undermined his health, but his persistence secured his posting to Port Arthur, where in spite of wounds and continuous illness he served with conspicuous gallantry until the fortress fell. On his return to Russia in 1905 a medical board found him unfit for service, and he spent the next few months putting in order the scientific results of his Arctic expeditions. He was awarded the Constantine Gold Medal, the highest scientific distinction in Imperial Russia. In 1906 he was sufficiently recovered to be appointed to the new Naval General Staff, and from then on (except for a short secondment to the Behring Straits) he was one of the small party of officers planning and attempting to implement the reorganization of the Russian Navy in the light of the lessons of the Japanese war. In World War I he served in the Baltic, took part in more than his share of fighting and throughout showed marked courage and professional competence. In July, 1916, to his surprise (for he was a man of great modesty), he was promoted Rear Admiral to command the Black Sea Fleet. Here he had to plan a projected operation against the Bosphorus and to safeguard the Russian coast and Russian shipping against raids from the fast cruisers *Goeben* and *Breslau*: on one such raid Kolchak in his flagship sighted the *Breslau* and opened fire at extreme range. There was uninterrupted work on the laying of minefields close up to the Turkish coast. Kolchak's resource in this branch of warfare won the admiration of a visiting American Naval Mission.

The February revolution came to Kolchak as a surprise rather than an overwhelming shock. He had been, inevitably, a monarchist. But the abdication of the Emperor and that of the Grand Duke Michael relieved him of his oath. As he was later to testify, 'After the overturn I assumed the standpoint on which I always stood, namely that I was after all serving not one form of government or another but my country, which to me was above all else.' He was one of the first senior officers to take the oath to the Provisional Government, which he hoped would provide a more effective leadership than its predecessor.

Kolchak was in some ways an embodiment of the simple faith of the old-fashioned officer. He believed that a crisis could be overcome by loyalty, decency, meticulous devotion to duty and good sense. During March, 1917, he visited the ships under

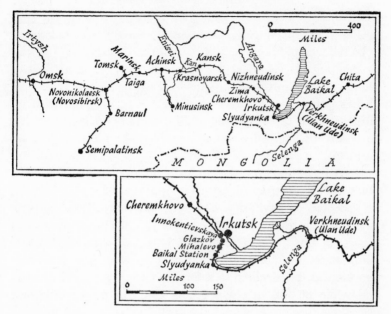

his command and made speeches to the ships' companies. He
co-operated with the Soviet of Sailors' Deputies. He considered
that 'at such a moment as we were then passing through we
needed institutions through which I could communicate with
the crews'. For the first few weeks things seemed to go well.
Then there came mass demands for leave, and increasing
trouble between officers and ratings; but even so the state of the
Black Sea Fleet was so much better than that in the Baltic that
in April (when Kolchak was called to Petrograd for discussions)
Guchkov, Minister of War, seriously considered offering him
the Baltic command. While in the capital Kolchak met a
number of politicians of various shades, and on his way south
again attended a conference of army commanders in Pskov.
He returned to Sevastopol profoundly depressed.

The position in his command deteriorated. In mid-May, for
the first time, a ship's company refused to obey orders to put to
sea. The original Seamen's Soviet, with which Kolchak had
successfully co-operated, lost influence, and a newly elected
Soviet was far more radical. Disaffection spread to the dock-

213

workers, and work on repairs and refitting came to an end. Feeling, perhaps, that the fault was in himself, Kolchak asked to be relieved of his command, but Kerensky urged him to stay on pending his (Kerensky's) visit. Kerensky, with his 'extraordinary belief in the omnipotence of words', came and went. Things got worse. Matters came to a head in June with an ultimatum for the disarming of all officers. At a mass meeting on board his flagship Kolchak described the ultimatum as an insult to himself, drew his sword and threw it overboard. This time the government agreed to his handing over his command. Once back in Petrograd, with the approval of the authorities, he accepted an invitation from the American Naval Mission to visit the States. He left at the end of July, spending a fortnight *en route* in London, where he met Lord Jellicoe and Admiral Hall, Director of Naval Intelligence. He was in America about two months. He decided to return to Russia via Vladivostock, and while he was at sea a report came in of the Bolshevik *coup d'état*.

He disembarked at Yokohama and tried to find out what was happening in Russia. In due course came news of the Russo-German armistice and peace negotiations. This he referred to afterwards as 'the heaviest blow—perhaps even worse than the one I received in the Black Sea Fleet'. After some heart-searching he felt his only course was 'to carry on the war, as the representative of the former Russian Government which had undertaken certain obligations to the Allies'. He called on the British Ambassador in Tokyo and asked to be accepted in the British Army 'on any conditions whatsoever'. The choice of ally is of interest in view of the persistent rumours of some special relationship between him and the British.

In due course the War Office accepted his offer and posted him to Mesopotamia. He left Japan via Shanghai and had got as far as Singapore where he was told that following a request from the Russian Ambassador in Peking the British authorities felt he would be of greater use to the Allied cause in the Far East. So he travelled north again, arriving in Peking in April at about the time of the creation of the Far Eastern Committee for the Defence of the Fatherland and the Constituent Assembly under General Horvath, General Manager of the Chinese Eastern Railway.

Kolchak was asked to co-ordinate the various anti-Bolshevik forces in the Chinese Eastern Railway area. It was an un-welcome assignment. He found himself with no means of enforcing his authority and without (he felt) adequate backing from Horvath. Semenov, leader of the largest of the little private armies, consistently snubbed him; and, it transpired, was doing so with the support of the Japanese. In July Kolchak left Harbin for Tokyo to see the Japanese General Staff. The Japanese were polite but entirely unhelpful. Once again he was conscious of failure.

He decided to make his way to South Russia and serve in the Volunteer Army under Alekseev; but the journey from the Far East to the Don was no easy matter. While waiting in Vladivostock he saw a good deal of General Knox, head of the British Military Mission. In September he went on to Omsk, and here he learned that both Alekseev and Kornilov were dead. Pressure was put on him to stay in Siberia and become Minister of War in the new All-Russian cabinet. At first he refused. He did not like what he had seen of Omsk, and he doubted whether he would be given powers to enforce the measures he felt were necessary. However, he let himself be persuaded. Almost at once he left for an extended tour of the front, returning to Omsk on November 16th. On the evening of the 17th some Cossack officers staged a *coup* and arrested the Socialist members of the Directorate. On the 18th, Kolchak acceded to a unanimous invitation of the Council of Ministers to accept the post of Supreme Ruler and Supreme Commander-in-Chief.

There is a great deal about the *coup d'état* at Omsk that we do not know and probably never shall. There is no hard evidence to disprove Kolchak's claim that the plot was con-ceived and carried out without his knowledge, or to sub-stantiate the rumours of British connivance. It is reasonably certain that it was his sense of duty rather than personal ambition that prompted his decision to accept. But all the same it was by his free and deliberate choice that he assumed a position which, for all his qualities, he was quite unfitted to hold. Apart from a few short-lived military successes Kolchak's twelve months as Supreme Ruler was a period of continued defeat at the front and of frustration and mismanagement at home. There were unending and inconclusive arguments with the Allied representatives, unceasing scandals in the Army and the administration. At no time did the Omsk régime under Kolchak succeed in establishing an effective hold over the far-flung empire it was supposed to govern.

Kolchak himself was not equipped to be a popular leader. There was little of the actor in him. His charm showed itself only in very small gatherings. In public he was brusque and awkward. He had no knack of kindling enthusiasm either in civilian assemblies or with troops on parade. He had little tinerest in or understanding of political problems. This would have mattered less had he possessed the flair for choosing the right men for the right posts; but his appointments, civilian as well as military, were arbitrary and capricious. They were frequently changed, as indeed were his decisions. The strain of the continued reverses told upon his nerves and he became moody, sometimes almost hysterical, smashing little objects on the table in front of him. At the same time he lacked the ruthlessness that his role demanded. That perhaps was his decisive failing. He was well aware of the rottenness all round him. But, as he was to tell his interrogators, 'I could never manage to get any results from my judiciary and investigating commissions.' Such an admission from a top Bolshevik would be unthinkable.

The same trait ran through the Omsk administration. Ruthlessness there was, very often, against civilians, peasants and prisoners. But in the case of the big offender or big problem little or nothing was done. The graft and incompetence at Omsk made it easy to forget that the makeshift cabinet offices and the swollen and top-heavy General Staff contained men of probity, intelligence and ant-like industry; but without the aggressiveness or the backing to get their way. And as the situation both of front and rear deteriorated, the cabinet, the ministries and the staff offices went more and more the way of all such bodies on the losing side of a war, with ever more meetings, drafts, reorganizations and recriminations and less and less grip upon the course of events. There had never been much contact between the Kolchak Government and the masses; by mid-October, 1919, when the loss of Omsk was seen to be inevitable, there was little contact even with government organs outside the capital. Those few who still dreamed of victory saw it only in terms of large-scale Japanese or German intervention.

By this time the First (Siberian) Army, under General Anatol Pepelyaev, had lost the will to fight and was in process of withdrawal for regroupment round Tomsk. The Second and Third Armies, under strength and ill-equipped, were endeavouring to delay the main Red advance. The semi-independent Cossack armies under Dutov, Annenkov and the like were no longer of much military importance. Semenov, now reconciled with Kolchak, was still a factor in his Japanese-backed private empire in Trans-Baikalia. But that was two thousand miles away from Omsk.

Of the foreign contingents, the two British battalions had left. The Japanese and the Americans were the other side of Lake Baikal. In Siberia proper by far the most important Allied force was that of the Czechs, who, with small detachments of Poles, Italians, Roumanians, Serbs and Balts, were under the command of the French General Janin, and were guarding the railway line between Taiga (the junction for Tomsk) and Irkutsk. The Czechoslovak unwillingness to go on fighting, which made necessary their withdrawal from the front, had provoked Kolchak's disgust at the time he was Minister of War; and his outspoken comments caused bitter resentment among the Czechs, who in any case disapproved of the *coup d'état* that brought him to power. There had also been friction with Janin; and this bad feeling between Kolchak on one side and the Czechs and their overall commander on the other was to have its effect on subsequent events. The Czechs, moreover, had no desire to remain in Siberia at all; the war was over, their country was independent and they wanted to go home. But as the Allies had decided they should stay the Czechs, as practical men, took full advantage of the practical opportunities offered them. Their auxiliary and technical services were perfected and they went into business in a big way, starting up factories and opening banks. With the vast distances involved the key to commercial success was transport: the Czechs acquired a dominating position on their twelve-hundred-mile stretch of the Trans-Siberian Railway and the relevant international commission set up in Vladivostock favoured them in the allocation of rolling-stock. Throughout Siberia and the Far East a good many Russians were combining public service with private profit, and it would be unjust to expect the Czechs to do otherwise. But they were better businessmen than the Russians and had more opportunity. The contrast between the Czech haves and the Russian have-nots became more and more marked. In any case most Russians were getting tired of Czechs just as the Czechs were getting tired of Russians, and the mutual antipathy grew.

The Czech National Council was at this time in Irkutsk. For the Council the political atmosphere there was more congenial. The Governor, who had held his office since pre-Kolchak days, was a Right-wing Socialist Revolutionary. The municipal council had an S.R.–Menshevik majority. For the last few months a number of socialist oppositionists (including, incidentally, Maisky) had been making their way to Irkutsk. In November, 1919, there met an All Siberian Congress of *Zemstvos* and Municipal Councils, which, in spite of the Omsk election laws, preserved a Socialist flavour. Out of this Congress a clandestine Political Centre was formed, predominantly S.R. and Menshevik, which aspired in due course to take over the government. The existence of the Political Centre was not a well-kept secret, but in view of the connivance of the Governor and the presence of Czech armed forces the local Kolchak military command was chary of quashing it.

One of Omsk's few successes had been the drastic suppression, in the spring of 1919, of the Communist Party's organization throughout Siberia. 'The Kolchak Government succeeded not only in stifling the Bolshevik underground organization but also in laying its claws on its most courageous and resolute leaders.' It was not till November that the Communists could once more set up a clandestine Siberian headquarters, again, naturally, in Irkutsk. So weak did the Party in Siberia appear that its local chairman, Krasnoshchekov, regarded a government of bourgeois moderates as the only feasible successor to Kolchak.

In the country areas were the partisans. Soviet historians estimate that by the late autumn of 1919 partisans in the Altai, Tomsk, Enisei and Irkutsk provinces numbered some 80,000 men. But even if this figure is correct the overwhelming majority of the men were very recent recruits. A number of unco-ordinated peasant partisan groups were active on either side of the railway. Their origins all follow a familiar pattern—orders from Omsk for the mobilization of men and the requisitioning of horses; peasant evasion and obstruction; the dispatch of a punitive enforcement squad. When arms were available and the local leaders resolute the peasants would take to the woods and fight back. Early successes against inadequate and ill-led White detachments brought an influx of recruits and great local prestige for the partisan leaders. It was not till June, 1919, that the government took serious steps to crush the movement. Large Russian and Czech forces were deployed (the Czechs, with their property to defend, were especially drastic); the partisan groups were decisively beaten and their leaders, with such few men as had not deserted them, driven far into the *taiga*. But with the Red victories of the summer and autumn the tide turned again. Omsk units were recalled, or lost the will to continue. The partisans rallied. Every rumour, true or false, of the Red advance brought in hundreds of peasant volunteers; and by early November, whole armies of them, numbering many thousands, were moving in on the main centres of Eastern Siberia.[1]

[1] An account of the various Siberian partisan groups is contained in the author's contribution to *St. Antony's Papers No. 1* (London, 1956).

Meanwhile, outside the partisan areas, the bulk of Siberian peasants retained their stubborn disinterest in matters political. As late as July, 1919, a member of the Omsk cabinet was disconcerted to find, within a few hours' drive of the city, a prosperous peasant who had barely heard of Admiral Kolchak and believed he was an Englishman.

Such were the human factors at this period. On all, the evacuation of Omsk—a public admission of catastrophic defeat —had its inevitable psychological effect. But we must also remember the physical factors. The final chapter of the story of the Kolchak régime took place in the depth of a Siberian winter. There were serious local shortages of food, fuel and clothing. Typhus was rampant, and frostbite was taking almost as great a toll as typhus. The setting was along fifteen hundred miles of the Trans-Siberian Railway, the *magistral*, with the main road, the *trakt*—a ridged and undulating ribbon of frozen snow—running parallel to it. All along the railway fuel was short; the pumps froze and the points and signals froze. If a locomotive was left unattended it froze up and the pipes and boiler burst. British officers who took part in the evacuation have left vivid details of the struggles round the pumping stations and the rows of stiff, naked corpses lining the track where they had been thrown out of hospital trains because their place and their clothing was needed by others. There was a huge floating population of foreigners, refugees, and wives and families of officers, who lived in railway cars on sidings for lack of housing. When the end came everyone pressed madly to go east and the railway could not carry them. Janin estimates that of the three hundred evacuation trains that left Western Siberia at this time only seventy got as far as Irkutsk. He excludes Czech trains from both these figures.

(ii)

Argument and uncertainty over the evacuation of Omsk continued to the last minute. Kolchak and some of his entourage were anxious to stand and fight. On November 4th, General Dieterichs, the Commander-in-Chief, who insisted on withdrawal, was replaced by General Sakharov, who cancelled the evacuation orders of his predecessor. Within forty-eight hours it was obvious that resistance was hopeless, and Kolchak gave the final order to withdraw. Once more the troop movement orders were reversed, and the confusion was accentuated by a freak of the weather. The river Irtysh had not yet frozen solid, and the armies on the west bank were unable to march across.

During the last few days the cabinet of the All Russian Provisional Government were working with a feverish intensity. There was the problem of a new Prime Minister: the mild and ageing Vologodsky was quite useless in the present crisis. There were urgent questions of local government and monetary reform; and there was a mass of legislation already drafted but not yet approved by the Supreme Ruler. Delegations of ministers would push their way into Kolchak's study to persuade him into signing, with an official of the State Printing Press waiting outside in an ante-room ready to rush off the decrees before the press was dismantled. On November 10th hard frost set in at last, and the troops were able to cross the river. That same night the cabinet left. Throughout their nine-day journey to Irkutsk they worked meticulously in the train. There was the problem of the reintegration of the civil servants, now being evacuated, and the more personal one of ministerial emoluments. From Denikin's area was a request for comments on a draft project for a legislative organ; and General Miller was protesting from Archangel at the limitations on his powers of promoting officers and awarding decorations.

Admiral Kolchak, with an imposing convoy of seven trains, whose cargo included the State Gold Reserve, left on the night of the 14th, twenty-four hours before the Red Army entered Omsk. Janin, who had left on the 8th with his Czechoslovak escort, stopped at various points along the line to discuss details of the Czech departure. He reached Novonikolaevsk— four hundred miles from Omsk—on November 18th. Here he found a message from Kolchak asking him to wait for him for consultations. But Janin had a reply sent back that he was unable to wait. At Taiga, the junction for Tomsk, he met Anatol Pepelyaev, Commander of the disaffected First Siberian Army. They found themselves in agreement on the impossibility of Kolchak continuing as Supreme Ruler. There was a large Czech contingent at Taiga, and Janin was disturbed to find them behind their evacuation schedule; freight trains with grain were due to arrive from the South and the Czechs did not want to leave without them. Janin did what he could to speed matters up and continued eastwards, reaching Irkutsk on the 29th.

The Omsk cabinet by then had been there for ten days. They had been made increasingly aware of the precarious position of their government. The atmosphere in Irkutsk was hostile. In Vladivostock there had been a *putsch*, albeit an abortive one (by the now unemployed Gajda) against the local Kolchak authorities. And the Czech National Council, now that the Whites were decisively beaten, had published on the 13th an open letter to the Allies expressing their profound disapproval of Kolchak and his government, their horror at the brutality and incompetence of his régime, and demanding for themselves immediate evacuation to their homeland. The cabinet were well aware of the need to find some broader backing. Urgent telegrams were sent down the line to Kolchak, and his assent was at last obtained to the appointment as Premier of Victor Pepelyaev, Minister of the Interior and brother of the general, in place of the negative Vologodsky.

The new Prime Minister, a Siberian Regionalist, endeavoured to induce local S.R. and Menshevik leaders to come into a coalition government. But they refused to take office under Kolchak, and the cabinet as finally constituted was a makeshift one. Its first act was to declare, on December 2nd, its intention to work in the closest harmony with the people and with the Czechs, to set up a Land Assembly as legislative organ, and to free the civilian administration from any kind of military interference. The Prime Minister then proceeded down the line to join his brother the general and to persuade the Supreme Ruler to agree to this new programme.

Meanwhile Kolchak and his convoy were proceeding slowly eastwards. Sakharov, the C.-in-C., was close behind in his own train, and touch was maintained with the retreating Second and Third Armies under Kappel and Voitsekhovsky. A flow of orders and proclamations were issued from the Supreme Ruler's train. On November 21st he announced the establishment of a Supreme Council (*Verkhovnoye Soveshchaniye*) which, had it ever come into being, would have made the cabinet redundant. By the 25th he had become aware of the Czech National Council's open letter of the 13th, and he confidentially instructed his cabinet to drop all contact with its authors and to press the Allies for their immediate removal. The Czechs were able to tap and decipher this telegram, and the harassed Prime Minister in Irkutsk could only entreat the Admiral to leave such matters to him. It is not clear whether Victor Pepelyaev did or did not then know that at about the same time Kolchak had telegraphed to Semenov in Chita requiring him to be prepared to stop Czech passage through Trans-Baikalia by occupying the Baikal tunnels, and that the Czechs had intercepted this telegram also.

Kolchak's train reached Taiga on December 7th, where the two Pepelyaevs were waiting for him. There was inconclusive argument and both parties dispatched a series of confused and angry telegrams to the cabinet in Irkutsk. In one of them Kolchak wired: 'I am willing to resign but Pepelyaev does not want this.' Sakharov's train arrived on the evening of the 8th, and the argument became more bitter. Sakharov demanded that Anatol Pepelyaev be relieved of his command and his troops put under Voitsekhovsky. Victor Pepelyaev demanded the dismissal of Sakharov. Kolchak, nervy and exhausted, announced he would give his decision next day. Sakharov has described how he woke up next morning to find the Admiral's train gone on and his own surrounded by troops of the First Siberian Army. An officer told him he was under arrest. He demanded to see Pepelyaev and walked across the frozen tracks to the latter's train. The two brothers, heavy, unshaven Siberians, were sitting in a Pullman littered with cigarette ends, remains of food and dirty glasses. They told him they had taken this measure because they considered him a bad influence on Kolchak. In due course Victor Pepelyaev went on to join Kolchak. Sakharov was kept on Taiga station for twenty-four hours when Kappel arrived and released him. Kolchak meanwhile was sending wires from telegraph offices along the line to find a new Commander-in-Chief. His first choice was Dieterichs, but Dieterichs refused. Then he contacted Kappel, and Kappel accepted. But any such real authority as the Supreme Ruler still possessed had evaporated in the incident on Taiga station.

(iii)

On December 10th Kolchak's trains were held up at Marinsk behind a congestion of Czech transport. His Quartermaster-General, General Zankevich, telegraphed to complain to Janin, and Janin referred the matter to General Syrovy, commanding the Czech forces. Syrovy gave orders that the Admiral's trains should be let through. But two days later, on the 12th, there was a far more serious jam at Krasnoyarsk, and Kolchak was immobilized there for six days.

We have already noted the difficulties along the railway. By mid-December things were worse. Typhus, frostbite, panic, the ferocity of the cold, the pressure from the Fifth Red Army and the threat from the partisans were all playing their part. On December 12th, Syrovy, down the line, telegraphed to Janin at Irkutsk that the position was extremely critical: unless the Czech trains were allotted first priority he could not accept responsibility. Janin approved any measures that Syrovy might take, and on December 15th the latter issued an order that no Russian echelon was to be let through to the East except on his, Syrovy's, specific order.

There ensued a scramble for rolling-stock and priorities

which has been the subject of bitter recrimination. The advantages were all on the side of the Czechs. They were in physical occupation of the railway stations and they had their own staff of technicians. In the end they all reached Vladivostock with their wives, their families, their girls and a considerable amount of property. It is true that a number of individual Russians owed their survival to being given a place on a Czech train, though others were refused owing to fears of typhus. It is certain that there were a number of ugly incidents: the circumstances were not such as to make for decency in human behaviour.

A stream of exasperated telegrams came from Kolchak at Krasnoyarsk, keenly conscious of the humiliation of being held up by a foreign authority on a Russian railway. Janin's nerves were also becoming frayed. 'I would be most pleased,' he testily remarked to Lampson—the Allied High Commissioners were then in Irkutsk to arrange for the evacuation of their nationals —'I would be most pleased to do all I am asked, if only not be pestered day and night. But there are the facts of the position on the railways.' He added, 'One must understand the feelings of men who think more of their own safety than of that of someone who has been publicly talking of them as enemies for the last year.'

The facts of the position on the railways affected the Second and Third White Armies, still far to the West. The troops themselves were moving along the *trakt*, but the sick and wounded, wives, families and dependants were packed into trains. These were now as good as lost; and Kappel sent a furious open telegram to Syrovy with a challenge to a duel on account of the insults offered to the Russian Supreme Ruler and the brutalities inflicted on defenceless Russian non-combatants. Syrovy replied accepting the challenge as and when total Czech evacuation had been finally completed.

Syrovy's attitude remained consistent throughout—to allow no consideration and no representation from any quarter to deflect him for one instant from his task of ensuring safe transit and safe departure for all Czechs. He did, however, give instructions on December 18th for Kolchak's trains to be passed through Krasnoyarsk. And on December 23rd he wrote a letter to the Entente representatives, published in the *Ceskoslovensky Dénik*, in which he stressed his responsibility for evacuation and the fact that the collapse of the Russian state machine made it necessary for the Czechs to look after themselves. He included the point—perhaps aimed at the British—that if there was delay in arriving at Vladivostock, 'the Czechoslovak Republic would be threatened with serious financial loss.'

Meanwhile the position of the Kolchak cabinet in Irkutsk was an unhappy one. News from down the line was bad; on December 18th, the day after Kolchak had left, the garrison in Krasnoyarsk revolted and the town was occupied by partisans, thus cutting off the Supreme Ruler from Kappel and his armies. There were also signs that the Great Powers were preparing to cut their losses; on December 10th Lloyd George announced in the House of Commons that the whole question of Russia was under review. All this time the cabinet was without leadership. Prime Minister Pepelyaev was still down the line and unlocatable. The Vice-Premier, Foreign Minister Tretyakov, had left for Chita to consult Semenov, and bets were laid by his colleagues that he would not return from the comfort and security of that city. There were still intermittent exchanges with the Admiral, tapped out in station telegraph offices between Krasnoyarsk and Nizhneudinsk, but these were becoming more and more unrealistic. There was an unsuccessful plea to Kolchak to agree to the inclusion of three Jews on one of the representative bodies provided for in one of the cabinet drafts.

The cabinet had no say in either of the two important announcements of this period. One was an open telegram from Semenov to the Czechs, demanding immediate passage for Kolchak and for all Russian evacuation trains. Failing which, he concluded, 'with sorrow in my heart I will take steps, with the whole of the armed force at my disposal, to compel you to fulfil your duty to humanity and to your martyred sister nation Russia.' The other was from Kolchak himself, appointing

Semenov as Supreme Commander of all armed forces in Eastern Siberia and the Far East. This, dated December 23rd, was the last communication passed freely by Kolchak to the outside world. Thereafter he could send no message except by favour of the Czechs. His train reached Nizhneudinsk on December 24th. The station, of course, was held by the Czechs, but two days previously the Russian garrison had revolted, and the town was in the hands of insurgents. Kolchak was to stay on a siding in Nizhneudinsk station for fourteen days.

(iv)

The appointment of Semenov and his undisguised threat to the Czechs made a profound impression in Irkutsk. The Ataman was, to Left-wing Russians and to Czechs, the arch-symbol of reaction and brutality. His private empire lay across the line to Vladivostock; and by occupation or destruction of the vulnerable chain of railway tunnels around the southern end of Lake Baikal he could effectively block any passage to the East. It is reasonable to assume that the Political Centre, in agreement with the Czechs, timed their revolt so as to be in possession of Irkutsk before Semenov could make his power felt there.

In any case the Political Centre may have felt the tide was in their favour. There had been the revolts at Krasnoyarsk and at Nizhneudinsk, and also a rising, on December 22nd, of the miners at Cheremkhovo, some eighty miles west of Irkutsk. There was evidence that the Great Powers were dropping Kolchak. And a Soviet historian suggests that the Centre wished to be in control of the city before the arrival of undisciplined armies of partisans. How the Political Centre planned to consolidate their power is another matter. They seem to have been confident of coming to terms with the Red Army, with Moscow and with the local Bolsheviks. It is true the latter refused to accept responsibility for the revolt or to participate in the régime that it was to set up. But they promised their goodwill and their assistance. As for the future, both the Socialist Revolutionaries (who were in the majority in the Centre) and the Mensheviks may well have believed that Bolshevik rule would not last long in Moscow. News was seeping through of peasant discontent and economic breakdown. And when the crash came it would be for a Socialist Siberia, with its Socialist local councils and co-operatives and its Socialist hold on education, to act as guide and mentor to the Socialist Russia of tomorrow.

The final decision to launch the revolt was taken on the evening of December 23rd, and a former officer of the First Siberian Army was appointed to command the Political Centre's armed detachments. On the same day the Kolchak Security Service, aware of the imminence of trouble, arrested seventeen leading Mensheviks and Socialist Revolutionaries. The Political Centre made a request, via the Czechs, for their release. General Sychev, commanding the garrison, replied that they could only be released against guarantees that the Political Centre would undertake no action against the government. This communication remained unanswered.

It should be noted here that Irkutsk lies on the east, or north-east, bank of the river Angara. The railway station is across the river in the suburb of Glazkov where, at this time, were Janin's headquarters, the Czechoslovak Legion's headquarters and, of course, the Allied High Commissioners in their trains. Irkutsk and Glazkov were connected in summer by a bridge of boats and in winter by a road across the ice. This year the Angara, like the Irtysh, froze late. On December 21st floating ice-floes had destroyed the bridge of boats, and it took some days before the ice on the river could take traffic. Shipping and barges were mostly on the Glazkov side and under Czech control.

On December 24th the 53rd Regiment in barracks at Glazkov declared for the Political Centre. The insurgents thus acquired Glazkov without fighting, and also the suburbs along the railway as far as Innokentievskaya. In Irkutsk the garrison, for the time being, remained loyal, and Sychev appealed to Semenov in Chita for help.

December 25th passed off quietly. The Angara formed an effective barrier between the bulk of the two opposing forces. The cabinet, now completely isolated, sat in their quarters in the Hotel Moderne in Irkutsk. The Allied High Commissioners ate their Christmas dinners in their trains; they had collected their nationals and were preparing to leave for Vladivostock. On the evening of the 25th Sychev gave notice to all concerned that he proposed to bombard the barracks of the 53rd Regiment. Janin's reaction was to forbid any firing at targets within a kilometre of Glazkov station. The bombardment did not take place. The reason given for Janin's order (with which the High Commissioners concurred) was that damage to the railway would indefinitely hold up evacuation. But at the same time it meant that the Kolchak authorities had now no hope of crushing the revolt. The cabinet protested, but on the 26th, realizing that they had no alternative, they appointed (in the absence of the Prime Minister and Vice-Premier) a Triumvirate of three of their members to negotiate with the Political Centre for the handing over of Irkutsk. The first condition was safe transit to the East for Kolchak himself and all members of his forces and administration. This was agreed. But no agreement could be reached on the second and third conditions, namely, that the State Gold Reserve be evacuated with Kolchak and that the Political Centre should undertake to resist the Bolsheviks. The talks came to an *impasse*. At the same time parallel negotiations were started between cabinet representatives and the High Commissioners with a view to the neutralization of the railway zone. Sporadic fighting continued between the garrison holding the town centre and parties of insurgents based on the suburbs. The Security Service made further arrests of oppositionists. On December 28th fuel gave out and the electric lighting ceased to function. Cabinet members huddled in their furs in the crowded dirty corridors of the Hotel Moderne. The Angara froze hard. On the 29th the insurgents brought reinforcements across the river, and fighting flared up round the northern fringes of the town.

On the 30th came news that a Semenov force with three

armoured trains under General Skipetrov had reached Mihalevo, twenty miles to the south-east. Behind them was a
detachment of Japanese. On the 31st Skipetrov advanced on
Glazkov. For a time there was near panic in the insurgent
ranks; it was only the arrival of partisan reinforcements that
prevented a disorderly retreat. Janin issued a further order
forbidding Sychev to use his artillery against insurgent positions.
A little group of partisan volunteers blew up a locomotive in the
path of one of the advancing armoured trains. And then the
half-hearted attack was called off. Skipetrov went back to
Mihalevo, and sent up one of his colonels to confer with the
High Commissioners.

It is a curious incident on which Semenov's memoirs throw
very little light. It is true that events were to reveal the poor
quality of Semenov's detachments, but at least they were better
organized and better armed than the Political Centre's motley
forces. The smallest show of resolution could have decided the
issue. It is reasonable to suppose that Semenov's Japanese
backers advised against a showdown. In any case, the Japanese
force accompanying Skipetrov remained entirely passive, both
at the time and later when, once the line was cleared, they came
on into Glazkov station.

The fiasco of the relief expedition was a further blow to the
prestige of the Kolchak cabinet and to the shaky morale of the
garrison units that still remained loyal. General Ogloblin,
commanding the Irkutsk Cossacks, addressed an ultimatum to
the Triumvirate, demanding to be told once and for all who
was coming to help them and what that help was going to
consist of; failing a satisfactory answer he proposed 'to act in the
light of his conscience and of Cossack interests'. The unfortunate
cabinet had no choice but to seek the High Commissioners'
help in new negotiations with the Political Centre. The issue
was to some extent simplified by the obvious fact that the
Kolchak régime was finished.

The High Commissioners were now also faced with the
problem of Kolchak himself. On December 31st the Czech
Commandant at Nizhneudinsk telegraphed to Syrovy and

Janin asking urgently for instructions; partisans, he reported, and bands of the local revolutionaries in control of the town had surrounded the station and were clamouring for the Admiral to be handed over. The High Commissioners, of course, had no force at their own disposal; in this respect they were dependent on Janin as C.-in-C. of the Allied troops, which for all practical purposes meant the Czechs. Janin was therefore brought into the discussion and, he tells us, emphasized that the principle of Czech neutrality in Russian affairs '*m'interdisait de promettre pour l'amiral l'emploi de la force, surtout s'il ne voulait pas se demettre*'. The final decision took the form of a directive to the C.-in-C. Allied troops in Siberia, dated January 1st and signed by the Japanese, American, British, French and Czechoslovak High Commissioners.

The directive laid down that 'all measures should be taken to assure the personal safety of Admiral Kolchak within the limits of the possible. If Admiral Kolchak should find himself obliged to appeal for the protection of the Allied forces there is no doubt that these forces should take Admiral Kolchak under their protection and take all measures necessary to assure his transfer to whatever destination the Allied Governments may decide. . . . If Admiral Kolchak should not feel that circumstances necessitate his invoking the protection of the Allied Forces, a situation might well arise where it would be difficult for the Allied forces to decide on their line of action. The matter would then become one of Russian internal politics, and it would be impossible to insist on the Allied forces taking military action. However, even in this event, these forces should take all possible steps to assure Admiral Kolchak's personal safety by means of conciliation.' A further note, also dated January 1st, laid down that the Allied forces should, for the time being, take over custody of the State Gold Reserve.

On January 4th Kolchak in his train at Nizhneudinsk gave formal notification of his decision to resign and to hand over his powers and command to General Denikin; and he requested the Allied authorities to make arrangements for the forwarding of his train and its personnel.

Meanwhile, in the renewed negotiations between the Cabinet and the Political Centre, the High Commissioners had made clear that they were in no position to act as arbiters; they were merely intermediaries. They could, of course, give advice, and did suggest to the cabinet that they hand over power to the Political Centre at once, apparently adding that Socialist Revolutionaries had nothing in common with the Bolsheviks, so that the Allies had no reason to oppose them. On January 2nd a temporary armistice was arranged between insurgents and garrison. On the 3rd the talks began. The parties were unwilling to meet round a table, so it was arranged that the Political Centre representatives should sit in the British High Commissioners' train and the cabinet delegates in Janin's, messages being passed from train to train. For both sides in that drab and frozen city these sessions were perhaps the only chance they had of keeping warm. The negotiations trailed on. There was no demand from the Political Centre for the handing over of Kolchak. The armistice was prolonged for another twenty-four hours. More partisan bands came in from the country. More soldiers of garrison units deserted. On the Glazkov siding the session of the evening of the 4th proceeded in an increasing atmosphere of unreality. There were sounds of firing from across the river. At midnight came news that General Sychev, after an abortive attempt to remove the contents of the State Bank, had left Irkutsk for the East. Even the shadow of the Kolchak régime had ceased to exist.

There was no handing over of power in Irkutsk. The Political Centre had merely to assume it. On the morning of the 5th, the Centre issued the first of its numerous manifestos. The Kolchak régime was overthrown. All freedoms were restored. There would be peace with the Bolsheviks and friendship with the Allies and the Czechs. A Siberian Council was to be summoned for the following week to hold power until the establishment of a Siberian Constituent Assembly.

The High Commissioners exchanged politenesses with the new masters of Irkutsk and prepared once more to leave. There was a further telegram about Kolchak from the Czech

Commandant at Nizhneudinsk, to which a reply was sent confirming the previous arrangement. There was an inquiry from the Political Centre about the hostages arrested by the Whites: it was reported that Sychev or Skipetrov had removed them. The High Commissioners could only refer the matter to Janin who referred it to Semenov who replied that he was not Janin's subordinate. There were further delays. There was the usual shortage of locomotives. And there was trouble on January 7th and 8th when some of Semenov's units tried to occupy points along the railway. But getting no support from the Japanese, the *Semenovtsi* were quickly ejected by Czech troops in the Baikal area and by the Americans further east. The High Commissioners were finally able to depart on January 9th.

(v)

Kolchak's arrival at Nizhneudinsk coincided with the beginning of the Irkutsk rising on December 24th, and for the next fortnight we have the account of General Zankevich. The local Czech Commandant, Major Gassek, reported that he had orders from Irkutsk that the Supreme Ruler and the Gold Reserve should remain at Nizhneudinsk pending further instructions. Kolchak attempted to contact Janin on the direct line from the station telegraph office, but was told that Janin was unavailable. Gassek then suggested that Kolchak's Russian escort should be disarmed, but when Zankevich flatly refused the suggestion was not pressed. On either January 1st or 2nd Gassek informed the Party that he had orders from Janin to the effect that the trains were under Allied supervision, and that when it was possible for them to proceed on to Irkutsk they would travel under the flags of the Allied nations. For the time being the Russian escort need not be disarmed, but the Czechs had orders to enforce a strict neutrality, and should any fighting break out between the escort and revolutionary bands the Czechs would disarm both parties.

233

On January 4th, as we have seen, Kolchak announced his decision to resign; though, as an afterthought, he issued a further order on the 5th appointing Semenov C.-in-C. of all forces in all Siberia and the Far East until such time as Denikin could take over. Following the promise of Allied protection he released his escort from their obligations and most of the rank and file left the train. Doubts persisted among some of the officers. On one occasion Zankevich urged Kolchak to do as a number of Russian officers were doing—remove his insignia and ask for a place on one of the eastward-bound Czech echelons. But Kolchak did not wish to be under an obligation to the Czechs. A more seriously considered project was to leave the train and trek southwards across the two hundred and fifty miles of frozen steppe into Mongolia. Gassek was sounded and raised no objections; his staff produced such information as they had on the location of partisan bands along the route. At a meeting to discuss the scheme there was some hesitation and a senior officer pointed out that the Admiral had a promise of Allied protection: they, the others, had not. He could in all confidence go on to Irkutsk; they could more safely make the trek without him. Kolchak asked: 'Are you deserting me?' The officer answered: 'No, we will go with you if you wish.' It was decided that all should proceed to Irkutsk.

On the 5th or 6th Gassek reported the receipt of new orders; if the Admiral wished to proceed he must travel in one railway coach and limit his entourage to such as this one car could hold. A second-class passenger car was produced and arranged for the journey. Kolchak occupied one *coupé*, together with Madame Timireva, his intimate companion for the past twelve months, who had refused to leave Omsk before him. Some sixty officers were accommodated in the other *coupés*. A second coach carried Prime Minister Pepelyaev and his suite. American, French, British, Japanese and Czech flags were affixed. The train, with its Czech guard, left Nizhneudinsk station on January 7th.

The last stage of their journey, the three hundred miles from Nizhneudinsk to Glazkov, took them eight days. At a number of stops there were hostile demonstrations and demands for their surrender. But it does not seem that the passengers were unduly apprehensive. There was the encouraging news of Japanese troops at Irkutsk; and now that they had faced, and digested, the bitterness of defeat their minds were set on the future. They wondered if their destination was to be Harbin or Vladivostock. Then there was the money problem: with all the graft and speculation that had been going on around him, the ex-Supreme Ruler's private fortune amounted to 30,000 depreciated Omsk roubles.

At Innokentievskaya, just outside Irkutsk, there was a long wait. Zankevich wished to go on and interview Janin, but the guard stopped him. He sent a note, which was returned with a message that Janin had left for Baikal station, thirty-five miles to the south-east. He tried to get information from the train commandant; the latter could only say that discussions were going on between Syrovy and Janin. He (the Czech) believed Vladivostock was the destination, but his own responsibility went only as far as Irkutsk. Zankevich made an attempt to contact Janin on the direct line, but was told he had already left Baikal station.

It was late at night when the train moved on again. Glazkov station was almost deserted except for a passive group of Japanese. The train commandant hurried off to report to Syrovy. A further wait, and he returned to say his instructions were to hand over the Admiral to the local authorities. Kolchak asked: 'In other words, the Allies are betraying me?' Representatives of the Political Centre arrived with an escort and took over the prisoners against a signed receipt. They were marched across the frozen Angara to the far bank, where a car was waiting to take Kolchak and Pepelyaev to the prison and Madame Timireva, by now in a state of collapse, to the prison infirmary.

(vi)

The Political Centre had soon been made aware that their hold on Irkutsk was extremely precarious. They had little popular backing. Their military force was of little account. The town was filling up with undisciplined and uncontrollable partisans. Food and fuel were short and the workers were more and more embittered. The Bolsheviks had more influence over the masses and once again they were pressed to join the government; they could only agree to help the Centre if it came to terms with Moscow, and on January 11th Krasnoshchekov, the local party boss, left for the West in a Czech train with three delegates from the Centre to contact the Fifth Red Army headquarters. The Czechs in Irkutsk, too, were insecure. They were two thousand miles from their port of embarkation. They had no sure friends. Their punitive operations of the summer had made them hated by the partisans; and they had no guarantee against attack by the advancing Red Army.

Meanwhile there was the question of the hostages removed from Irkutsk by the Whites. On the 7th ugly rumours began to spread. On the 8th and 9th *Semenovtsi* prisoners captured in the brushes along the railway revealed that the hostages had been killed on board a ship on the lake on the morning of the 6th.

This mass murder was carried out by a Semenov security squad including a certain Sipailov (later responsible for the more gruesome bestialities of Ungern-Sternberg's Mongolian campaign). The news was taken up by the Czech publicists and a full account printed in the *Ceskoslovensky Dénik* of the 10th. It created enormous feeling and a bitter clamour for revenge. The issue became the condition of the Political Centre's further existence. Skipetrov, Sipailov and their colleagues were, of course, out of reach. Kolchak was not. And so, in the words of the Soviet historian, Parfenov, 'the Political Centre, whose leaders had recently assured the Allies that no harm would come to the person of Kolchak . . . were now categorically forced to come to Janin with the demand for the handing over of Kolchak to their prosecutors.'

Janin's memoirs tell us that by January 7th his staff officers were worried about his health and were pressing him to go eastwards to rest. He yielded and on the 10th he reached Slyudyanka, and Verkhneudinsk on the 13th. On the following day there occurred what, he tells us, he had been gloomily anticipating. He was called to the direct wire by Syrovy who reported that conditions in Irkutsk were critical. The workers were on strike. Preparations were being made for armed attack. The Czechs were in danger. It was not possible to convey Kolchak beyond Irkutsk. Janin replied: '*Je n'ai pas le droit d'enfreindre les ordres reçus, et de te prescrire une intervention mettant l'armée en danger. Fais ton mieux en sauvegardant le nom tchèque. Je t'approuve.*'

In the polemic that followed this episode, obscured by all manner of political and personal issues, General Knox emphasized 'the French Commander's failure to discipline properly the Allied contingents' under his command. The charge is pertinent, though how far it had ever been in Janin's power to discipline the Legion is quite another matter. The Legionaries' record, as well known to Janin as to Syrovy, was never to fight except for their own security or for their own advantage. In January, 1920, anti-Kolchak feeling in the Czech units in Irkutsk was running high, and may well have been deliberately fostered by certain Czech propagandists. The Soviet historian, Parfenov, has noted with a certain complacency: 'It appeared that the Czech troops were demanding the handing over of Kolchak. Quite apart from the advantage of raising Czech stock in the eyes of the working masses, it gave a good guarantee of their being able to travel on eastwards. Finally, Kolchak had never been on good terms with the present Czech command . . . They (i.e., Janin and Syrovy) came to an agreement with the one condition that the ceremony of handing over should take place after Janin had left. It would have been disagreeable.' And finally: 'The Allies might have saved him. They certainly possessed sufficient armed forces.

But without a government he no longer represented any advantages to them, and his handing over gave undoubted advantages, especially to the Czechs.'

(vii)

On January 21st the first session was held in Irkutsk prison of the interrogation of Kolchak by a special committee of the Political Centre's Extraordinary Commission, consisting of two S.R.s, one Menshevik and one Bolshevik.

Meanwhile a good deal was happening along the railway line to the west. On January 4th Kolchak's Second and Third Armies under Kappel reached the outskirts of Krasnoyarsk. The Whites attacked but were repulsed by the local insurgent garrison. On the 6th, after more fighting, they by-passed the town, crossed over the ice of the Enisei river and continued their march to the East along the *trakt*.

On January 8th the advance guard of the Fifth Red Army reached Krasnoyarsk, pressed forward along the railway, and made contact with a weak Polish division which formed the rearguard of the Allied contingents. The Polish commander appealed to Syrovy to allow two Polish hospital trains to pass through the Czech echelons in front. Syrovy refused. The Reds attacked, the Poles were overrun, and there now remained only a small Roumanian contingent between the Red Army and the Czechs. Shots were exchanged between Czechs and Roumanians; it was alleged that the Czechs were seizing Roumanian rolling-stock. Then the Red Army overran the Roumanians, and fighting broke out between the Red Army's advanced patrols and the Czech rearguard. On January 13th the last Czech train passed Kansk.

On the 15th the Kappel armies arrived outside Kansk. Once again a frontal attack failed. Again it was decided to by-pass the town. There was a sharp engagement, the Whites captured some arms and ammunition—they were taking no prisoners—and crossed over the frozen Kan. Five days later they defeated a combined Political Centre and partisan force at Uk, and went on to capture Nizhneudinsk, ten miles further east.

Meanwhile Krasnoshchekov and the Political Centre delegates who had left Irkutsk on January 11th reached Tomsk on the 19th, and at once started talks with I. N. Smirnov and Eiche, representing the Soviet Government. Krasnoshchekov propounded his scheme of an East Siberian buffer state with its capital at Irkutsk, with the Political Centre as its government, but with a permanent Soviet representative (i.e., Krasnoshchekov) holding special powers. Kolchak and the Gold Reserve, it was explained, would be handed over to Moscow. The proposal was referred to the Kremlin and its approval by Lenin and Trotsky (including Krasnoshchekov's appointment) was received back in Tomsk on the 21st.

It was, of course, impossible for Lenin and Trotsky to know that already on the day they approved the proposals the idea of a buffer state round Irkutsk had become meaningless—though the scheme was later to be successfully put through in the Far Eastern Republic further east. On January 20th Irkutsk became an integral part of the Soviet empire; on the 17th, the Political Centre's military commander had told his masters that the position was quite out of control, and the latter had no choice but to hand over to a Bolshevik Revolutionary Committee (*Revkom*) headed by Shiryamov.

This new development was in itself no disadvantage to the Czechs. What they required was some stable authority with whom they could make firm arrangements for their evacuation, and this the Political Centre had signally failed to become. *Revkom* on their side were anxious to get the Czechs out of their area, and an agreement was rapidly reached under which the Czechs should be evacuated with their arms, and the Gold Reserve handed over to *Revkom*. Very soon, however, there was friction. A minor Czech official was murdered by a partisan on January 26th. There were protests, demonstrations and counter-demonstrations. This coincided with serious news from down the railway. Red Army advanced detachments had caught up with the rear Czech echelons, there had been sharp fighting and the Czechs had lost four armoured trains before they could disengage. There were urgent discussions between the Czech command in Irkutsk and *Revkom*, and it was agreed to send off a Lieutenant Gub as Czech delegate, with two *Revkom* representatives, to negotiate direct with the Fifth Red Army headquarters. The party had an adventurous journey owing to the trouble down the line, and the fat and talkative Gub did not make a good first impression on the hard-bitten Bolshevik leaders. But negotiations were started.

Kappel by now had learned of Kolchak's arrest and was pressing ahead to effect his rescue. His force left Nizhneudinsk on January 23rd, marching in two columns under Voitsekhovsky and Sakharov along the roads on either side of the *magistral*. That the Whites should in such circumstances retain so much discipline and cohesion was in itself a considerable military feat. Typhus was still rampant, and losses from frostbite very high: Kappel himself was badly affected in both legs. After Nizhneudinsk the Whites on the *trakt* were moving parallel with the rear Czech echelons on the railway. Relations seem to have been not unfriendly. The Czechs were willing to sell food for gold and a Czech doctor attended Kappel. When it was realized how ill he was he was offered a place on a Czech train. He refused on account of the Czech behaviour over Kolchak. The frostbite affection spread to his whole body. On the 25th he was just able to sign an order appointing Voitsekhovsky as his successor. On the 27th he died. The Czechs paid their tribute to his character by transporting his body for burial in Chita.

The Whites continued to press ahead. *Revkom*, seriously alarmed at the threat to Irkutsk, dispatched a hastily assembled force to Zima, half-way from Nizhneudinsk. There was a battle in the course of which the Czech station guard at Zima came in on the side of the Whites, and the Irkutsk force was routed. The incident caused consternation at Czech headquarters in view of the negotiations down the line, and Syrovy took urgent steps to enforce conformity. The Whites went on to capture Cheremkovo, and, on February 2nd, Innokentievskaya.

(viii)

All this time the interrogation of Kolchak was taking place in Irkutsk prison. The interrogators originally appointed by the Political Centre were maintained in their function by the *Revkom*, Popov, the chairman, being a Bolshevik. 'The Commission,' Popov subsequently wrote, 'wanted to reconstruct, through this examination, not only the history of the Kolchak régime as described by its supreme head but also the autobiography of Kolchak, in order to have a more complete picture of this leader of the counter-revolutionary offensive against the young Soviet Republic. This plan was correct but it was not carried to its completion.'

The reason, of course, was the approach of the White Army. On February 3rd, Voitsekhovsky issued an ultimatum from Innokentievskaya demanding the handing over of Kolchak and his party and also the Gold Reserve; the evacuation of Irkutsk by all Red troops; and rations for 50,000 men to be left in the city. On his part Voitsekhovsky promised that his forces would leave Irkutsk within two or three days. Strict neutrality was to be observed *vis-à-vis* the Czechs.

No answer was returned to this ultimatum. On the 4th and 5th the Whites advanced, and there was fighting in the suburbs. The position of *Revkom* was a difficult one. The Red Army was too far away to help them. They had no illusions about the quality of their troops. Furthermore, in hiding in the town were large numbers of White officers whom their security squads had not yet laid their hands on; there was thus a serious risk of an internal rising. But there seems to have been no question of yielding, and no wavering of the determination that Kolchak must not be recovered by the Whites. On the night of the 4th/5th, *Revkom* decided on his execution, subject to the approval of Smirnov at Fifth Red Army Headquarters.

The final session of the Interrogation Commission took place on February 6th. The prison authorities had intercepted a note which Kolchak had tried to smuggle to Madame Timireva in the solitary confinement block: this showed he was aware of Voitsekhovsky's ultimatum, but felt that its probable effect would be to hasten his own end. At this last session both Kolchak and his examiners showed signs of considerable nervous strain. Nevertheless, Popov records, Kolchak 'showed great caution in testifying. He steered clear of even the least chance of supplying material for the indictment of persons who had already fallen, or might fall, into the power of the re-established Soviet rule'. His general bearing 'was that of the captive commander of a defeated army; and from this standpoint, it was entirely dignified'.

Smirnov, now in Krasnoyarsk, had a difficult decision to take. Moscow was thinking of staging a show trial, and was insisting that Kolchak should be sent back to the capital alive. There had been telegraphic instructions to this effect from Lenin. But Smirnov felt the position in Irkutsk was such that he must give a free hand to the men on the spot. His approval was received by *Revkom* on the evening of the 6th. That same night Kolchak and Pepelyaev were removed from their cells and shot, and their bodies pushed under the ice of the frozen Angara.

Throughout February 7th sporadic fighting continued on the outskirts of Irkutsk. On that day, down the railway line, the Czech delegate Gub signed a detailed agreement with Smirnov to cover the final evacuation of all Czech personnel, with their arms, dependants and property. When news of this reached Czech Headquarters, on the morning of the 8th, an ultimatum was issued to Voitsekhovsky to keep away from Glazkov. The White commanders were aware by now that Kolchak was dead, and held a council of war. Sakharov strongly pressed for an all-out attack to take revenge; but he was overruled by Voitsekhovsky. On the night of the 8th/9th the White forces disengaged, and twenty-four hours later they were making their precarious way eastward across the uncertain ice-floes of Lake Baikal.

(ix)

The collapse of Kolchak's empire meant that it was no longer necessary to maintain a British High Commissioner in Siberia; and on March 8th a Foreign Office suggestion that the post be abolished was sent up to Lord Hardinge. Hardinge minuted: 'So ends a not very creditable enterprise', and passed the file to Lord Curzon. Curzon drew a line through the 'not very' of Hardinge's minute, and substituted 'highly dis-'.

The main sources for Chapter V are:

Gins, G., *Sibir, Soyuzniki i Kolchak* (Peking, 1921).

Grondijs, L., *Le Cas Koltchak* (Leyden, 1949).

Janin, Gen. M., *Ma Mission en Sibérie* (Paris, 1933).

Klante, M., *Von der Wolga zum Amur* (Berlin, 1931).

Konstantinov and Shiryamov, *Posledniye Dni Kolchakovshchiny* (Moscow–Leningrad, 1926).

Parfenov, P. S., *Borba za Dalni Vostok* (Moscow, 1928).

Parfenov, P. S., *Grazhdanskaya Voina v Sibiri* (Moscow, 1924).

Sakharov, K., *Das Weisse Sibirien* (Munich, 1925).

Smirnov, I., in *Borba za Ural i Sibir*.

Varneck and Fisher, *The Testimony of Kolchak and Other Siberian Materials* (Stanford, 1935).

Zankevich, Gen., in *Beloe Delo*, Vol. II (Berlin, 1927).

Other works consulted include:

Argunov, A., *Mezhdu Dvumia Bolshevizmami* (Paris, 1919).

Documents on British Foreign Policy 1919–1939, First Series, Vol. III.

Gutmann-Gan, A., in *Beloe Delo*, Vol. III (Berlin, 1927).

Knox, Gen. A. W., in *Slavonic Review*, Vol. III (March, 1925).

Krol, L. A., *Za Tri Goda* (Vladivostock, 1922).

Makeev, A. S., *Bog Voiny* (Shanghai, 1934).

Maksakov and Turunov, *Partizanskoe Dvizhenie v Sibiri* (Moscow-Leningrad, 1925).

McCullagh, F., *A Prisoner of the Reds* (London, 1922).

Melgunov, S. P., *Tragediya Admirala Kolchaka* (3 vols., Belgrade, 1930–1931).

Semenov, G., *O Sebe* (Harbin, 1938).

Vining, L. E., *Held by the Bolsheviks* (London, 1924).

CHAPTER VI

Makhno

(i)

T here are a number of reasons why a study of the Russian Civil War should take account of Nestor Makhno. He was a guerrilla leader of quite outstanding ability, and made an important military contribution both to the Bolshevik defeat in South Russia in the summer of 1919 and to the subsequent collapse of Denikin and later of Wrangel. His was one of the very few revolutionary movements to be led and controlled throughout by members of 'the toiling masses'. He provides one of the very few instances in history where for a period of months and over a wide area supreme power was in the hands of men who professed themselves Anarchists. And the story of his movement throws light on the feelings and aspirations of the Russian peasant, and on the difficulties that the Bolsheviks had to face in imposing their régime on the rural areas.

(ii)

Makhno was born, in October, 1889, of an almost destitute peasant family at Gulyai-Polye in the Southern Ukraine. From the age of seven he earned a little money minding cattle. At twelve he became a full-time agricultural labourer, but three years later he left the land to work at a local foundry. A year or two afterwards, as a result of the local repercussions of the 1905 revolution, he became concerned with politics.

Anarchists of various groups were then comparatively numerous in the Ukraine. There were Anarchist-Communists, Anarchist-Syndicalists and Anarchist-Individualists (the Anarchist-Universalists appeared later), but their ideological differences were blurred. The group to which Makhno adhered were nominally Anarchist-Communists, but first and foremost fighting revolutionaries. Their aims were to 'dispose of the myths of the other parties and lead the social revolution'. At Gulyai-Polye the immediate task was to fight, by terrorist means, against the police repression following the disorders of 1905–1906. Before he was nineteen Makhno was arrested and sentenced to life imprisonment for his share in the murder of a police officer. The next nine years, up to March, 1917, he spent in the Butyrka Prison at Moscow.

Here he made friends with a fellow-prisoner, one Arshinov from Ekaterinoslav, an ex-carpenter in a railway workshop and editor of an illegal Bolshevik news-sheet and subsequently a militant Anarchist, who had arrived in the Butyrka at about the same time as Makhno. Arshinov was a man who had taken great pains to educate himself, and such political and general education as Makhno ever acquired was due to his fellow-prisoner. Not that he was an easy or an apt pupil. He never learned to speak Russian correctly. All the same, he was always writing, and his fellow-prisoners were 'bombarded' by his endless manuscripts. When not writing he was arguing. He was consumed by a restless and turbulent vitality, that earned him the sarcastic nickname of *Skromny* (modest). He was always in trouble with the prison authorities, and spent much of his time in irons or in the freezing punishment cells—where he probably contracted the tubercular trouble that eventually helped to kill him. He was intensely proud of being an Anarchist. He conceived a lasting horror of prisons, and at the height of his success on capturing a town one of his first acts would be to free the prison inmates and destroy the building.

(iii)

On the release of the political prisoners following the February revolution of 1917 Arshinov stayed on in Moscow. Makhno remained only three weeks in order to polish up his ideological equipment and to meet the leading Moscow Anarchists. Then he returned home to carry on the work of the revolution. His ultimate aims were simple. All instruments of government were to be destroyed. All political parties were to be opposed, as all of them were working for some or other form of new government in which the party members would assume the role of a ruling class. All social and economic affairs were to be settled in friendly discussion between freely elected representatives of the toiling masses.

Makhno was the one political prisoner that Gulyai-Polye possessed and he returned as a hero. There was still a small Anarchist group in the village and they arranged a reception for him. Here he issued a firm demand for organization. This occasioned some demur: to the more meticulous Anarchists organization as such was suspect. Mass action should be spontaneous and the only permissible activity was propaganda. However, Makhno had his way, and by the end of March the Gulyai-Polye Association of Peasants was founded, with himself as chairman.

Before long he had made himself the effective political boss of the district. In August the Kornilov affair and the appeal of the Petrograd Soviet provided just the lead he had been waiting for. A Committee for the Defence of the Revolution was formed with, inevitably, Makhno as chairman, and the expropriation of all large land holdings, factories and workshops was taken in hand. The representatives of the Provisional Government at Ekaterinoslav were powerless to interfere. By comparison the Bolshevist *coup d'état* of October created little stir. It took some weeks before it was possible to form a clear idea as to what had happened; and, of course, much longer before the new Petrograd régime could exercise effective control in the provinces. But the slogans 'Land to the Peasants' and 'Factories to the Workers' were perfectly acceptable. To Makhno's peasants it seemed that the inhabitants of Petrograd were doing just what they themselves had done a few weeks before.

At Gulyai-Polye the toiling masses proceeded, more or less peacefully if untidily, to consolidate their revolution. The little factories functioned, or failed to function, under the control of the workers. The estates were split up, without much incident, among the peasants. Most of the peasants, having got their land, took no further interest in outside affairs. But under the drive of a few idealists a certain number of agricultural communes were formed, where an elected committee of elders would allot the work, and then themselves work alongside their colleagues. Makhno himself became a member of one of them.

Relations with the Soviets of Aleksandrovsk and Ekaterinoslav remained friendly if somewhat reserved. They were dominated by Bolsheviks and Left S.R.s, and it was proper to support these revolutionary parties against the Whites on the Don and also against the Kiev Rada (regarded by Makhno as a gang of bourgeois chauvinists). Arms were obtained, with Bolshevik assistance, and a Gulyai-Polye militia was recruited and sent off to support the Red forces. At the same time Makhno's visits to the neighbouring towns filled him with misgivings for the future. From what he had seen of the Bolsheviks and Left S.R.s in action he felt that they were not loyal to the spirit of their slogans. There were too many arrests. Whichever of the two parties attained ascendancy—he was convinced that sooner or later one would squeeze out the other —was likely to endeavour to impose its authority 'in the harsh sense of the word'. Lack of unity and lack of organization among the local Anarchists prevented them from being more than 'the tail of the Bolshevik-Left S.R. bloc'. He set his hopes on the Anarchist movement in the capitals; but his letters to them asking for advice and guidance remained unanswered.

Meanwhile there arose the problem of putting into practice the basic principle of Anarchist economy—the exchange of commodities freely arranged between free organizations of free producers. The South Ukrainian peasants had plenty of grain: what they needed was manufactured goods. Accordingly, a Gulyai-Polye comrade was sent on a tour of the towns. He seems to have been cordially received by the workers everywhere, and in Moscow he met with tangible success. Two Moscow trade union representatives arrived at Gulyai-Polye to fix details. The grain was loaded on rail cars, sent off under a Gulyai-Polye guard and duly arrived. The Moscow workers held to their part of the bargain, and a consignment of textiles and other manufactured goods was dispatched to the south. It was held up at Aleksandrovsk. There was intense indignation among the Gulyai-Polye peasants, who threatened to march on the town. The threat was enough. The Aleksandrovsk Soviet gave way, and the consignment was duly released and distributed among its rightful recipients.

The implications of the Brest-Litovsk Treaty were not immediately apparent in Gulyai-Polye. The Kiev Rada propaganda could be countered without much difficulty. But towards the end of March Ukrainian troops were across the

Dnieper, with, apparently, German and Austrian detachments
in support, and there was no evidence that the Red forces were
putting up an effective resistance. The fainter-hearted in the
region began to waver. At a mass meeting at Gulyai-Polye,
Makhno declared that they could now rely only on themselves
and must fight for their freedom. There was a rush of volunteers.
Makhno was elected Commander-in-Chief. Local intellectuals
were gingered into organizing a medical service. More arms
were obtained, and a sizeable detachment was moved up to
reinforce the Red garrison of Aleksandrovsk.

Meanwhile it was becoming more and more apparent that
there was no cohesion among the Red units. Each was acting
on his own, 'often in those sectors where there was no enemy.'
When they did meet the enemy they were liable to panic.
Makhno was summoned for consultation to the headquarters
of Yegorov, the Commander of the Red forces. When he
reached the rendezvous he found that headquarters had moved
eastwards, so for the next forty-eight hours he followed, over
country cluttered with refugees and stragglers and drunken
bands of Red sailors, after the ever-receding headquarters staff.
On his way news reached him that Gulyai-Polye had been
occupied by the enemy. He made desperate efforts to rally some
groups of stragglers to come back with him and liberate the
village. But far too few were willing, and his only course was
to go on east again to Taganrog, the point for which all the
stragglers seemed to be making, and collect any of his people
he could find. He went on, he records, full of grief and shame at
the collapse of his revolution.

Taganrog was crowded with Red Army detachments,
stragglers, deserters and civilian refugees. A fortnight previously, on April 13th, Moscow had staged its anti-Anarchist
drive. The *Cheka* had raided their premises and arrested
several hundred members; and haphazard arrests of Anarchists
were taking place in Taganrog. Makhno himself was not
molested; he found a number of refugees from Gulyai-Polye
and neighbouring villages, and in late April they held a
congress to decide on future policy.

It would be wrong to consider these refugees as typical of the South Ukrainian population. The bulk of the peasantry (and, indeed, the townsmen) stayed where they were. They had their land. They were not particularly interested in politics. A few felt themselves good Ukrainians and welcomed the Rada. Others hoped that the new régime would mean the establishment of peace and order. It was mainly the convinced revolutionaries and those whose recent activities marked them out for reprisals that had evacuated. The unanimity and bellicosity of the Taganrog congress are therefore not surprising.

They were determined to re-establish their revolution in Gulyai-Polye. They now realized that they had little to hope either from the Bolshevik Government or from the Bolshevik higher command: they must fight their own battles themselves. After discussion of ways and means it was decided that late June and early July, the harvest season, was the best time for subversive work among the peasants. It was therefore agreed that the congress participants should infiltrate back to the area at that season singly or in twos and threes. Once back they would re-establish contacts; spread propaganda; organize clandestine groups of potential fighters; collect arms; and urgently and conspiratorially prepare the ground for a general peasant revolt.

The time chosen for action meant an interval of nearly eight weeks; and Makhno decided to spend this period going round the big centres of Soviet Russia. He wanted to find out for himself what had happened to the Anarchists, and what they were intending to do. He wished to see what Bolshevik supremacy meant in practice, and what was the position and attitude of the workers in the big factories. He needed to know at first hand what help and what obstruction he might expect for his coming revolution in the south. The account of his Odyssey, which takes up the second volume of his memoirs, affords a fascinating worm's-eye view of Bolshevik Russia in the spring of 1918.

(iv)

Makhno arrived in Moscow in early June after a tour that had included Tsaritsyn, Saratov, Astrakhan and Tambov. While *en route* he heard news of the dispersal of the Ukrainian Rada and of the installation of Skoropadsky with German backing— which convinced him of Lenin's error in accepting the Brest-Litovsk Treaty. Later came news of the Czech revolt and the establishment of the S.R.-dominated Government at Samara. In all the cities Makhno visited administration was confused if not chaotic. In Saratov, for instance, there was a large force of Red sailors (from both Kronstadt and the Black Sea) engaged in constant friction and intermittent shooting with the Saratov *Cheka*—each side branding the other as counter-revolutionaries. A third irreconcilable element was the 'Detachment of Odessa Terrorists', two hundred and fifty strong, who arrived about the same time as Makhno and who refused either to be disarmed or to go back and fight the Hetman.

A depressing feature of his tour was to note the general eclipse of the Anarchist movement. In some centres the groups had disintegrated. Such groups as still existed had no funds, no organization, no will to action. Members were in constant fear of arrest by the *Cheka*; and Makhno himself found it wiser to conceal his political affiliation and only to display his card as Chairman of the Gulyai-Polye Committee for the Defence of the Revolution. To the young man from Gulyai-Polye Moscow appeared as 'the capital of the Paper Revolution', a vast factory turning out empty resolutions and slogans while one political party, by means of force and fraud, elevated itself into the position of a ruling class.

Here again the Anarchists seemed cowed and demoralized, largely concerned with keeping out of trouble. His old friend Arshinov had taken on the post of Secretary of the Society for the Ideological Propagation of Anarchism. Makhno was present at some of their meetings, and was impressed by their cultural and theoretical range. But there seemed no urge for action. Again and again in his memoirs he comes back to his phrase 'paper revolution'. He attended a conference of Anarchists including a few like himself from the south, but no one present seemed to intend to go back there and fight for his convictions. The meeting would not even accept the proposal to ask Bolshevik permission to set up an organization for underground work in the Ukraine. There seemed an unbridgeable gap between what Makhno was burning to do and the general mood of the movement. Afterwards, when his revolution had flared up and been extinguished, his historian was to suggest that the Anarchist leaders 'had overslept' the Makhno movement.

During his three weeks' stay in Moscow he went to the All Russian Congress of Textile Unions, where 'were concentrated the flower of the Socialists then living in the centre of the paper revolution. They got up one after another, talked, waved their arms and screamed, each louder than the one before.' He also attended some Left S.R. meetings. He felt sympathy with the Left S.R.s: they had, he believed, not approved of the drive against the Anarchists in April, and they were ashamed of their impotence *vis-à-vis* Lenin. He was impressed with Kamkov and with Spiridonova. But, like the Anarchists, they had 'good will in plenty but not enough strength to tackle the enormous task of reorientating the course of the Revolution'.

One episode of Makhno's Moscow visit gave him pleasure. As a boy in prison his great hero had been the veteran Anarchist, P. A. Kropotkin, and in spite of all his disappointments with the present Anarchist leadership the admiration remained. He made a number of attempts to see the old man, and at last succeeded. They had a long conversation. No practical guidance was forthcoming; he was told that even the issue of his return to the Ukraine was one which he, Makhno, alone could decide. But he met with a sympathy that he had not before experienced. As he was leaving Kropotkin said: 'One must remember, dear comrade, that there is no sentimentality about our struggle. But selflessness and strength of

heart and will on our way towards our goal will conquer all.'
Years later, long after the defeat of his revolution, when
Makhno himself was a dying man in the humiliation and
penury of emigration he was to write: 'I have always remembered these words of Petr Alekseevich. And when our
comrades come to know all that I did in the Russian Revolution
in the Ukraine and then in the independent Ukrainian
Revolution—in the vanguard of which revolutionary *Makhnovshchina* played so outstanding a role—they will recognize in
my activities that selflessness and that strength of heart and will
about which Petr Alekseevich spoke to me. I hope this precept
will enable them to develop these traits of character in themselves.'

His meeting with Lenin was unplanned and unexpected. He
went to the Kremlin to get himself a billeting card, blundered
into Sverdlov's office; and Sverdlov found the young revolutionary from the south sufficiently interesting to arrange an
appointment with Lenin for the following morning.

Makhno was received with a paternal simplicity. Lenin
patted his shoulder, put him down in one chair and Sverdlov
in another, told his secretary they were not to be disturbed for
an hour. All through the interview he talked slowly and clearly,
with frequent repetitions to make sure there was no misunderstanding in question or answer.

Lenin asked what the Ukrainian peasants made of the slogan
'All power to the local Soviets'. Makhno replied that they took
it literally—assuming they were to have complete control of all
affairs affecting them, and added, when Lenin asked him, that
he himself felt this was the correct interpretation.

Lenin: 'Then the peasants are infected with anarchism.'

Makhno: 'Do you think that is bad?'

Lenin: 'I did not say that; it may be to the good if it speeds
up the victory of Communism.'

Lenin went on to observe that mere peasant enthusiasm
would burn itself out—it could not survive serious blows from
the counter-revolution. Makhno said that a leader should not be
pessimistic or sceptical. Lenin pointed out that the Anarchists

had no serious organization, they were unable to organize either the proletariat or the poor peasants, and thus unable to defend the Revolution.

Lenin showed particular interest in the military performance of the Red Guards, and questioned Makhno in very great detail. Then he asked about the propaganda in the villages, and Makhno explained that, on the revolutionary side, there was little of it and what there was was ineffective.

Lenin turned to Sverdlov and said that the true path to victory was the reorganization of the Red Guards into the Red Army. Then he asked Makhno his plans, and when Makhno said he was going home, illegally, commented that the Anarchists had plenty of fanaticism and self-sacrifice but they were short-sighted; they neglected the present for the far-distant future. Turning back to Makhno he said he must not take this too hardly: he (Makhno) was a good man, and if only a third of the Russian Anarchists were like him the Bolsheviks would 'on certain conditions' be prepared to go a long way with them in the free organization of production.

Makhno records that he was uncomfortably conscious of coming under the spell of Lenin's personality: he was beginning to feel reverence for the man he knew to be most responsible for the drive against the Anarchists. He protested that Anarchists were thorough revolutionaries. Lenin said, 'We know the Anarchists as well as you. They all think only of the distant future and pay no regard to the practical problems of the present.' Makhno replied that he was a simple, ill-educated peasant. He could not properly argue with a man like Lenin. But it was quite untrue that the Anarchists did not concern themselves with present realities. The whole revolutionary struggle in the villages against the Kiev Rada had been carried on by the Anarchists and a few S.R.s. There were no Bolsheviks in the villages and if there were any they had no influence. It was the Anarchists who had done the fighting.

Makhno records his feeling of frustration at this interview— he realized the enormous opportunities offered to him and he could not take them. He could not properly express himself.

Finally Lenin asked if he would like help for his journey home; Makhno said he would, and Sverdlov on Lenin's instructions telephoned to a certain Karpenko. Lenin told Makhno to take this as evidence that, after all, he was not so ill-disposed towards the Anarchists; he should go and see Karpenko who would help him across the frontier.

Makhno: 'What frontier?'

Lenin: 'Don't you know that a frontier has been established between the Ukraine and Russia?'

Makhno: 'And you consider the Ukraine as Soviet Russia?'

Lenin: 'To consider is one thing, to see is another.'

In due course the Bolshevik organization in charge of illegal frontier crossings provided Makhno with a false passport in the name of Ivan Yakovliev Shepel, school-teacher and reserve officer from near Taganrog. On June 29th, Arshinov came with him to the station and saw him off. After a long, slow journey the train reached Kursk, and then Belenikino, which was the terminal. The little station was crowded with refugees, one or two from Gulyai-Polye who told Makhno that in his absence his mother's house had been burned down, one of his brothers executed and another lodged in Aleksandrovsk gaol. He hired a cab to take him across no-man's-land and reached Belgorod without incident. He found a secluded spot and put on the Ukrainian officer's uniform that had been given to him to match his passport.

(v)

Events had seen to it that the date Makhno had fixed back in Taganrog for his rendezvous with the Ukrainian Revolution was well timed. As has been mentioned, the bulk of the peasantry, in spite of Makhno's brave words to Lenin, had offered no resistance to the Rada and the German armies. In a large number of villages the invaders had been welcomed. Even the return of the landlords in their wake did not in itself make for large-scale disturbances. Reports reaching Soviet

Russia tended to show that most of the peasants could have been induced to pay a small rent for the land they had taken over. But the landlords were greedy: they wanted the harvest, and the peasants were firmly convinced that the crops they had themselves sown and harvested were their personal property. On top of this came the special agreements between Kiev and the Central Powers for the bulk delivery of grain and other foodstuffs. The peasants tried to cheat. When that failed they started burning barns and sabotaging transport. There were isolated cases of small bands offering armed resistance.

In their occupation of western Russia, German troops held the northern and central areas, the whole of the territory bordering on Soviet Russia as far as the Don, and the Crimea and Tauride province in the south. The Roumanians were west of Odessa. In between, holding most of the Ekaterinoslav and Kherson provinces, were the Austro-Hungarians. It was with the latter that Makhno had mainly to do during the first few months of his activity.

The final stages of his journey back were precarious. The authorities got wind of his return and he had to jump the train to avoid arrest. He made his way on foot to a village some twenty kilometres from Gulyai-Polye where he had friends who would hide him, and there established his conspiratorial head-quarters. On July 4th he issued his first secret circular, made out in ten copies and passed by safe hand to peasants he knew he could trust: in it he announced his return and warned recipients to be ready to act. An immediate reply from Gulyai-Polye urged him not to come back to the village. There was an Austrian garrison. The place was full of spies and all members of the former Soviet were under arrest. The Jews had betrayed the village back in April, and now it was the young Jews who were hunting down the revolutionaries and the Jewish bourgeoisie was encouraging them.

Makhno was worried at this evidence of anti-Semitism. His people were making the Jews to be the scapegoat of past misfortunes and the excuse for present inaction. He wrote that while the rich Jews would naturally side with the invaders against the Anarchists the poorer Jews were the peasants' friends and allies. He also composed a second circular, dated July 2nd, outlining the programme to be undertaken. Peasants must first organize, so that every small village and every quarter of each big village had its own proper fighting squad. When the squads were formed they should watch for the opportunity to start small-scale action against isolated landowners.

He continued to receive messages warning him against coming to Gulyai-Polye; his presence would inevitably become known and provoke reprisals on the poorer peasants. But he was tired of inaction. One night, escorted by two armed peasants, he arrived at the cottage of a widow on the outskirts of Gulyai-Polye. Children were sent round with messages, and all through the small hours his old friends collected in the cottage. There were many absentees—dead, deported or in prison. Of those that turned up most were dispirited; some of them urged him to leave; a few were anxious to help. He remained in hiding for three or four nights and organized some 'initiatory groups' of three to five men under his own orders. But then came news that in some of the neighbouring villages the recipients of his first circular had understood it to be a signal to act: peasants had staged some premature and ineffective attacks on landowners' houses. The authorities were alerted and there was a wave of arrests and house-searches in Gulyai-Polye itself. The pessimists seemed to have been justified. Makhno was smuggled out of the village and went into hiding with some distant cousins at Ternovka, a village fifty miles away.

(vi)

If Gulyai-Polye was the Mecca of the Makhnovite movement Ternovka has some claims to be its Medina. There was plenty of fighting spirit in the village; also a small stock of arms, left behind in the spring by the retreating Red Guards and carefully hidden. Makhno organized the young men into squads. A few weeks later, as more and more evidence came in of peasant unrest, he issued the slogan 'Death to all who with the aid of German-Austrian-Hetmanite bayonets remove from peasants and workers the conquests of their Revolution', and initiated a series of attacks on landlords' country houses. Some landlords were killed, as were any guards who might be stationed there; others abandoned their properties and went off to the garrison towns to await the restoration of order. Makhno's raids covered an ever wider range, more and more volunteers joined up with his band and in mid-September he felt his resources were adequate for an attack on Gulyai-Polye. On the march towards the village he surprised and disarmed two Hetmanite detachments and thus came into possession of sufficient Hetmanite army and militia caps and overcoats to disguise his little army. For four days the Makhnovites operated in a circle of about thirty miles round Gulyai-Polye. The Austrian authorities were warned of their approach. Punitive expeditions came after them, missed them, took reprisals on the villages and the young villagers ran away to join up with the insurgents. One night Makhno with a fighting patrol ran into a company of Austrians, who took them to be Hetmanite militia so that they were able to withhold their fire until point-blank range. The Austrian company commander was among those killed. The prisoners included three Galicians who were sent back to their battalion with a letter dictated by Makhno and addressed to the Austrian rank and file: these were told to shoot their officers and make their way home to start a revolution there—otherwise they would be killed by the Ukrainian revolutionaries. A problem after this little battle was the disposal of the Austrian corpses, which, if found, would provoke reprisals on the local villagers; so a squad of peasants was called out to cart them and dump them on the nearest landlord's property.

Peasants were now rallying to Makhno in hundreds, some with rifles, some without. There were continual councils of war as to the next move, and a wide variety of opinion. Some wanted to launch an attack on Gulyai-Polye, others to disperse and instigate a general rising in the villages all round. The very uncertainty and constant change of insurgent plans added to the difficulties of the Austrian Intelligence, and in the event on the night the attack was staged most of the troops had been sent off on various false scents. The attack was successful: only the garrison headquarters staff managed to get away in the darkness and confusion. The Makhnovites seized the post office, the printing press and the railway station (which was some miles out of the centre of the village). Old scores were paid. Hundreds of leaflets were rolled off calling on the peasants to rally to the revolution.

It was one thing to seize Gulyai-Polye, but quite another to hold it. Some of the hotheads wished to hold on at all costs, but Makhno realized he had no prospect of successfully defending the village against regular troops. When news was received from the local stationmaster of the approach of enemy troop trains, Makhno moved out his little army; fought a successful rearguard action; undertook a forced march of eighty miles and then paused to refit.

The successful seizure and evacuation of Gulyai-Polye was Makhno's first important military operation. The second was the engagement at Dibrivka which took place a few days later. While at rest in the forest near this village he was joined by another insurgent force under one Shchus, whom he had met during the fighting in the spring and who had attended the Taganrog congress. The combined army now totalled nearly 1,500 men. Makhno planned a long-range raid (of which he was later to conduct so many) across the southern Ukraine to the Sea of Azov. One problem was that a number of Shchus's men were wounded, but these had found girls in the village, and when the girls heard of the proposed expedition they all volunteered to ride with their men with the army on peasant carts and look after them *en route*.

There were busy days of preparation. It was here that the Makhnovite pattern of feeding the army first took shape. At a mass meeting the peasants would indicate the richest households. These (not unnaturally) would agree to provide one sheep each. All peasants gave bread, according to their capacity.

There was recruiting: but no volunteers were accepted over and above those for whom arms were available; the others were put on a register. And there were continuous mass meetings and speeches at which Makhno was at pains to emphasize the danger not only from the Hetman and the Germans but also from the White generals in the south-east.

And then one night the Austrians attacked. A few partisans held up their advance while the wounded were loaded on to carts and taken off to the forest. The villagers panicked and implored Makhno not to retreat, but he knew that withdrawal was essential. All that night and most of the next day his men hid in the forest. Then, when the enemy were reported to be on parade in the main square they launched their counter-attack. They moved in surreptitiously, in small groups. One girl tried to give the alarm, but she was caught and knocked on the head to stop her screaming. The partisans climbed over the back walls and occupied the shops and houses overlooking the square. The enemy troops were resting. Their rifles were stacked; some men were lying down. Makhno opened fire at eighty yards' range. It was a massacre rather than a battle. Some of the enemy got away. Some barricaded themselves in houses, and the houses were set on fire. The village woke up 'like an ant heap'. Peasants swarmed out of the houses with axes and hammers, chasing after the fugitives and beating the prisoners. There had been one Austrian battalion, detachments of Hetmanite and German colonist volunteers and a contingent of militia. Makhno saved some twenty Austrians from lynching, tied up their wounds, fed them and sent them off to tell the story to their companions. All other prisoners were killed, as was the girl who had tried to give the alarm. Next day Austrian reinforcements arrived with a number of field guns. The *makhnovtsi* were shelled out of the village and shelled again when they took up positions in the forest. Makhno and Shchus were both hit, Shchus seriously. Frightened peasants streamed after them out of the village. But Makhno had no means of helping the peasants. He had no alternative but to withdraw again, this time right out of the area. Next night, already miles away, he could see the glow in the sky from the burning houses of Dibrivka.

(vii)

In the next three weeks Makhno's raids covered many hundreds of miles, and were marked by an extreme ferocity. The slogan was 'Death, death, death to all on the side of the Hetman'. He wrote afterwards that this was 'not a slogan thought out by those that sit in offices . . . but dictated by factual reality'. His detachments operated round Berdyansk, Maryupol and Pavlograd, exterminating landlords and militia. His main force once came up against a Hungarian battalion and was badly mauled; he told his partisans they would have to learn to fight like Magyars. But mostly he was able to avoid the occupying armies who were tending more and more to concentrate in the urban centres and big railway junctions.

The sphere and scope of his operations widened. He felt himself no longer a mere guerrilla leader but, once again, the instrument of a social revolution. The policy of vengeance and destruction was ceasing to be adequate. The revolution must build up its stores of arms, horses, money and essential supplies. Measures were thought out, and approved at a mass meeting of the insurgent army, for a system of organized requisitions. Revolutionary Tribunals were set up; public enemies were no longer to be shot out of hand but to be executed publicly after some show of court proceedings. The main insurgent army came to be followed by a long column of carts carrying cash and stores, and it was now possible to offer immediate relief to any destitute villages on the route.

In early October the Austrians evacuated Gulyai-Polye and the insurgent army marched in, this time to stay there, except for one brief interval, for some months. Makhno's first act was to send an ultimatum to the (Hetmanite) Town Commandant of Aleksandrovsk, demanding the release of all the prison inmates. When, eventually, the Gulyai-Polye Anarchists (including Makhno's brother) came back home they were given a resounding welcome and afforded a much-needed reinforcement of the military and administrative staffs.

Makhno was in the field when the momentous news came from Kiev that Hetman Skoropadsky was no longer in power and that a Directory, of the same political colour and largely of the same personnel as the former Rada, had assumed the government of the Ukraine. There was much jubilation among the peasants, but Makhno had misgivings. He regarded the Directory, as he had regarded the Rada, as an instrument of bourgeois chauvinism. At the same time there was need for caution: his infant revolution had already a great many enemies and not nearly sufficient armed forces. When he returned to Gulyai-Polye there were days of anxious delibera-tion as to the policy to be adopted. Makhno's own account of this period is incomplete; he was a dying man when he reached this stage of his memoirs and there are long gaps in his record. But it is certain that at one stage a decision was made to main-tain, for the moment, an attitude of cautious neutrality; and that a few days later the decision was reversed in favour of war. Makhno's memoirs give no indication of the reason for this change. It may have been the hope of coming to some working alliance with the Bolsheviks.

In the late autumn and winter of 1918 the Red Army's counter-offensive on the Eastern front of the Civil War carried Bolshevik power as far as Ufa and Orenburg. But in the south the Red offensive against the Cossacks and the White Volunteer Army petered out: there were disturbances in the Red rear and disaffection among certain subordinate Red commanders. In addition the Red troops were badly hit by typhus. In November, Denikin captured Stavropol and a few weeks later the north Caucasian Red army was completely broken.

In the Ukraine the withdrawal of the German and Austro-Hungarian occupation armies meant the removal of the one force capable of enforcing some kind of order. In the coastal area and the Crimea a number of weak and transient local authorities came into being; Denikin sent his representatives to the main centres, and the French were soon to land in some force. At Kiev the Directory made desperate efforts to raise and maintain an army capable of defending its existence. The Bolsheviks made ready to stage a second invasion. In the interior, throughout the countryside, there operated a wide variety of petty war lords and band leaders, some with nationalist or political slogans and some mere bandits. Makhno's position was exceptional on account of the strength of his army, of the hold he had established on the loyalty of the peasants of his area, and of the nature of his political ideals and programme.

The German-Austrian retirement offered Makhno a unique opportunity to build up a reserve of arms and stores, and his memoirs are full of incidents with German retreating units. There was some fighting. There was a good deal of negotiation, and a fair amount of doublecrossing. These few weeks saw an appreciable increase both in the effective strength of the Makhnovite Army and in Makhno's own personal reputation. This last was no longer merely local. In the Soviet Russian Press he came to be frequently and favourably featured as a true revolutionary fighter. In mid-December, 1918, he received and accepted an invitation from the underground Bolshevik committee at Ekaterinoslav to take part in an attempt to seize the town from the Petlurist garrison and to assume command of all the insurgent forces.

Makhno brought up his troops at night to a working-class suburb on the west bank of the Dnieper, and they came into town, their arms concealed under their great-coats, on an early morning workmen's train. The station was seized at once. Some Bolshevik workers' detachments and a few S.R.s also came into action. A Petlurist artillery officer changed sides, with a number of his guns and gun teams. After three or four days of confused fighting the insurgents had occupied the greater part of the town. Makhno seized the prison and released the inmates; he arrested and shot the prosecutor who had secured his conviction ten years before; and he issued proclamations forbidding looting. A new Soviet was installed as the

governing authority, but it functioned for only twenty-four
hours as the Petlurists brought up reinforcements and the
Makhnovites were forced to withdraw. A few days later the Red
Army pressed out the Petlurists.

We have an account of the fighting in Ekaterinoslav from a
professor of law at the University, who with his wife occupied
one floor in a house overlooking a square that became a
no-man's-land between the opposing forces. Shells screamed
overhead, and spent bullets pattered down on the roof. The
unbellicose occupants of the professor's house gathered together
in the first floor, which seemed to them to be the least unsafe,
and 'waited in silence for death'. On the evening of the fourth
day the shooting died down. Then there was knocking, and
some ten men pushed in through the street door, insisting that
they required the house. The landlord pleaded and argued:
eventually they agreed to take the front rooms and leave the
back to the residents. So the residents retired to the back, but
their visitors pushed in after them and more crowded in from
the street. A meal had been laid on the table and the partisans
sat down to it; the ladies of the house made haste to serve
them.

They were members of a Makhnovite machine-gun section.
Their dress was varied—uniforms of every kind, peasant dress;
some wore expensive civilian fur coats. All were armed to the
teeth and hung about with hand-grenades. One, who was very
drunk, kept giving accounts of the bourgeoisie he had shot.
'They were very stupid,' he said. 'They squeaked all the time.'
The men were not unfriendly. One produced a pair of stockings
which he offered to the professor's wife. She was convinced
they had just been pulled off a dead woman's legs and refused
in horror: there was an ugly moment, but the landlord accepted
them on behalf of his daughter. One elderly peasant was
awestruck at the splendour of the first urban interior he had
ever seen, and offered formal thanks between each mouthful.

The commander of the detachment joined them. He would
not eat or drink, but he sat at the table and talked. He was
anti-Semite. He described his leader Makhno as 'a real

Communist, not like the Petlurists who have sold themselves to the Jews'. He went on to explain that when they occupied a town Makhno allowed his men to take one pair of whatever he needed, provided the man could carry it himself. Whoever took more than that was shot. Peaceful inhabitants need not be frightened, as the Makhnovites only killed Germans and Jews; these, after all, were the main bourgeois.

In due course the squad went on to relieve their companions. The commander gave permission for the door between the front and back rooms to be bolted. During the night men came in and rattled at the inner door. In the square in front there was intermittent shouting and bursts of machine-gun fire. Next morning all was quiet with the men at their posts in the square. In the front room a cupboard had been broken open and all the linen stolen, and a sack of hand-grenades was lying under a bed. The landlord called to a partisan who came and collected the bombs. When, later, firing began again it was from the Petlurist reinforcements, and the Makhnovites retreated.

(viii)

After the fighting at Ekaterinoslav the *Makhnovtsi* went back towards Gulyai-Polye. For the first few weeks of 1919 the advancing Red Armies by-passed this area, where Makhno and his staff went ahead with their work of military and social organization. This period saw the beginnings of what might be called the Makhnovite Government in that two Congresses were held, the first in January at Velikaya Mikhailovka and the second three weeks later at Gulyai-Polye. They were composed of delegates of peasants, workers and of the insurgent army, and were intended to clarify and record the decisions of the toiling masses and to be regarded as the supreme authority for the liberated area. This area, for the time being, was exclusively rural and the workers' representation was insignificant. Peasant delegates, however, came in from thirty-two *volosts*.

There were rousing revolutionary speeches, and tirades

against European and American imperialists and their instruments such as Denikin, Kolchak and Petlura. There was also in the general resolution a warning: 'With deep regret the Congress must also declare that apart from external enemies a perhaps even greater danger, arising from its internal shortcomings, threatens the Revolution of the Russian and Ukrainian peasants and workers. The Soviet Governments of Russia and of the Ukraine, by their orders and decrees, are making efforts to deprive local soviets of peasants and workers' deputies of their freedom and autonomy.' The Bolshevik Party, the resolution went on, was 'demanding a monopoly of the Revolution'.

The main civil achievement was the establishment of a Regional Revolutionary Military Soviet of Peasants, Workers and Insurgents, a permanent committee with no powers to initiate policy but designed merely to implement the decisions of the periodic congresses. Otherwise the re-establishment of the former agricultural communes was approved. A resolution was passed urging the setting up of 'free', i.e. non-political, Soviets of toilers in all districts; and another urging 'direct union' between peasants in the country and workers in the towns. This last remained academic; communications were too bad and there was too great a variety of military occupation to allow any real contact between villagers and big town labour. But the Makhnovites did at least make the considerable gesture of dispatching a large consignment of grain to the hungry factory workers of Petrograd and Moscow.

However, the main emphasis of the two Congresses was upon defence. Makhno had learned the lesson of the spring of 1918: a social revolution must have an effective military force to protect it. All through the early weeks of 1919 Makhnovite detachments were fighting the Whites in the south, and this continuous campaigning was bringing home to Makhno the shortcomings of volunteerism. The flow of volunteers did not dry up: sometimes there were more than he could arm. But it was spasmodic and unpredictable. Individuals and groups were apt to get tired of the war and return to their homes. It was essential to put the manpower question on a regular basis.

Accordingly, at Makhno's insistence, the second Congress passed a resolution in favour of 'general, voluntary and egalitarian mobilization'. The orthodox Anarchist line, expressed at an Anarchist gathering of this period, was that 'no compulsory army . . . can be regarded as a true defender of the social revolution', and debate ranged round the issue as to whether enlistment could be described as 'voluntary' (whatever the feelings of individuals) if it took place as the result of a resolution voluntarily passed by representatives of the community as a whole. Makhno gained his point. A Soviet writer (Kubanin) suggests that the issue proved that Makhno knew his peasants better than did the Anarchist intellectuals: peasants held back from volunteering because they knew that the Whites shot all Red volunteers. As mobilized men they would be safer.

The first contact between Makhno's staff and that of Dybenko, the local Red Army commander, took place at the end of February. Relations were friendly. Each side needed the military alliance. Makhno continued to be featured in the Soviet Press as a champion of the toiling masses. When the Red Army proposed, in March, a unification of military forces against Denikin (now in supreme command of all the Whites in the south), it took little time to come to an agreement.

This first of the three agreements to be negotiated by Makhno with the Bolsheviks laid down that the Makhnovite Army was to maintain its own internal organization, but would be subordinate for operational purposes to the Red Army Higher Command, and would furthermore accept Red Army nominees as Political Commissars down to regimental level. It was to receive, from the Bolsheviks, arms and supplies on the same level as the neighbouring Red Army units. It was to keep its name of Insurgent Army [later it was to adopt the title of 'Insurgent Revolutionary Army of the Ukraine (Makhnovites)'] and to retain its (Anarchist) black flags. Nothing was said about the civil administration of the areas of Makhnovite occupation.

The agreement with Makhno marked the beginning of a

number of Red successes in the south. In late March, Grigoriev
(an ex-Tsarist officer who had served the Petlurists and then
defected with his partisan army to the Bolsheviks) captured
Kherson. In April the French hurriedly evacuated Odessa and
the Reds marched in. The same month the Red Army occupied
the Crimea. But, in spite of this, the Bolsheviks were meeting
difficulties in their attempts to assimilate and reintegrate the
newly reoccupied southern provinces. Bolshevik policy, while
approving the distribution to the poorer peasants of some of the
landowners' estates, laid down that the rest was to be
administered as State farms. Vineyards and sugar-beet planta-
tions were to be State property, as was all livestock and
equipment belonging to the dispossessed gentry. The peasants,
on the other hand, maintained that all property of the former
landlords was now by right their own, as had been arranged at
Gulyai-Polye (Makhno's agricultural communes had been
entirely voluntary). Furthermore, the Red Armies lived off the
country and that meant requisitions and mobilization orders.
Red commissars and *Cheka* officials (who often happened to
be Jews) soon became objects of hatred. Bolshevik Party
organization and propaganda was weak enough in most of the
towns, and non-existent in the rural areas. Attempts were
already being made to form committees of poor peasants, but
these were ineffective. Poor peasants had no time for committees which were often packed with *kulaks*. In any case there
was little incentive for the poorer peasant to co-operate with
his new rulers. The villagers, rich and poor alike, were united
in their opposition. Some of them believed that a new party had
come into power in Moscow. They were, they proclaimed, for
the Bolsheviks who had given them the land, but they were
against the Communists who were now trying to rob them.
Recent experience seemed to have shown that authority could
be successfully resisted and throughout the area there were
refusals to deliver, arsons, lynchings, and action by armed
bands. Trouble began to spread to the locally recruited Red
units. The Second Ukrainian Red Army Division was confidentially reported to be riddled with indiscipline, drunkenness,

card-playing, anti-Communism, anti-Semitism, pro-Makhno and Black Flag slogans.

The reference to the Black Flag is not isolated. Anarchist influence was reported from Aleksandrovsk and other centres. Anarchists were holding a conference in Kursk at about this time and in one of their resolutions it was stated that 'the Ukrainian Revolution will have great chances of rapidly becoming Anarchist in its ideas'. The position called for renewed Bolshevik measures against the Anarchists. *Nabat*, the main Anarchist newspaper in the Ukraine, was suppressed, and its editorial board dispersed under threat of arrest. Some of them came to Makhno at Gulyai-Polye; Voline, the most eminent intellectual, was delayed *en route* but arrived there in the summer and was elected chairman of the Revolutionary Military Soviet. Arshinov had already arrived (in April) from Moscow and had assumed charge of Makhnovite education and propaganda. There was some justification for suspecting Gulyai-Polye of becoming a centre of ideological opposition.

(ix)

Relations between Bolsheviks and Makhnovites were already deteriorating when in April the Revolutionary Military Soviet at Gulyai-Polye convoked the Third Congress of Peasants, Workers and Insurgents. When the Congress was in session a telegram was received from Dybenko denouncing it as counter-revolutionary. Makhno was away at the front; but the newly arrived intellectuals sent back a long reply, arguing out that the Congress was the expression of the will of the toiling masses. Meanwhile military co-operation continued. Antonov-Ovseenko paid a friendly visit to the Makhnovite headquarters on April 29th, and S. S. Kamenev on May 4th. Kamenev suggested that it might be wise to dissolve the Revolutionary Military Soviet; he was told that unlike similarly titled bodies elsewhere, which were instruments of a political party, the local R.M.S. was the creation of the people themselves.

It was now that favourable mention of Makhno ceased to appear in the Soviet press; an increasingly critical note became apparent. Supplies failed to get through to Makhnovite units and areas. It may be significant that Trotsky (to whom Makhno's ideas and methods were bound to be anathema) was now paying more personal attention to the southern front. But in May the whole military position was completely changed when Grigoriev, main Soviet commander in the south-west, staged a revolt against his Bolshevik masters and proclaimed himself Ataman of Kherson and the Tauride.

Red garrisons in some centres remained true to Moscow; in others they declared themselves neutral. Many Soviet troops came over to Grigoriev. The peasants (in so far as they counted) were anti-Bolshevik. The Soviet south-western front collapsed, and it seemed possible that if Makhno defected the south-eastern front would collapse as well. On May 12th Kamenev telegraphed the news of Grigoriev's revolt to Makhno: 'The decisive moment has come—either you stand with the workers and peasants of all Russia, or you in fact open the front to the enemy . . . I rely on your revolutionary honour.' Makhno replied that he did not know what were Grigoriev's intentions: if he were trying to set up a government he was a common adventurer. Meanwhile, the Makhnovite Army remained 'unchangeably true to the Revolution of the Peasants and Workers, but not to instruments of violence like your Commissars and *Chekas*'. At the same time he issued a general order to his troops facing Denikin: all at the front should stand fast, without regard to the quarrels between the Bolsheviks and Grigoriev. However, it soon became apparent that Grigoriev was not an important factor. His troops carried out savage pogroms and considerable looting; but he had no constructive ability and was unable to keep his army together. Within a few weeks he was little more than a bandit leader with some two or three thousand guerrillas. The Bolsheviks once more felt able to take a firmer line.

In the latter part of May the *Cheka* sent over two agents to assassinate Makhno; one lost his nerve and confessed to the

Insurgent *razvedka*. Both were executed. By this time the secret services both of the Makhnovites and the Soviet authorities were busy penetrating the opposite party—a state of affairs which lasted till 1921. Makhno received warning not to venture into any Bolshevik-held town. The Red hold-back of supplies for the Insurgents developed into a blockade of the area. Makhnovite units at the front ran short of ammunition. (Makhno's people, incidentally, never learned to conserve their arms or munitions; despite the huge stocks they acquired by one means or another they were always running short.)

The cause of the open break was a decision to convoke a Fourth Congress of Peasants', Workers' and Insurgents' Representatives at Gulyai-Polye. The deterioration in relations with the Bolsheviks had coincided with the onset of Denikin's big spring offensive: and the R.M.S. announced on May 30th that the situation was such that 'it could be handled only by the toiling masses themselves and not by individual persons or political parties'. The rank and file of the Red Army were publicly invited to send representatives on the same basis as the Makhnovite units.

Trotsky, then at Kharkov, may or may not have been informed of the text of the convocation when he wrote the denunciation of *Makhnovshchina* in his train newspaper *Na Puti* on June 2nd. In any case, the approach to the Red Army rank and file (whose dubious loyalty had been shown up in the Grigoriev affair) called for far more drastic measures. Order No. 1824, signed by Trotsky at Kharkov on June 4th, forbade the holding of the Congress, declared that any participation amounted to high treason against the Soviet State and ordered the arrest of all delegates and all concerned with the distribution of the invitations. There is reason to believe that a further (secret) order called for the arrest of Makhno.

No copy of Order No. 1824 was sent direct to Makhno. Meanwhile, the White offensive was gathering momentum. Gulyai-Polye was captured by Cossacks on June 6th. The following day a Red Army armoured train was sent to Makhno as a reinforcement, with a message that his units were expected to resist to the end; and he himself received an invitation to come and confer with Voroshilov and Mezhlauk at their head-quarters. By this time Makhno was in possession of Order 1824 and of a subsequent order under which he was to hand over his command. On June 9th he sent off a long telegram to Voro-shilov with copies to Lenin and to Trotsky. He rebutted the charges made against him, maintained that the Bolsheviks found Insurgent methods to be incompatible with their dictatorship, but added that in view of the gravity of the situation and of Bolshevik hostility to himself he proposed to resign from his command.

It is difficult, on the evidence available, to trace the exact sequence of events in this confused period. But in any case Makhno went to Aleksandrovsk and handed over his command to a Red Army officer temporarily out of touch with Kharkov. He instructed the commanders of his units in Red Army formations to remain at their posts. He himself with a small force of picked cavalry crossed the Dnieper. While on the east of the river the Bolsheviks were losing successively Ekaterinoslav and Kharkov, Makhno, on the right bank, was fighting small engagements with any Red units that opposed him, liquidating Bolshevik and *Cheka* organizations in the villages, and en-couraging the peasants to form free Soviets. Towards the end of the month he came into contact with Grigoriev.

Makhno believed Grigoriev to be an adventurer, and there-fore a counter-revolutionary (as all adventurers were *ipso facto* counter-revolutionary). At the same time he was more than ever obsessed with the necessity of building up his army and he felt the Grigoriev force contained good potential material. He therefore agreed to hold a conference, and in mid-July Grigoriev arrived at Makhno's headquarters. He made a bad first impression by commenting adversely on the Jews there, and followed this up by his attitude throughout the conference. The Makhnovites held that the object of joint action was to fight against the Whites and the Bolsheviks, but that to fight the Bolsheviks was a counter-revolutionary act unless this was done in the name of the Social Revolution. Grigoriev's line was that the Bolsheviks and the Petlurists were swine: he had had experience of them and he knew. He implied it would be admissible to join up with any ally against the Bolsheviks. As for the Whites, he had had no experience of them and so did not know what they were like.

The association was a brief one. Two White Army emissaries called at Makhno's headquarters with a letter for Grigoriev. The emissaries were discreetly liquidated, and a few hours later Grigoriev and his bodyguard were shot at a private meeting by members of Makhno's staff. A subsequent joint congress of both armies was harangued by Makhno and his senior officers, and approved of what had taken place on the ground that it was 'historically necessary'. All partisan detachments formerly under Grigoriev were incorporated in the common Insurgent Makhnovite Army.

The Makhnovite propagandists gave the fullest publicity to the execution of Grigoriev, and a copy of the circular telegram announcing the event was sent to the Kremlin in Moscow. The accretion of military strength was not, however, as great as Makhno had hoped. The *Grigorievtsi* had seen little serious fighting for many weeks, and unlimited looting, pogroms and drunkenness had demoralized them. As Voline puts it 'they were ignorant, and, having contracted bad habits during their time with Grigoriev, they were unable to raise themselves to the moral level of the Makhnovite partisans'.

(x)

The summer of 1919 was one of sustained military disaster for the Soviet Armies in the south. Denikin's advance was continuous. In July the Red Army had to be pulled out of the Crimea. In August Denikin captured Kherson, Nikolaev and Odessa along the Black Sea coast, and Kiev to the north. Further east, General Mamontov started his spectacular raid behind the Red lines. Arshinov records Makhno's 'disgust' at Bolshevik feebleness. Indeed, the general picture was reminiscent of the early months of 1918 when the Germans were advancing. The Red Armies in the south, ineffective and demoralized, seemed to be disintegrating. In July Makhno sent messages to his former units now with the Red Armies that they should return. Most of them joined up with him near Elizavetgrad in August. A number of Red Army soldiers came with them. Makhno spent a few days reorganizing his force, which now amounted to more than 15,000 with four infantry brigades, one cavalry brigade, a detachment of artillery and a special machine-gun regiment equipped with five hundred machine-guns.

The inception of this new phase of his activities was marked by the issue of his Order No. 1 of August 5th, 1919. This laid down the general principles for Insurgent conduct. Their enemies were listed as the rich bourgeoisie—whether Russian, Ukrainian or Jewish—furthermore, all those who upheld an unjust social order of a bourgeois nature such as Bolshevik Commissars, the *Cheka*, or members of punitive detachments. All these last were to be arrested and sent to headquarters or shot on the spot if they tried to resist. Insurgents must renounce any consideration of personal profit: there must be no beating up or robbing of peaceful Jews; there must be no arbitrary or independent requisitioning. Behaviour must be orderly and disciplined. Drunkenness was a crime, especially to be seen drunk in the streets. An insurgent must always be ready for battle; but he must be considerate to the local population. Following the issue of this order the Insurgent Army captured Elizavetgrad from the Whites and pressed on towards Odessa.

There is good evidence that the Whites soon came to regard Makhno's new army as their toughest immediate opponent. Special troops were detailed for use against him—officers' battalions and picked cavalry, whose fighting qualities earned Makhno's respect. There was a set battle to the north of Odessa and the Insurgents were beaten: their opponents were in too great strength, and, as always, they themselves ran short of ammunition. White pressure increased, and Makhno was forced to retire northwards and then north-westwards.

Voline, who took part in it, has left a vivid picture of the retreat of the main column through the heat and dust of an exceptionally dry autumn. The cavalry were away to the rear or on the flanks, in almost continuous brushes with White patrols. The infantry were carried in two-horse peasant carts (*tachankas*)—two partisans and a driver on each—the first cart of all bearing the black flag with the slogans 'Liberty or Death' and 'Land for the Peasants, Factories for the Workers'. There were innumerable carts carrying wounded, and the column was swelled by peasant families, with all their belongings and livestock—refugees from White brutalities.

One attempt was made to make a stand, but the enemy was too strong and the retreat continued. In late September the column made contact with a strong Petlurist force near Uman and Peregonovka. The Whites were hard on their heels and the position was critical. Negotiations were started with the Petlurists, with the inevitable reserves and suspicions on both sides. An agreement was reached by which the Petlurists undertook to take care of Makhno's wounded and to observe neutrality as between him and the Whites. The Makhnovites at once attempted to win over the Petlurist rank and file, and leaflets were hurriedly printed on the portable press and distributed. But before any effect became apparent Makhno received secret information that the Petlurists were negotiating behind his back with the White Command. He was completely surrounded.

On September 26th he launched a counter-attack with all his force against the White positions. It was the bloodiest engagement of all Makhno's campaigns. After twenty-four hours of fighting the Whites were beaten (they lost twenty guns and a hundred and twenty machine-guns), and the Insurgents were driving westwards. The speed of their advance, through the thinly held White rear, is almost incredible. Within a fortnight they successively captured Krivoi Rog, Nikopol, Aleksandrovsk, Gulyai-Polye; and Melitpol, Berdyansk and Mariupol on the Sea of Azov. On October 20th they took Ekaterinoslav. There is some justification for the claim that Peregonovka was one of the decisive battles of the Civil War in the south.

(xi)

The three or four months from October, 1919, marked the peak of Makhno's career. Denikin's White armies were committed to the supreme gamble of the drive towards Moscow, reaching Orel, their furthest point north, shortly after Makhno's breakout at Peregonovka. But the Whites had failed to build up reserves, and there were no troops available effectively to hold the rear areas. To dislodge Makhno from one centre entailed withdrawing the garrison from another. During these weeks many towns changed hands several times. The operations covered almost the whole area of the White communications. Huge stocks of stores were seized when Makhno captured the big railway junctions, and the supply lines from the Black Sea ports to the Whites in the north were cut again and again.

Makhno was not the only guerrilla leader operating against Denikin; there were a number of smaller bands, some proclaiming themselves pro-Makhno, some pro-Petlurist. But these were insignificant in comparison with the Makhnovites, who for some months constituted what amounted to a free republic covering most of the southern Ukraine. The peasants were solidly behind Makhno; the State farm system and the enforced grain collections had made them anti-Soviet, and the behaviour of the Whites had made them even more anti-Denikin. Soviet attempts to split the peasantry and isolate the *kulak* had so far failed. Back in February the Gulyai-Polye Congress had declared 'it is essential not to split the toilers into parties and into mutually hostile groups . . . ways and means of our new agricultural order must be devised by the free and natural decision and initiative of the peasantry as a whole'. The existence of *kulachestvo* was recognized, but that, it was felt, was a problem that would solve itself in the course of time. At the end of the year the general feeling in the villages was still very ready to support this Makhnovite line.

Makhno and his Revolutionary Military Soviet had no need for misgivings regarding the villagers. The towns, however, presented a more complicated, but extremely important, problem. In early October when Makhno's partisans were approaching Berdyansk he issued an order: 'Comrade Insurgents! Every day that passes sees an extension of the area of activity of the Revolutionary Insurgent Army. Probably the hour is not far distant when the Insurgents will liberate some or other town from the grip of Denikin. This will be a *town* [underlined in the original] set free by the Makhnovite Insurgents from any kind of government. This will be a town in which, under the protection of the Revolutionary Insurgents, a free life will spring into being, in which there will grow up a free organization of Workers in union with the Peasants and Insurgents.' A fortnight later, in front of Ekaterinoslav, there appears perhaps to be a note of anxiety in the order of the day: 'The nature of our behaviour in the towns we capture is a question of life and death for the whole of our movement.' In all towns captured notices were posted up to inform the inhabitants that the place was, for the time being, occupied by the Makhnovite Insurgent Revolutionary Army, a force in the service of no government, no political party and no dictatorship. The Army's sole aim was to protect the liberty of the toilers against all. This liberty of the toilers was their own possession and subject to no restriction whatever. It was now for the peasants and workers to organize themselves as they wished. The Army was willing to help and to advise, but would not govern and would not give orders.

The most serious Makhnovite attempt to sponsor free organizations of industrial workers took place at Aleksandrovsk, where two trade union conferences under Insurgent auspices were held in mid-October, 1919. Both Voline and Arshinov, who were there at the time, admit that their practical results were negligible. Arshinov suggests that the workers were bewildered at the novelty of the ideas put to them; also that the town was too near the front. Voline speaks of fears that the town would soon be recaptured either by the Whites or by the Bolsheviks. But in fact the workers were primarily concerned with wages. The railwaymen on the line from Aleksandrovsk to Melitpol had had no pay for weeks. Makhno advised them to come to an equitable understanding with those that used the railway, and recoup themselves out of the proceeds. In point of fact, Makhno did later allot certain funds seized at Ekaterinoslav to paying the railwaymen, but workers in other branches were less fortunate; it was pointless to exhort them to organize a free economic order from below. The only union that made a serious attempt to work on Makhnovite lines was that of the bakers (in which the Anarchists had long had a strong footing) : the union appointed a committee of five to draw up a scheme for the socialization of bread grains and for the baking of bread for the whole population.

There was plain speaking at the workers' conferences in Aleksandrovsk and at a further meeting held in Ekaterinoslav. Menshevik speakers were so critical of the Insurgent handling of affairs that Makhno referred to them as 'bourgeois mongrels'. The Mensheviks then left the meeting, the S.R. representatives with them, and a number of trade unions passed resolutions protesting at the insult to the working class. Makhno explained that he was referring only to the Menshevik Party.

Makhnovite ideas on industrial affairs were, of course, utopian nonsense; but they accentuated their difficulties with the workers by their financial measures. The villages could subsist for long periods on what they produced themselves; but the worker, unless in receipt of rations, must be paid a sufficient wage in an acceptable currency to enable him to cover his basic needs. It was the general practice of the opposing sides in the Civil War to refuse to recognize the enemy's currency (though the Bolsheviks for a time accepted Ukrainian Petlurist roubles). Makhno proclaimed all Russian currencies as valid, and when he levied contributions on monied classes and institutions he would accept currencies annulled by the previous occupant. The result, accentuated by the manœuvres of the black bourse operators, was a fantastic wave of inflation in which the town worker was the main sufferer.

(xii)

At the end of October there took place in Aleksandrovsk a General Congress of Peasants, Workers and Insurgents. To prevent manœuvres by the political parties, election campaigning was forbidden. It was hurriedly convened, and the representation could not claim to cover the whole of the area under Makhnovite influence. Some three hundred delegates were present of whom a hundred and eighty were peasants. There were seventeen worker delegates including eleven Mensheviks and two Bolsheviks (one of the latter was subsequently shot by the *Cheka* on a charge of spying for Denikin). The workers' delegates played little part in the proceedings.

Matters dealt with included the perennial question of manpower; there was the old argument as to whether or not a 'voluntary' enlistment should be enforced. In the end this Congress also accepted Makhno's plea for a general mobilization in all liberated areas. The maintenance of the Army was discussed, and it was agreed that supplies be obtained by means of free contributions, requisitions from the rich, and war booty. It was decided to hold a further General Congress at an early date in Ekaterinoslav. Finally a resolution was passed to speed up by every means, and in every town and village, the establishment of free Soviets and of free associations and committees for the unconstrained and amicable settlement of all social and economic problems. There were a few doubting voices. A peasant from the Melitpol area asked: 'If there is a bridge between two of our villages and the bridge gets broken, who is to repair it? If neither village wishes to do the work, then we will not have a bridge and we will not be able to go to town.' But such objections did not seem worth taking into account. Voline had laid down months before (in the Kharkov *Nabat* of March 2nd, 1919) that for Anarchists there was 'no such thing as determined possibility or determined impossibility', and the simple revolutionaries of the Aleksandrovsk Congress were flushed with victory and filled with the vista of their community of free associations spreading ever wider, over the whole Ukraine, over Soviet Russia, over the West.

At the final session delegates were invited to raise any questions they wished, not excluding grievances or complaints against the Insurgent Army. One delegate pointed out the unsatisfactory state of the medical arrangements; a commission was appointed to inquire and to suggest means of improvement. Another, after some hesitation, complained of irregularities on the part of the Makhnovite *razvedka*; again a commission was appointed. A third speaker went so far as to complain against no less a person than the commandant of Insurgent troops in Aleksandrovsk, one Klein, who, after pasting the town with notices demanding sobriety, had himself got publicly and riotously drunk. A message was sent to ask Klein to appear before the Congress. Those who knew Klein's forceful and violent personality felt anxious. But when Klein arrived he at once confessed to the charge and expressed his regrets. He was, he said in mitigation, a simple soldier; an administrative post in a town made him bored and frustrated; he wished to go back to the front. The Congress accepted this explanation, and passed a resolution requesting the Makhnovite staff to transfer Klein to a combatant post.

The Makhnovites implemented their promises of freedom of the Press, and soon after their capture of Ekaterinoslav a number of papers began to appear, including organs of Right S.R.s, Left S.R.s and Bolsheviks (*Zvezda*). The only restriction was in the military field: all papers had to follow the communiqués of the Makhnovite *Put k Svobode*. But while expression was free 'the preparation or organization of enforcement on the masses of any régime affecting their complete freedom' was forbidden. Any serious work by the local Bolshevik cells had thus to be conducted conspiratorially.

That such work was, in fact, undertaken we know from the record of one Miroshevsky, a Communist Party official sent to Ekaterinoslav shortly before the Insurgent Army arrived. Underground work was based on the editorial office of *Zvezda*. The task was twofold: to work on 'neutral' industrial workers and win them over to the Soviet cause, and to split the Makhno-vites. The policy of instigating class struggle in the villages, of setting the poor peasants against the *kulaks* was being vigorously and not unsuccessfully pursued in Soviet Russia, and it was for the little group of Bolsheviks in Ekaterinoslav to prepare the ground, not only in the surrounding villages but also in the ranks of the Insurgent Army. Some progress was made : secret Bolshevik cells were formed in the Insurgent Iron Division, and the Divisional Commander himself, Polonsky, was won over. But the Makhnovite *razvedka* discovered what was happening and Polonsky and others were arrested. The Bolsheviks insti-gated an appeal for their trial in open court. This was refused and all were summarily shot. It was the first serious case of treachery that the Makhnovite movement had experienced.

Altogether Makhno's brief stay in the provincial capital was an unhappy one. His hold on the town remained precarious : the Whites were still on the opposite bank of the Dnieper and the town was intermittently shelled by their artillery. The project of a Second General Congress had to be abandoned. The town remained throughout under the control of the officer commanding the troops and the *razvedka*. Only negligible progress was made with the formation of free associations. But the main feature of the occupation was the full impact of the typhus epidemic upon troops and civilians alike. Makhno himself was soon to fall sick of it. Doctors were pressed into service and desperate attempts were made to organize hospitals : but survivors had nightmare stories to tell of the filth, confusion, lack of medicines and equipment, and appalling death-rate. On the approach of the retreating White armies from the north it was decided to evacuate.

Makhnovite apologists like Arshinov and Voline are ex-tremely sensitive to Bolshevik jibes that neither in Ekaterinoslav nor anywhere else did the movement show any constructive achievement. Their answer is that they never had time for it : they were always being forced out of their centres by some greatly superior enemy army. Military considerations were paramount, and often incompatible with civilian aspirations :

Voline, with his strict Anarchist conscience, went so far as to lay down that 'Every army, of any kind, is an evil'.

As we have seen, the movement now included some Anarchist intellectuals. Arshinov had arrived early in 1919 and started the newspaper *Put k Svobode*. In June the Federation of Anarchist Organizations in the Ukraine, much harried by the Bolsheviks, had decided to shift their headquarters to Makhno's area. This coincided with the Bolshevik break with Makhno and with Denikin's summer advance. Voline did not reach Makhno till August, and some of his colleagues never got through at all. Of those that did succeed in arriving only Voline and Arshinov remained loyal to Makhno to the end; the others, in a few months, found it impossible to reconcile Anarchist theory with partisan practice and left him. But for a time at least the weekly journal *Nabat*, the most important Anarchist organ in the Ukraine, was edited at the Insurgent headquarters and the new arrivals did much to improve the quality of the Makhnovite papers and leaflets.

In one or two areas some progress was made towards the establishment of schools. The aim was to put into practice the educational ideas of the Spanish Anarchist, Francisco Ferrer. Schools were to be the possession of the toiling masses themselves and to be entirely independent of any influence from Church or State. Teachers were to receive their livelihood from the communities they served. We hear of commissions being appointed, who were to work out plans. There is no available evidence to show whether such schools actually started to function.

Makhnovite opposition to any form of racial or national discrimination was frequently and clearly expressed. The Petlurists were opposed because they were bourgeois. Makhnovite ideas on Ukrainian independence were defined by the Revolutionary Military Soviet in a declaration of October, 1919: independence meant the free association of workers and peasants, and had nothing to do with 'independence of a nationalistic type'. Jews held leading positions in the movement throughout its existence, and anti-Semitism was regularly denounced in orders and proclamations and in articles in

Put k Svobode. Some anti-Semitism, of course, persisted, but cases of ill-treatment or of incitement against Jews were on occasion severely punished. We hear of Makhno himself shooting a partisan of long service who had chalked up a notice: 'Defend the Revolution! Long Live Makhno! Down with the Jews!'

The Makhnovite attitude to the administration of justice was laid down in a declaration of the Gulyai-Polye Congress of February, 1919: 'On the question of the need to organize a judicial administrative apparatus we suggest as a basic principle that any rigid permanent court and police machinery and any definitive codification of laws constitute infringements of the population's rights of self-defence . . . True justice cannot be administratively organized but must come as a living, free, creative act of the community . . . Law and order must be upheld by the living force of the local community, and must not be left to police specialists.'

It seems irrelevant to argue the question of Makhnovite capacity for constructive achievement. Many of their ideas made sense to Ukrainian peasants whose one political obsession was to be rid of any outside interference. Most of their ideas make nonsense when applied to any larger or more developed administrative unit. If left to themselves, Makhno and his advisers might, by trial and error, have so modified their ideas so as to make possible some more or less workable social order. But they had too many enemies and were always on the run. They had no constitutional apparatus. Their supreme authority was the Congress, but they were often chased out of their centres before the Congress sessions could be held. The Revolutionary Military Soviet was merely the instrument of the Congress, and in point of fact the R.M.S. was largely ignored by the military staff. In the emotional and physical circumstances of the time *Makhnovshchina* could not be an organized political movement. It was an army—an outstanding partisan army—with great powers of arousing peasant enthusiasm and a number of rather muddled ideas.

(xiii)

There were very wide fluctuations in the numerical strength of the Insurgent Army. The peak period was late 1919 when Makhno's prestige was at its highest and when he had a very wide area from which to draw recruits. Soviet estimates at this period vary from 40,000 infantry and 15,000 cavalry to 14,000 infantry, 6,000 cavalry, 5,000 gunners and machine-gunners: Makhno then possessed 48 field guns, 4 armoured trains, 4 armoured cars and 1,000 machine-guns. In any case, his force represented at least the same effective fighting strength as an average Soviet army on the Southern front.

No posts of command were held by former Tsarist officers, or by anyone of middle- or upper-class birth. Voline lists thirteen of Makhno's principal subordinate commanders, of whom eleven were peasants and two workers. A similar list of eighteen given by Arshinov breaks down into fourteen peasants, three workers and one village school-teacher. Voline gives the racial composition of the Army as 85 per cent Ukrainian, 8 per cent Great Russian, and the remainder Jews, Greeks, Tartars and Germans from the southern Ukraine. It is agreed that a high proportion of both officers and men came from Gulyai-Polye and the surrounding areas. The main weapons were sawn-off rifles and machine-guns—the latter for the most part mounted on *tachankas*. Dress was very variegated. A man would wear what he had till he could take something better. At Ekaterinoslav, Miroshevsky saw many insurgents dressed in British uniforms captured from the Whites. He noted that morale at that time was high and bellicose: the men were determined to liquidate Denikin, then to liquidate the Moscow Commissars, and then march westwards against the European bourgeois. The Insurgents were pitiless fighters and gave no quarter to the Whites, unless there was reason to believe that the prisoners were willing to change sides. There were incessant orders against looting and drunkenness, and intermittent drastic punishments: a Brigade Commander was shot for looting in

October, 1919, and a Regimental Commander in the summer of 1920. But the trouble was never eradicated: the peasant insurgents had been brought up to regard townsmen as their enemies and conceived it their right to take what they wanted from towns.

The Army was organized into divisions of three brigades, with three regiments to a brigade and three battalions to a regiment. Each unit had a Political Commissar, elected by the rank and file. Makhno nominated the officers commanding independently operating task forces. Other commanders were sometimes elected, sometimes nominated. Makhno retained the right to annul an election if he disapproved of the candidate selected; at the same time, if a unit was dissatisfied with a nominated commander the man was usually transferred. In late 1919 in the war against Denikin the Army operated mostly as a whole; in 1920 the circumstances of the fighting against the Bolsheviks brought about an increasing tendency to detach independent task forces; when these had completed their mission they would return to a given rendezvous, or await further orders by courier.

The enforcement of discipline was a matter of ever-recurring difficulty, in particular the problem of how to make units obey unwelcome orders. Here, of course, the personality of the commanding officer was of enormous importance: Makhno issued an order in December, 1919, laying the blame for certain lapses upon the commanders. There were cases in which units were punished for disobeying orders by having their horses and arms taken from them. Regimental and battalion mass meetings played a certain role. We hear of a regimental meeting which passed a resolution against all card-playing and against the issue of hard liquor either to partisans or to their commanding officers. The same meeting passed a resolution that all orders must be obeyed provided that the commanding officer was sober at the time of giving it.

Makhno must have shown remarkable judgment in his selection of his subordinate commanders. The qualifications were exacting. Apart from acquiring and keeping the absolute confidence of their troops they needed initiative, resource, flexibility and indefatigable physical toughness. Speed and surprise were the essence of Makhnovite tactics. Infantry were carried in carts and both infantry and cavalry could move at twice the speed of regular army troops. Makhno would seize every opportunity of getting behind his enemy. If attacked he would retreat, leave a small unit in front of the enemy to act as decoy, pass his main body round the flanks, and counter-attack from the rear. The partisans made use of every trick that peasant cunning could devise—ambushes, use of enemy uniforms, pretended surrenders. If surrounded with no chance of a break-out a unit would bury its arms and stores and disappear, as peasants, into the surrounding villages, waiting to re-form as soon as the enemy had passed on. At the peak of Makhno's hold on village loyalties it was almost impossible for the enemy to locate Insurgent formations: the peasants would not talk. Intelligence and communications were comparatively simple matters for the Insurgents.

Though the question of supply was always appearing on the agenda of Makhnovite Congresses it does not appear that any serious attempt was made to establish an organized supply department. There is no record of the setting-up of repair shops or S.A.A. factories as was done by the Red Army, and even by most of the partisan movements in Siberia. For one thing the Insurgents were too frequently on the run; for another, small amateur workshops could have done nothing to make good the enormous wastage of small arms and ammunition. In the course of his career Makhno captured huge quantities of stores of all kinds from his various enemies. Much was distributed to the local villagers. Of the rest, Makhno's habit was to bury, in great secrecy, such arms as it was not feasible or convenient to carry away. Later on the Bolsheviks dug up a number of these caches. We also hear of Makhno burying gold. Food and horses were provided by the villages. One secret of Makhnovite speed was that his men could always exchange tired horses for fresh ones *en route*. Later on, when the incessant passage of fighting bands and armies had drained the Ukrainian villages of their resources, the question of food and horses became more difficult. Throughout their campaigns the Makhnovites showed extreme concern for their sick and wounded, and long trains of carts of wounded and typhus cases followed the main body of the Army: but their circumstances allowed no opportunity for the setting up of any effective medical service.

Of the Makhnovite security services—the *Razvedka* and the *Kommissiya Protivmakhnovskikh Del*—we know very little. Their excesses were violently arraigned by the Bolsheviks, and the Soviet historian, Kubanin, cites them as proof of Makhnovite hypocrisy in vilifying the *Cheka*. Makhno's later campaigns are among the most vindictive and bloody in history, and in the circumstances one can safely assume that these services were responsible for frequent injustices and atrocities. Voline is witness to the fact that they were under no effective control. But, like their opposite number the *Cheka*, they seem to have been not unsuccessful in carrying out the task which they were set.

(xiv)

Makhno himself at the height of his power retained many of the characteristics of the young man who, three years before, had come home from the Butyrka Prison to make the Ukrainian revolution a reality. He retained his remarkable physical vitality. In spite of his lung affection and the aftermath of typhus and many wounds he could outride and outwork any of his colleagues. He would never go to bed till the task he had set himself was finished, and two hours later he would be tapping at the windows of his sleeping staff to bring them back to their work. He lived like a peasant himself and was always accessible to his peasants. He would always make time to talk to peasants, drink with them, take a hand with a flail. He would book the date two weeks in advance for a village wedding. Hence his enormous popularity. It was said that some of his subordinates, Kurilenko in particular, were at least as good soldiers and probably better administrators than Makhno; but no one could carry the countryside as he could.

He became increasingly engrossed in military matters, and it was harder and harder to keep him away from the front line when military operations were in progress. When sick or severely wounded he insisted on being carried in a cart with the front troops till he was well enough to ride a horse again. He was daring, persistent and resourceful; whatever the crisis that faced him he was never nervy or panicky. Nerves only became apparent in his office. As time went on he grew impatient of administrative details, and also of the theoretical disquisitions of his articulate Anarchist friends. He could not be bothered with the wordy resolutions of the Revolutionary Military Soviet. Voline, in his deposition when in Bolshevik hands, wrote that 'Makhno's personal attitude to the R.M.S. was partly to ignore it'. The *Nabat* Anarchists who left him in 1920 carried a resolution at their conference later that year to the effect that 'Bat'ko Makhno, as leader of the *Makhnovshchina*, while possessing many valuable revolutionary qualities, belongs, unfortunately, to that class of person who cannot always subordinate their personal caprices to the good of the movement'. Voline in later years was to say of him that 'he had no theoretical or historical political knowledge; he was thus unable to make the necessary revolutionary generalizations and deductions.' Arshinov makes the same complaint.

Makhno was a heavy drinker, increasingly so as time went on. Kubanin quotes a number of extracts from the diary of his 'wife', Fedora Gaenko (which was alleged to have been captured by the Red Army and preserved in the archives at Kharkov), giving instances of his drunkenness. Arshinov disputes the diary's authenticity, pointing out that his legal wife, Galina Andreevna (who escaped abroad with him), neither kept nor lost a diary. There is, however, plenty of independent evidence of his drinking habits. Voline considers the influence of alcohol to have been deplorable. 'It had little effect on his physical constitution. But alcohol made him ill-disposed, bad-tempered, excitable, unjust, intractable, violent. How often during my time with the Army I was in a state of despair when I left him, having been able to get no sense out of the man because of his abnormal state. Indeed, at certain periods it almost became his normal state.' Voline goes on: 'The second failing of Makhno and of many of his close associates was their attitude towards women. These men, especially when intoxicated, could not refrain from behaviour that was improper—disgusting would often be the correct adjective—amounting almost to orgies in which certain women were obliged to participate.'

Makhno became less and less inclined to take advice. As he became increasingly dictatorial he developed a false sense of security. His decisions were capricious, made on the spur of the moment. He refused to think things out or to calculate possible future developments. It would have been easy to foretell the Bolshevik attack at the beginning of 1920, and their second attack at the end of that year. But in neither case did Makhno make any counter-preparations.

(xv)

The Red Army captured Kharkov and Kiev in December, 1919. They marched into Ekaterinoslav a month after Makhno withdrew. A few weeks later they took Tsaritsyn and Rostov. The Whites were decisively beaten: by the end of March they had been driven into the Crimea, and Denikin was about to hand over to Wrangel.

The Red Army advance guard first contacted the Makhnovite Army in Aleksandrovsk in December. Relations at first again were friendly: there was a sense of solidarity in the victories over the Whites, and there were fraternal meetings and greetings. But shortly afterwards, at the turn of the year, the headquarters of the Fourteenth Red Army (under Voroshilov) sent Makhno formal instructions that he should proceed with the whole of his Army to take up positions on the Polish frontier. It is true that there were military reasons for reinforcing this sector, though the Polish war was not to break out for another four months. But it is admitted on the Soviet side that this order was primarily 'dictated by the necessity' of liquidating *Makhnovshchina* as an independent movement. Only when he was far removed from his home country would it be possible to counteract his influence, and to split up and integrate his partisans into various Red Army formations.

There were other occasions (notably in Siberia) of the Soviet authorities solving the problem of difficult partisan leaders by sending them off to fight on distant fronts. Makhno and his staff, however, were perfectly aware of the underlying Soviet motives. A reasoned reply was sent to the Fourteenth Army: the Insurgent Army, more revolutionary than any other army, would stay in the Ukraine where it belonged; the proposed transfer to the Polish frontier was pointless, and in any case impossible until the typhus had abated. At the same time an appeal was made, over the heads of the Red Command, to the Red Army rank and file that they should not be party to this 'provocation'. There was no immediate response from the Bolshevik side. But in mid-January the Central Committee of the Ukrainian Communist Party declared Makhno and his force to be outside the law, and the Red Army attacked. There followed eight months of the most savage fighting in which the Makhnovites were ever engaged.

In their new campaign to assimilate the southern Ukraine the Bolsheviks were in a far stronger position than they had been in the spring. With Denikin beaten and the Polish War not yet started they had far more troops at their disposal. Trotsky's reconditioning of the Red Army had had time to take effect. Subsidiary services, not least the *Cheka*, had been reinforced and improved. Experience of the White Armies had made the peasants less hostile towards the Reds, and the Soviet Government were now in a better position to work to a set policy rather than on a series of hasty improvisations. In February regulations were passed to assure a further distribution of land to the poorer peasants, and within a few months the unpopular State farms had been cut down by half in numbers and by two-thirds in acreage. More land was taken from the richer peasants and handed over to the poorer. An intensified drive was undertaken to split the peasantry and to secure the active co-operation of the *bednyaks* against the *kulaks*.

The war of 1920 was not a war of large-scale battles. There were a few engagements, and Gulyai-Polye changed hands several times with considerable bloodshed. Insurgent strength at this period was certainly less than in late 1919, and Makhno's offensives were necessarily confined to surprise attacks on isolated Red formations. The Bolshevik objective was twofold— to round up Makhno, and to eradicate his influence in the countryside. In the first they failed; in the second by weight of numbers and consistent ruthlessness they achieved a partial success. One of the first Makhnovite casualties was Voline: he was lying sick with typhus when overrun by the Reds and sent back to prison in Moscow.

On the occupation of a village by the Red Army the *Cheka* would hunt out and hang all active Makhnovite supporters; an amenable Soviet would be set up; officials would be appointed or imported to organize the poor peasants and to arrange for the deliveries of produce; and three or four Red militia men left as armed support for the new village bosses. This method did not always work. Though the Sovkhoz system had been appreciably modified, War Communism remained. There were requisitions, mobilization and forced labour. The enforced deliveries of produce were harsh, haphazard and bitterly resented. Peasant obstruction and resentment again came into play. Newly appointed members of Soviets (and even of poor peasant committees) would sometimes reveal themselves as *kulaks*. Bolshevik nominees would be murdered, driven out, or terrorized into refraining from carrying out their jobs. At any moment a Makhnovite band might appear, out of the blue, and all the new bosses would be rounded up and shot.

It is impossible to estimate the casualties involved. Voline and Arshinov give a figure of 200,000 peasants killed by the Reds—a large proportion being *Cheka* executions. The Makhnovites killed all Bolshevik Party activists they could catch, all *Cheka* and Militia members, and all officials of forced delivery and poor peasant organizations. In the military operations the Bolsheviks shot all prisoners. The Makhnovites shot all captured officers unless the Red rank and file strongly interceded for them. The rank and file were usually sent home, though a number volunteered for service with the Insurgents. Red Army reports complain of poor morale; certain Red commanders and political commissars were arrested for the unsatisfactory showing of their units. It is certain that numbers of the Red Army rank and file had little heart in this particular phase of the Civil War. The Reds used a number of Lettish and Chinese troops to decrease the risk of fraternization.

The outbreak of the Polish War did not cause a serious depletion of the Red Army in the southern Ukraine. Red superiority in numbers continued to be overwhelming. Makhno and his main body were pursued hither and thither across the country. On occasion he was brought to fight and was beaten; but always he would elude his opponent, re-form and reappear to strike a blow when least expected. We hear of his capturing half a battery, a supply train, a whole Red infantry regiment. All the resources of Bolshevik propaganda and misinformation were called into play. There were frequent reports of his death or capture. The *Cheka* staged further abortive attempts to assassinate him.

However, Bolshevik strength and methods began to tell. Makhno was appreciably weaker in the late summer of 1920 than he had been in the spring. The successive occupation of village after village by the Red Army and the *Cheka* meant the successive elimination (or terrorization) of all anti-Bolshevik activists. Furthermore, the continued years of fighting and requisitions had left the villagers exhausted and destitute. They wanted peace, any sort of peace. They had no supplies or horses left for even the much-reduced Makhnovite armies. They had nothing to give, and they resented demands made on them. The question of horses was all-important for Makhno's tactics were based on speed, and speed depended on fresh horses.

(xvi)

As opposed to the Polish War, the Wrangel campaign directly affected the Insurgent Army. Wrangel was determined to make use of any available ally. As early as May 13th, 1920, he issued an order that his troops should, where possible, co-ordinate with Makhno and other anti-Bolshevik groups, whereupon Bolshevik papers published allegations of Makhno-Wrangel collaboration. On June 18th the White Command dispatched a couple of emissaries (a colonel and a captain) with formal proposals to Makhno for joint operations against the Reds. The matter was considered at a meeting of the Insurgent Command on July 9th: the colonel was shot and the captain hanged with a placard bearing the legend 'There never was and never will be any association on the part of Makhno with White-Guardists, and if any other White Headquarters wish to send a further envoy he will meet with the same fate as this one.' Makhno issued a proclamation stating what he had done, as refutation of Bolshevik slanders.

It is agreed that the initiative for joint action against Wrangel came from the Makhnovites. Proposals to this end were telegraphed by Makhno to Kharkov and Moscow in July and again in August. Soviet historians suggest that Makhno was forced to make this approach by the pressure of general peasant opinion; and Arshinov makes the rather significant remark that if Makhno had to choose between Wrangel and the Bolsheviks the important factor was that the masses would prefer the Bolsheviks—it was true that the Bolsheviks had lied to them and cheated them, but the main enemy of the masses was still Wrangel. Kubanin suggests that Makhno's aims in making the approach were firstly to ensure the defeat of Wrangel, and secondly to have the chance to infiltrate into the Red Army, and subvert and win over an appreciable portion of the Red troops. The second point may be true. But by this time Makhno was less than ever inclined to work out a long-term programme; he may just have blindly relied on his luck. In any case, it is certain he would have run any risk in order to annihilate Wrangel. He remained to the end the implacable enemy of the Whites.

Makhno's approach to the Reds was left unanswered till September. Then Wrangel staged his big offensive: Berdyansk was overrun, then Gulyai-Polye, Aleksandrovsk, Sinelnikovo and Ekaterinoslav. Towards the end of the month a Bolshevik representative arrived at Makhnovite headquarters; then two Makhnovite delegates were sent to Kharkov and an agreement was negotiated between October 10th and 15th.

The agreement was in two parts, military and political. The Military Section contained four clauses. (i) The Insurgent Army would retain its own internal organization, but would be subordinate operationally to the Red Higher Command. (ii) The Insurgent Army would not recruit or accept as volunteers any Red Army deserters. (iii) Makhno was to issue a signed proclamation to be published and distributed by the Soviet authorities, calling upon the population to take no action detrimental to the Red Army or to the Soviet Government. (iv) The families of members of the Insurgent Army living in Soviet-held areas were to enjoy the same rights as Red Army families.

The Political Section contained three clauses. (i) All Makhnovites and all Anarchists under arrest in Soviet hands were to be set free forthwith. (ii) Makhnovites and Anarchists were to have full liberty of expression, subject to the requirements of military censorship and provided that nothing was expressed that tended towards the overthrow of Soviet Power. The Soviet authorities would provide Makhnovites and Anarchists with technical facilities for the expression of their views. (iii) Makhnovites and Anarchists were to enjoy full rights of participation in elections to local Soviets, including the right to be elected. They were to have the right to participate in the organization of the forthcoming Fifth All-Ukrainian Congress of Soviets.

There was, in addition, a fourth clause in the Political Section, which occasioned a great deal of argument, and which the Bolshevik negotiators refused to sign, but referred back to their higher authorities. It was to the effect that in areas occupied by the Insurgent Army the population was to create and maintain its own free and autonomous social and economic order—these areas subsequently to be federated with Soviet Russia by means of agreements to be freely negotiated with the appropriate Soviet Government organs.

The Makhnovites pressed for the full agreement to be published at once. The Military Section appeared in the Bolshevik papers fairly promptly, but the Political Section only after some delay. Nothing more came of the draft fourth political clause which, as Kubanin points out, was obviously quite unacceptable to the Bolsheviks. But an official Soviet communiqué was issued to the effect that Makhno had never helped Wrangel and that allegations that he had done so had been untrue. And a start was made with the implementation of the rest of the Political Section. A number of Makhnovites and Anarchists in Soviet prisons were, in fact, released. These included Voline, who came to Kharkov, started up *Nabat* again and made preparations for another Anarchist conference to be held in Kharkov at the end of the year.

The Bolsheviks obviously felt these measures necessary in order to ensure the full co-operation of the Makhnovite Army. They did not underestimate Wrangel and they wished to rally all the resources available for what might prove to be a hard and prolonged campaign. A Soviet historian writes that the agreement with Makhno was 'justified by the strategic conditions'. But, as Kubanin states flatly, there was never the slightest intention on the Bolshevik side of keeping to the agreement once its military value had passed. Months later, when Voline was in prison again, he was told by his *Cheka* interrogator: 'When we had need of Makhno we knew how to make use of him, and when we no longer had need, when in fact he was becoming a nuisance, we knew how to get rid of him once and for all.'

It would be idle to pretend that there was good faith on the Makhnovite side. They were all perfectly aware that a further clash would come, and they were determined that their own ideas, and not the Bolsheviks', should in the end prevail. But they do not seem to have made any practical plans. The loudly voiced Bolshevik accusations of treachery may well be justified on the score of ultimate intention, but not on the score of serious conspiratorial work. Makhnovite hopes seem to have laid on a crescendo of popular feeling in their favour both in the villages and in the rank and file of the Red Army. But this needed time, and events moved much too fast for them.

Makhno did not on this occasion accompany his units to the front. He went back to Gulyai-Polye—his first chance of returning home in any security after nine months of hard fighting. With him went his headquarters staff and some 3,000 Insurgents.

The Red Army counter-offensive against Wrangel was spectacular in its speed and success. By early November the Whites had been driven off the mainland and the Perekop positions defending the Crimea had been forced. In mid-November news reached Gulyai-Polye that the Red Army, together with some Insurgent units under Karetnik, were marching on Simferopol; and a member of Makhno's staff remarked: 'This is the end of the agreement. Within a week the Bolsheviks will be attacking us.'

The importance that the Bolsheviks attached to Makhno is evidenced by the scope, the speed, the thoroughness and the secrecy of the preparations they made for his liquidation. (Voline, on seemingly good authority, reproduces copies of telegrams showing Lenin's personal interest.) On November 23rd, nine Bolshevik security service agents were captured by the *razvedka* in Gulyai-Polye. They confessed under interrogation that they had been sent by the commander of the 42nd (Red Army) Division, with the assignment to locate and watch the place of residence and movements of Makhno and his principal officers: they were to remain there till the arrival of the Red Army which was expected in a couple of days. Makhno's Chief of Staff contacted Kharkov on the direct telegraph line, made a strong protest and demanded the arrest

of the O.C. 42nd Division and any others responsible. Kharkov
replied that there must be some misunderstanding: they would
institute inquiries. In a further telegraphic conversation a day
or two later Kharkov promised that the incident would be
settled to Makhnovite satisfaction. When pressed on the matter
of Clause 4 of the Political Agreement (the Makhnovites were
impatiently awaiting its approval by Moscow), Kharkov replied
that here too a satisfactory solution was imminent.

In Kharkov on November 25th Voline secured an interview
with Rakovsky, head of the Ukrainian Soviet Government.
There had been some police persecution of *Nabat* readers,
contrary to the agreement of October. Voline also pressed for
a speedy approval of Clause 4. Rakovsky promised early satisfaction on both counts. That night Voline, together with other
Anarchists, was arrested and *Nabat* suppressed. The Makhnovite negotiators of the October Agreement, who were staying on
in Kharkov pending settlement of Clause 4, were seized,
removed to Moscow and there executed.

At Red Army Headquarters at Melitpol on November 23rd
Frunze signed Order 00149 requiring complete integration in
the Red Army of all Insurgent units. This order was not made
public till mid-December. On the 25th or 26th the commander
of the Makhnovite forces in the Crimea was invited to a Red
Army command post where he was seized and shot. The
Makhnovite units were surrounded, but 250 cavalry broke
through and eventually joined up with Makhno.

On November 26th the Red Army attacked Gulyai-Polye in
force. Makhno was completely surrounded. But he fought his
way out, collected some reinforcements, counter-attacked and
recaptured the village. In this engagement the 42nd Red Army
Division was routed, losing (according to Arshinov) 6,000
prisoners, of whom 2,000 agreed to serve under Makhno and
the rest sent to their homes. Three days later Makhno defeated
two further Red divisions, again with a huge haul of prisoners
of whom a large proportion volunteered to join him. This
development caused serious concern to the Red Army authorities, and a special catchment corps was organized, with firing

squads, to pick up stragglers and prevent news spreading. For a few days there was considerable optimism at Makhnovite headquarters: it was felt that all that was needed was another victory or two and the war against the Bolsheviks would be won. But the Red Army continued to bring up further reinforcements: twice again the Insurgent Army was encircled and had to fight its way out, and each time the victory was more dearly won. Reports brought by peasants made it apparent that no less than four Red Army Corps were being assembled. At a meeting of the Soviet of Revolutionary Insurgents it was agreed that there was no prospect of being able to hold the Gulyai-Polye area, and the Makhnovite Army retreated northwards.

It was an extremely severe winter. The Red Army held all important road junctions in force, and for the most part the Insurgents moved over the frozen fields. Up north, not far from Kiev, they had to abandon their artillery and heavy baggage in the snow. In the following eight months of almost continuous fighting, Makhno covered the whole of the Ukraine. From the Kiev province he struck east, skirting Poltava, Kursk and Khartov. It was at this period that, a thousand miles to the north, the Kronstadt sailors were fighting under slogans somewhat similar to his own; but we do not know whether news of Kronstadt ever reached him. He was badly wounded and when, in early March, he came south again he had to be carried in a cart. He passed through the Gulyai-Polye area, reached the Black Sea coast and turned east along the Sea of Azov. On his way north again he was wounded once more near Gulyai-Polye; but was sufficiently recovered to ride a horse at the rendezvous of his troops he had fixed for April in the Poltava province.

In 1921 the Soviet Armies were still on a war footing, and there was no external enemy. The whole of the military machine in south Russia was available for the elimination of Makhno, and for the support of the State and Party organizations and *Cheka* in their work on the integration of the Ukrainian villages. It was the story of 1920 all over again, but this time with the scales weighted far more heavily on the side of the Soviet Power. It is remarkable too that, in spite of the introduction, in early 1921, of the N.E.P. measures to remove most of the peasants' grievances, Red Army reports should still complain of the support afforded to Makhno by the villagers.

Arshinov reproduces a letter written later by Makhno to a friend in which he describes the 'nightmare' of those last few months. There were victories; more often than not he got the better of his brushes with the Bolsheviks. Now and then he captured a small town, when his first move would be to seize the local printing press and run off leaflets demanding free Soviets. There were moments of encouragement, as when a delegation of Chernigov peasants came to one of his columns to offer their support. But in the unequal struggle his resources progressively dwindled. He himself in this last period was wounded six times, twice seriously. Of the thirteen principal subordinate commanders listed by Voline (who included Makhno's closest personal friends), four were dead before the final break with the Bolsheviks in November, 1920. During the next six months Makhno lost all the nine survivors: two were seized and shot in the Crimea; two were taken prisoner—their subsequent fate unknown; one was executed by the *Cheka* and the remaining four killed in battle. Casualties among the rank and file were very heavy.

Owing to the intensity of the pursuit and the difficulties of supply it became necessary to operate in ever smaller units. Small detachments were sent off to operate independently— and mostly disappeared. In early August, Makhno realized he could do no more, and on August 13th he crossed the Dnieper for the last time, between Orlik and Kremenchug, making for the West. On the 16th he was cornered by the Reds but fought his way out, capturing thirteen Maxims and three Lewis guns. His own losses were seventeen men. There was another battle on the 22nd when he was hit again, this time badly, and had once more to be carried on a cart. On the 26th, almost in sight of the frontier, there was a final engagement. On the evening of the 28th the survivors, numbering two hundred and fifty men, crossed the Dniester into Roumania.

(xvii)

Arshinov did not accompany Makhno to Roumania. He went back to the Anarchist undergrounds of the Ukraine and Great Russia where he wrote his history of the Makhnovite movement. In due course the manuscript was smuggled out for publication in Berlin.

Voline meanwhile was lodged in the Taganka Prison in Moscow. In the summer of 1921 he staged a hunger strike which came to the knowledge of an international Red Trades Union Congress then in session in Moscow. French and Spanish Anarchist delegates made representations on his behalf, in consequence of which the Soviet Government released him and expelled him from Soviet territory.

Makhno and his little force were disarmed and interned by the Roumanians, and there followed a series of acrimonious diplomatic notes from Moscow demanding his extradition. There is reason to believe that the Roumanian authorities connived at his escape across the Polish frontier. Here he was arrested and brought to trial on a charge of 'anti-Polish activities' in the Ukraine. He was acquitted, went on to Danzig and was arrested again. All this time international Anarchist organizations had been vocal on his behalf, and he was eventually allowed to move to Paris and settle there.

His final period was an unhappy one. He was miserably poor. Before leaving the Ukraine he had dug up one of his hidden stocks of gold, but that was soon spent. His turbulent life had worn him out and his health was broken. He never learned to speak any French. Voline speaks of his 'difficulty in adjusting himself to circumstances so very different from his former way of life'. He was moody, quarrelsome, subject to fits of extreme depression. He started to work on his memoirs and Voline attempted to help set in order his illiterate manuscript. A first

volume was completed and issued during his lifetime, but then
he quarrelled with Voline, and two further parts, edited by
Voline, appeared only after his death. He died in 1935 and
his ashes were buried in the Père Lachaise Cemetery.

The main sources for Chapter VI are:

Antonov-Ovseenko, V. A., *Zapiski o Grazhdanskoi Voine* (Moscow, 1933).
Arshinov, P., *Istoriya Makhnovskovo Dvizheniya 1918–1921 gg.* (Berlin, 1923).
Grazhdanskaya Voina 1918–1921 gg. Vol. III (Moscow, 1928–1930).
Kubanin, M., *Makhnovshchina* (Leningrad, n.d.).
Makhno, Nestor, Vol I: *Russkaya Revolyutsiya na Ukraine* (Paris, 1929).
    Vol. II: *Pod Udarami Kontrrevolyutsiye* (Paris, 1936).
    Vol. III: *Ukrainskaya Revolyutsiya Iul-Dekabr 1918* (Paris, 1937).
Voline, V. M. (Eichenbaum), *La Révolution Inconnue* (Paris, n.d.).

Other works consulted include:

Igrenev, G., in *Arkhiv Russkoi Revolyutsii*, Vol. III (Berlin, 1921),
Miroshevsky, V., in *Proletarskaya Revolyutsiya*, Vol. IX (Moscow, 1922).
Yaroslavsky, *History of Anarchism in Russia* (London, n.d.).

Conclusion

One feature of the Russian Civil War is, surely, the relatively small number of Russians—let alone foreigners—who had any wish to take an active part in it. Campaigning in Russia was a grim and unpleasant business with the killing cold of the winter, the quagmires of the spring thaw and autumn rains and the plague of mosquitoes in the swamps and forests of the northern summer. And, in the Civil War, there were factors that made for all manner of beastliness in its conduct—the vindictive hatred of the fanatics on either side, the absence of control that opened the way for thugs and sadists, the lust for reprisals that early atrocities let loose. There was plenty of subconscious motivation for the wish to 'declare neutrality'. In spite of the respective appeals of Revolution and of Russia—both spelt with a very capital R— for the common man, the non-fanatic, it was a war to keep right out of.

It has been easy to forget the features common to the two parties in the struggle. At the top, on both sides, were men of middle and lower middle class origin (the very rich and noble were, throughout, more prominent in the drawing-rooms of emigration than in the field). In both 'democracy' was tried; found not to work; and dropped. Both sides were embarrassed by the antics of their S.R. and other allies of convenience. The composition of the armies was not dissimilar. There were, it is true, more workers in the Red ranks, and more Cossacks in the White; but as and when substantial forces came to be deployed the bulk of them on both sides were peasants, with a majority of former officers in posts of command. They were unwieldy armies: in spite of the numbers available on paper it was an almost insuperable problem to get enough men together in the right place at the right time.

Both sides set hopes on raising volunteer armies; and, as these hopes faded, there were all the difficulties of enforced mobilization. The incidence of desertion on either side was huge. There were mutinies and mass defections. The efforts to build up auxiliary services meant, for both parties, a continuous battle against muddle, dishonesty and waste. Both sides, in course of an advance, were hailed as liberators; and, as occupation continued, attempts to gear the population into the war effort met with a mounting tide of peasant obstruction, hostility and resistance.

The numbers on both sides were roughly equal, and the military command on about the same level of professional competence. As against the Red advantage of interior lines the Whites had large stocks of Allied stores at their disposal. In an attempt to explain why it was that the Red victory was so complete one should perhaps first consider the personal quality of the respective leaders. Lenin (and also Trotsky in his sphere) had a grip on men and events that none of the White leaders could ever acquire. And they were realists. Trotsky's flaming rhetoric never obscured the practical difficulties to be overcome. No small part of Lenin's genius was to couple tenacity with the power to judge where and when a temporary concession could bring a double dividend. As against this, Kolchak, Denikin, Miller (and Chernov after his fashion) were romantics, whose conceptions of loyalty left no scope for tactical manœuvre.

And in the Communist Party the Bolshevik leadership fashioned an instrument with a corporate spirit and a discipline to stand up to the exhaustion and frustration of civil war. It kept alive a spirit of dedication: but under the guidance of its leadership and in the hard school of war it learned to prune away the costly survivals of revolutionary romanticism and Utopianism. Red ruthlessness came to acquire a method and effectiveness far beyond the spasmodic brutalities of the Whites. The Party brought a cohesion to the Red war effort that was lacking on the other side, a co-operation between front and rear and between leaders and led, a spur and an example on every level, a constant vigilance against softness, treachery or dishonesty. It won its experience by trial and error, and with the false starts, setbacks and human failures that the times and conditions made inevitable. But it held on to its task. Trotsky in his account of the Civil War has written 'in the unstable poise of a scale only a small weight is enough to decide'. That small weight was probably the Party.

Bibliographical Note

The principal authorities used in compiling this book are listed at the end of each chapter.

Source material on the Russian Civil War is voluminous, incomplete and often difficult of access. British, French and Soviet archives have not been made generally available; and, in the case of the U.S.S.R., this includes not only the Soviet official, Party and Security Service records but also the records from the various White headquarters overrun by the Red Army. A considerable mass of material concerning the Socialist Revolutionaries and the Czechoslovak Legion was removed from Prague to Russia after World War II.

Even so, there is far more relevant material available to the West than Western scholars have so far been able to process. There are the German Foreign Office (and other German) documents, of which a large proportion are on microfilm in the Public Record Office in London; and, to take the example of a comparatively minor sector, there are some hundreds of not yet examined files on the Yudenich campaign in the Hoover Institute in Stanford, California, and the Columbia Russian Archive in New York. Valuable work on the documents available was carried out by American scholars between the wars, resulting in such publications as Bunyan and Fisher's *The Bolshevik Revolution* (Stanford, 1934), Varneck and Fisher's *The Testimony of Kolchak and Other Siberian Materials* (Stanford, 1935) and J. Bunyan's *Intervention, Civil War and Communism* (Baltimore, 1936). But much remains to be done.

A number of histories and memoirs by participants have been written by Russians in emigration, many of them of considerable interest and value. Most of them were published in small editions and are now hard to come by. Emigré historical journals, notably *Arkhiv Russkoi Revolyutsii* and *Beloe Delo* (both Berlin) contain much material essential to the study of the subject. The same holds good of Soviet historical reviews, in particular *Proletarskaya Revolyutsiya* (Moscow, 1921—). Valuable work on the Civil War published in Russia during the twenties includes a number of monographs, local and regional collections and such compilations as *Grazhdanskaya Voina 1918–1921 g.g.* (3 vols., Moscow, 1928–30) and *Borba za Ural i Sibir* (Moscow-Leningrad, 1926). From about 1930, however, Soviet historical writing became more and more rigidly subjected to the Stalinist line.

The best general account of the Civil War in English (or indeed in any language) is Vol. II of W. H. Chamberlin's *The Russian Revolution* (New York, 1935, revised 1952). Both this and *The Testimony of Kolchak* contain good bibliographies. The most important works on certain aspects that have since appeared include George F. Kennan's *Russia Leaves the War* (London, 1956) and *The Decision to Intervene* (London, 1958); also James W. Morley's *The Japanese Thrust into Siberia, 1918* (New York, 1957). On the minor fronts, the only easily available account of the Transcaspian episode is C. H. Ellis' contribution to *St. Antony's Papers No. VI* (London, 1959). For the background to the all-important role of the Bolshevik Party there is Leonard Schapiro's *The Origin of the Communist Autocracy* (London, 1955) and *The Communist Party of the Soviet Union* (London, 1960).

Recent Soviet work on the Civil War has been disappointing. The publication of documents shows a high degree of selectivity, and the elaborately produced and illustrated *Istoriya Grazhdanskoi Voiny v SSSR* now appearing is an exercise in propaganda rather than history. This work is a product of the Moscow Institute of Marxism-Leninism, one of its principal editors and contributors being S. F. Naida, director of the section for the history of the Civil War in that Institute. An apposite comment has been made by George F. Kennan in the *American Historical Review* of January, 1960. After listing a number of Naida's factual errors, Professor Kennan goes on: 'Naida calls for "a merciless struggle . . . against bourgeois objectivism in science". He defines "bourgeois objectivism" as something that occurs "when certain authors, ignoring the concrete historical setting, attempt to argue this or that proposition, arbitrarily selecting isolated factlings [*faktiki*], citing them out of context, without relation to the whole". One suspects that for Naida "facts" are historical circumstances, or alleged or suggested circumstances, which serve a preconceived ideological interpretation of the historical process and are therefore to be treated with respect, whereas "factlings" are circumstances which, though they may be marked by the awkward quality of having actually occurred, fail to serve this preconceived interpretation and are therefore to be despised.'

Relevant Dates

1917

March	7th	First large-scale demonstrations in Petrograd.
	12th	Formation of Committee of State Duma.
	,,	Formation of Petrograd Soviet.
	14th	Order No. 1 issued by Petrograd Soviet.
	15th	Abdication of Emperor Nicholas.
	,,	Formation of Provisional Government.
	16th	Abdication of Grand Duke Michael.
	27th	Appeal of the Soviet to Peoples of the World for Peace.
April	16th	Return of Lenin to Russia.
May	1st	Milyukov's note to Western Allies.
	3rd–5th	Anti-Government demonstrations in Petrograd following Milyukov's note.
	8th	Resignation of Milyukov.
	18th	Reorganization of Provisional Government.
June	16th	First Congress of Soviets.
July	2nd	Start of July offensive.
	16th–18th	The July days: suppression of anti-Government rising.
	21st	Formation of new Government with Kerensky as Prime Minister.
August	1st	Kornilov appointed Commander-in-Chief.
	25th–28th	State Conference in Moscow.
September	6th	Kornilov initiates advance on Petrograd.

September		
	10th–12th	Collapse of Kornilov movement.
	14th	Arrest of Kornilov and fellow-generals.
	19th	Bolshevik majority in Moscow Soviet.
October	6th	Trotsky Chairman of Petrograd Soviet.
	23rd	Decision by Bolshevik Central Committee to organize armed rising.
	25th	Formation of Military Revolutionary Committee.
November	7th	Bolshevik seizure of power in Petrograd.
	13th	Collapse of Kerensky's counter-move against Petrograd.
	15th	Bolsheviks establish their power in Moscow.
	„	Beginnings of Volunteer Army in the Don Province.
December	1st	Left S.R.s enter Government after agreement with Bolsheviks.
	2nd	Escape of Kornilov and fellow-generals from prison in Bykhov.
	3rd	Bolsheviks occupy Supreme Headquarters at Mogilev.
	15th	Armistice agreement signed with Central Powers.
	20th	Establishment of *Cheka*.
	22nd	Peace negotiations begin in Brest-Litovsk.

1917—*continued*

1918

January	18th	Opening of Constituent Assembly.
	19th	Constituent Assembly dispersed.
	23rd	Dissident Cossacks repudiate Don Government of Ataman Kaledin.
February	8th	Red Army occupies Kiev.
	9th	Ukrainian Rada concludes separate peace with Central Powers.
	10th	Brest-Litovsk negotiations broken off.

1918—*continued*

February	19th	Germans initiate advance through Ukraine.
	22nd	Volunteer Army evacuate Rostov.
	24th	Red Army occupies Rostov.
	25th	Collapse of Don Government.
	26th	Red troops occupy Novocherkassk.
March	2nd	Germans occupy Kiev.
	3rd	Brest-Litovsk Treaty.
	12th	Soviet Government moves from Petrograd to Moscow.
	13th	Trotsky becomes Peoples Commissar of War.
	14th	Ekaterinodar occupied by Reds.
April	5th	Allied ships and marines arrive in Murmansk.
	,,	Germans occupy Kharkov.
	13th	Repulse of Volunteer Army at Ekaterinodar; Kornilov killed in action.
	,,	Bolshevik drive against Anarchists in Moscow and elsewhere.
	,,	Germans occupy Odessa.
	14th	Germans and White Finns occupy Helsinki.
	29th	Germans establish puppet Ukrainian government with Skoropadsky as Hetman.
May	6th	Anti-Soviet Cossacks occupy Novocherkassk.
	8th	Germans occupy Rostov.
	11th	Krasnov elected Ataman of Don.
	14th	Czech-Soviet incident at Chelyabinsk.
	25th	Revolt of the Czechoslovak Legion: collapse of Bolshevik authority along the Trans-Siberian Railway.
	29th	Partial conscription for Red Army.
June	1st	West Siberian Commissariat formed at Omsk.
	8th	Czechs occupy Samara. Formation of Samara Peoples Government.
	23rd	Allied reinforcements arrive in Murmansk.
July	6th	Assassination of German Ambassador in Moscow.

1918—*continued*

July 11th Anti-Bolshevik mutiny and liquidation of Muraviev, commanding Red forces on the Volga.

14th Anti-Soviet revolt in Transcaspia. Formation of anti-Bolshevik Government at Ashkhabad.

16th Execution of Imperial family at Ekaterinburg.

25th Czech forces occupy Ekaterinburg.

August 2nd Establishment of anti-Bolshevik Government at Archangel.

3rd Allied troops land at Archangel.

6th Czech and Samara forces take Kazan.

14th Dunster-force lands in Baku.

15th Denikin captures Ekaterinodar.

19th Agreement between Ashkhabad Government and British Military Mission.

26th Volunteer Army captures Novorossisk.

September 10th Bolsheviks capture Kazan.

13th Dunster-force leaves Baku.

23rd Ufa Conference sets up Directorate as All Russian Provisional Government.

October 8th Red Army captures Samara.

9th Directorate fixes capital at Omsk.

November 9th Revolution in Germany.

11th Armistice concluded between Allies and Germany.

13th Soviet Government denounces Brest-Litovsk Treaty.

18th Directorate suppressed at Omsk. Kolchak assumes supreme power.

December 14th Collapse of Skoropadsky régime in the Ukraine.

17th French land in Odessa.

25th Kolchak's Northern Army captures Perm.

1919

January	3rd	Red Army occupies Riga and Kharkov.
February	6th	Red Army occupies Kiev.
	15th	Resignation of Krasnov: Denikin assumes supreme command in S.E. Russia.
March	2nd–7th	First Congress of Communist International in Moscow.
	13th	Kolchak launches spring offensive.
	21st	Allied decision to withdraw forces from Russia.
	,,	Soviet régime set up in Hungary.
April	5th	Departure of British and Indian troops from Transcaspia.
	8th	French evacuate Odessa.
	10th	Soviet troops enter Crimea.
	26th	Frunze's counter-offensive against Kolchak.
May	7th	Ataman Grigoriev, commanding Soviet troops in the South-East, turns against the Bolsheviks.
	19th	Start of Denikin's spring offensive.
	23rd	Von der Goltz's troops take Riga.
June	4th	Partisan leader Makhno breaks with Red Army.
	9th	Decisive defeat of Kolchak in centre and south.
	25th–30th	Denikin captures Kharkov, Tsaritsyn and Ekaterinoslav.
July	1st	Soviet troops reoccupy Perm.
	15th	Red Army occupies Ashkhabad.
	25th	Red Army takes Chelyabinsk.
	27th	Grigoriev killed by Makhno.
August	23rd	Denikin occupies Odessa.
	31st	Denikin occupies Kiev.
September	7th	Start of Soviet-Estonian peace negotiations.
	26th	Makhno defeats Whites at Peregonovka.

1919—*continued*

September	27th	Allies evacuate Archangel.
	28th	Yudenich starts offensive against Petrograd.
October	14th	Denikin's troops reach Orel.
	20th	Red Army reoccupies Orel: general retreat of White Armies.
November	9th	Capture of Ekaterinoslav by Makhno.
	14th	Final defeat of Yudenich.
	,,	Red Army occupies Omsk.
December	12th	Red Army occupies Kharkov.
	16th	Red Army occupies Kiev.
	24th	Anti-Kolchak revolt in Irkutsk.
	30th	Red Army occupies Ekaterinoslav.

1920

January	3rd	Red Army occupies Tsaritsyn.
	4th	Abdication of Kolchak as Supreme Ruler.
	8th	Red Army takes Rostov.
	15th	Kolchak handed over to the Political Centre, now in control of Irkutsk.
	16th	Allies end blockade of Soviet Russia.
	18th	Bolshevik Revolutionary Committee takes over from Political Centre in Irkutsk.
February	2nd	Soviet-Estonian peace agreement.
	7th	Execution of Kolchak.
	19th	Fall of Northern Government at Archangel.
March	17th	Red Army occupies Ekaterinodar.
	27th	Red Army occupies Novorossisk.
April	4th	Denikin succeeded by Wrangel.
	24th	Outbreak of Russo-Polish War.
May	6th	Polish forces occupy Kiev.
June	6th	Wrangel starts offensive.
	12th	Red Army recaptures Kiev.
July	11th	Red Army takes Minsk.
	14th	Red Army takes Vilna.

1920—*continued*

August	17th	Polish counter-offensive.
September	21st	Start of Russo-Polish peace negotiations.
October	12th	Russo-Polish provisional peace treaty.
	25th	Red Army offensive against Wrangel.
November	2nd	Wrangel retreats to Crimea.
	11th	Red Army storms Perekop Isthmus.
	14th	Evacuation of Crimea by Wrangel forces.
	26th	Red Army drive against Makhno.

Index

DATE DUE

AUG 23 '63			
MAY 1 '64			
APR 22 1969			
MAR 15			
MAY 5 1970			
APR 2 7 1973			
NOV 1 4 1973			
NO 10 '83			
GAYLORD			PRINTED IN U.S.A.